The Original Torah

REAPPRAISALS IN JEWISH SOCIAL
AND INTELLECTUAL HISTORY
General Editor: Robert M. Seltzer

*Martin Buber's Social and Religious Thought:
Alienation and the Quest for Meaning*
LAURENCE J. SILBERSTEIN

The American Judaism of Mordecai M. Kaplan
EDITED BY EMANUEL S. GOLDSMITH, MEL SCULT,
AND ROBERT M. SELTZER

On Socialists and "the Jewish Question" after Marx
JACK JACOBS

Easter in Kishinev: Anatomy of a Pogrom
EDWARD H . JUDGE

*Jewish Responses to Modernity:
New Voices from America and Eastern Europe*
ELI LEDERHENDLER

Rabbi Abraham Isaac Kook and Jewish Spirituality
EDITED BY LAWRENCE J. KAPLAN AND DAVID SHATZ

The Americanization of the Jews
EDITED BY ROBERT M. SELTZER AND NORMAN J. COHEN

Russia's First Modern Jews: The Jews of Shklov
DAVID E. FISHMAN

The "Other" New York Jewish Intellectuals
EDITED BY CAROLE S. KESSNER

*The Nations That Know Thee Not:
Ancient Jewish Attitudes toward the Religions of Other People*
ROBERT GOLDENBERG

*The Original Torah:
The Political Intent of the Bible's Writers*
S. DAVID SPERLING

S. DAVID SPERLING

THE ORIGINAL TORAH

The Political Intent of
the Bible's Writers

NEW YORK UNIVERSITY PRESS
NEW YORK & LONDON

NEW YORK UNIVERSITY PRESS
New York and London

© 1998 by New York University

Library of Congress Cataloging-in-Publication Data

Sperling, S. David
The original Torah : the political intent of the Bible's writers /
S. David Sperling.
p.   cm. — (Reappraisals in Jewish social and intellectual history)
Includes bibliographical references and index.
ISBN 0-8147-8094-6 (cloth : alk. paper)
First published in paperback in 2003
ISBN 0-8147-9833-0 (pbk : alk. paper)
1. Politics in the Bible. 2. Bible. O.T.—Criticsim, interpretation, etc.
I. Title. II. Series.
BS1171.2.S65   1998
222'.106—dc21   97-45378
CIP

New York University Press books are printed on acid-free paper,
and their binding materials are chosen for strength and durability.

Manufactured in the United States of America

10 9 8 7 6 5 4 3 2 1

Contents

Acknowledgments   vii

Abbreviations   ix

Chronological Table   xiii

Introduction   1

1. It Says in the Torah   11

2. History and Allegory   27

3. The Allegory of Servitude in Egypt and the Exodus   41

4. Yahweh's *Berît* (Covenant):
   Which Came First—Sex or Politics?   61

5. Abraham   75

6. Jacob, Jeroboam, and Joseph   91

7. Aaron   103

8. Moses   121

Afterword   135

Notes   137

Bibliography   165

Index   179

About the Author   185

Acknowledgments

My work on this book would not have been possible without the encouragement and support of several people and institutions, and I would like to thank them all. First, I want to thank my daughter Deborah Lewis Sperling who came home from Temple Israel Religious School one day at the age of eight and posed the following question about the stories in the Torah: "Since no one could have known what really happened, why were these stories made up?" *The Original Torah* is my attempt to answer Deborah's question.

In the course of writing this book, I relied heavily on the staff of the library of the New York School of Hebrew Union College–Jewish Institute of Religion, especially Mr. Henry Resnick and Mr. Julius Sperling (no relation). Thanks to these dedicated gentlemen, I was spared a great deal of time in hunting for materials and double-checking references.

I am also very grateful to two groups of students who served as audiences for much of the material presented here. As is the case with many academics, I had the opportunity to try out scholarly theories in my classes, at both HUC-JIR and New York University. In addition, however, I had a fringe benefit reserved for some fortunate rabbinic spouses, a willing audience of intelligent and critical laics. The members of Temple Israel of the City of New York, where my wife Judith Lewis serves as senior rabbi, provided an extraordinary venue for me to test hypotheses, communicated sometimes by me and sometimes, always with attribution, by my wife.

I owe a great deal to several academic colleagues. Professor Leonard Kravitz who, over the years has brightened my lunch hours at HUC–JIR, shared with me his extensive knowledge of the ways in which the medieval Jewish philosophers read the Bible. Professor

Elaine Pagels of Princeton and Professor Robert Seltzer of CUNY generously took the time to read early drafts of this manuscript. My special thanks go to Professor James R. Russell of Harvard for his detailed criticisms and annotations. I have probably erred in not accepting them all. I owe a similar debt of gratitude to Dr. Barbara Nevling Porter, also of Harvard, for her thorough reading and acute suggestions.

Had it not been for Professor Robert Seltzer's personal direction, this manuscript might never have reached the editors of the New York University Series, Reappraisals in Jewish Social and Intellectual History, a series in which I am honored to have this book included.

Thanks to the efforts of Jennifer Hammer, associate editor of New York University Press, the Lucius Littauer Foundation generously provided a grant to cover the initial production costs of this volume. Their support is gratefully acknowledged.

I dedicate this book to my wife Judith Lewis and my children Sharon Sperling-Silber, Deborah Lewis Sperling, and Benjamin Lewis Sperling.

New York, New York
Shavuot, 1997

Abbreviations

The names of books of the Bible are abbreviated according to the system of the *Journal of Biblical Literature (JBL)*. Primary and secondary sources in Assyriology are abbreviated according to the system of the *Assyrian Dictionary of the Oriental Institute of the University of Chicago* (CAD).

AB	Anchor Bible
ABD	Freedman, David N., Gary Herion, et al., eds. *The Anchor Bible Dictionary*. New York: Doubleday, 1992.
AHw.	von Soden, Wolfram, ed. *Akkadisches Handwörterbuch*. Wiesbaden: Harrassowitz, 1965–1981.
ANET	Pritchard, James B., ed. *Ancient Near Eastern Texts Relating to the Old Testament*. 3d ed. with supplement. Princeton, N.J.: Princeton University Press, 1969.
ASOR	American Schools of Oriental Research
BA	*Biblical Archaeologist*
BAR	*Biblical Archaeologist Reader*
BASOR	*Bulletin of the American Schools of Oriental Research*
BO	*Bibliotheca Orientalis*
BZ	*Biblische Zeitschrift*
CAD	Gelb, Ignace, A. Leo Openheim, Benno Landsberger, and Erica Reiner, eds. *The Assyrian Dictionary of the Oriental Institute of*

	the University of Chicago. Chicago: Oriental Institute, 1956-.
CBQ	*Catholic Biblical Quarterly*
DDD	van der Toorn, Karel, Bob Becking, and Pieter W. van der Horst, eds. *Dictionary of Deities and Demons.* Leiden: Brill, 1995.
EncIslam	Gibb, Hamilton A. R., Johann Hendrik Kramers, Évariste Lévi-Provencal, and Joseph Schacht, eds. *Encyclopedia of Islam.* New ed. Leiden: Brill, 1960.
EncJud	Roth, Cecil, and Geoffrey Wigoder, eds. *Encyclopaedia Judaica.* Jerusalem: Keter Publishing, 1972.
EncRel	Eliade, Mircea, ed. *Encyclopedia of Religion.* New York: Macmillan, 1987.
ErIsr	*Eretz Israel*
HUCA	*Hebrew Union College Annual*
ICC	International Critical Commentary
IDB	Buttrick, George A., ed. *Interpreter's Dictionary of the Bible.* Nashville: Abingdon, 1962.
IEJ	*Israel Explanation Journal*
JANES	*Journal of the Ancient Near Eastern Society*
JAOS	*Journal of the American Oriental Society*
JBL	*Journal of Biblical Literature*
JCS	*Journal of Cuneiform Studies*
JEOL	*Jaarbericht van het Vooraziatisch-Egyptisch Genootschaap "Ex Oriente Lux"*
JJS	*Journal of Jewish Studies*
JNES	*Journal of Near Eastern Studies*
JQR	*Jewish Quarterly Review*
JSOT	*Journal for the Study of the Old Testament*
JSOTSup	Journal for the Study of the Old Testament Supplement Series
LCL	Loeb Classical Library
NEB	New English Bible. Oxford: Oxford University Press, 1961–1970.
NJV	New Jewish Publication Society Version
OCD	Hammond, Nicholas G. L., and Howard H.

	Scullard, eds. *Oxford Classical Dictionary*. 2d ed. New York: Oxford University Press, 1970.
OED	Burchfield, Robert W., ed. *Compact Edition of the Oxford English Dictionary*. New York: Oxford University Press, 1987.
OLA	Orientalia Lovaniensia Analecta
OTS	*Oudtestamentische Studiën*
PEQ	*Palestine Exploration Quarterly*
RA	*Revue d'Assyriologie et d'archéologie orientale*
RB	*Revue biblique*
REB	Revised English Bible with the Apocrypha. Oxford and Cambridge: Oxford University Press and Cambridge University Press, 1989.
RSV	Revised Standard Version
SAA	State Archives of Assyria
TDNT	Kittel, Gerhard, and Gerhard Friedrich, eds. *Theological Dictionary of the New Testament*. Grand Rapids, Mich.: Eerdmans, 1974–76.
TDOT	Botterweck, G. Johannes, and Helmer Ringgren, eds. *Theological Dictionary of the Old Testament*. Grand Rapids, Mich.: Eerdmans, 1974–.
UF	*Ugarit Forschungen*
VT	*Vetus Testamentum*
VTSup	*Vetus Testamentum Supplements*
Whiston, *Josephus*	Whiston, William, ed. *The Complete Works of Josephus*. Grand Rapids, Mich.: Kregel, 1981.
ZA	*Zeitschrift für Assyriologie*
ZDMG	*Zeitschrift der deutschen morgenländischen Gesellschaft*
ZDPV	*Zeitschrift des deutschen Palästina-Vereins*

Chronological Table

All dates are B.C.E. and approximate.

1750–1700:	Letters from Mari in Syria.
1700–1550:	Hyksos rule in Egypt.
1355–1325:	Letters from the Egyptian capital Akhetaten (el-Amarna) in Egypt.
1220:	Victory hymn of Pharaoh Merneptah containing the first historical attestation of a people "Israel."
1198–1166:	Reign of Rameses III, king of Egypt. Philistines begin to settle in Canaan.
1100:	Earliest settlement of Beersheba.
1020–1000:	Reign of Saul, first king of Israel.
1000–961:	Reign of David, king of Israel and founder of the dynasty of Judah.
961–922:	Reign of Solomon.
922:	Revolt of Jeroboam, the division of Israel into a northern kingdom Israel and a southern kingdom Judah.
922–901:	Reign of Jeroboam I, king of Israel, the northern kingdom.
840:	The Moabite stone written by King Mesha of Moab.
786–746:	Reign of Jeroboam II, king of Israel, the northern kingdom. Activity of prophets Amos and Hosea.
720:	Fall of Israel, the northern kingdom.
704–681:	Reign of Sennacherib, king of Assyria.
640–609:	Reign of Josiah, king of Judah.
622:	Religious reform of King Josiah.

587:        Fall of Judah to the Babylonians.
587–539:   Babylonian exile.
515:        Prophecies of Malachi begin.
539–333:   Jews under Persian rule. "Postexilic" period.

Introduction

In 1980 the Society of Biblical Literature, the oldest professional society of Bible scholars in the United States, marked its centennial with the publication of a volume of essays entitled *Humanizing America's Iconic Book*. By characterizing the Bible as an "iconic book," the editors called attention to the power exerted by the image of the Bible on American life, an image that has often overshadowed the very Bible it is supposed to represent. In his essay "America's Iconic Book," which provided the title for the entire volume, the prominent sociologist Martin Marty quoted a fascinating statement by the former U.S. president Grover Cleveland:[1]

> The Bible is good enough for me, just the old book under which I was brought up. I do not want notes or criticisms or explanations about authorship or origin or even cross-references. I do not need them or understand them, and they confuse me.

The man who served the United States as its twenty-second president and then again as its twenty-fourth did not wish to be confused by "notes or criticisms or explanations." He just wanted the "old book," the Bible as an icon, a symbol to be revered, rather than a collection of writings to be understood. The president's attitude was not unlike that of many Christians of his day or, for that matter, of many contemporary Christians and Jews.

For Jews, the first five books of the Bible hold a special iconic status. Neither the English term "Pentateuch," based on a Greek word for a case containing five scrolls, or the more descriptive "Five Books of Moses" adequately conveys the emotive content of the Hebrew word "Torah," which literally means "teaching," "instruction," and "law." On one hand, Jews use "Torah" in an extremely broad sense to refer to the whole body of sacred Jewish lore, rooted ultimately in the Bible but including the vast body of talmudic literature and its commentaries and supercommentaries. Indeed, students in the pre-critical Jewish academies known as *yeshivahs* routinely describe their studies as "Torah" when, in fact, their curriculum includes virtually no Pentateuch and certainly no other part of the Hebrew Bible. On the other hand, "Torah" is used narrowly to refer to the *sefer torah*, a ritual object found in every synagogue, a setting in which it functions mainly as an icon. The *sefer torah*, a copy of the Five Books of Moses, is written on a scroll, even though the far more convenient book format has been available for almost two millennia. It is written in ancient Jewish orthography without the vowel signs that have been available since late antiquity. As if this were not enough, the *sefer torah* continues to be handwritten with a quill pen on parchment in an age when many private homes have laser printers.

The iconic aspect of the *sefer torah* becomes most obvious in its liturgical use. Every synagogue houses the scroll in a "Holy Ark" at the front of the sanctuary where it, like the cross in a church, is designed to be visible to the entire congregation and, at appropriate points, to be veiled. In many congregations the *sefer torah* is paraded around the sanctuary before and after sections of it are publicly read. In recent years it has become common at bar and bat mitzvah ceremonies for the grandparents of the thirteen-year-old celebrants to pass the scroll ritually to their own children, the parents of the bar or bat mitzvah. They, in turn, hand the scroll to their son or daughter, the bar or bat mitzvah, who—thanks to more recent religious school experience—may be the only one in these three generations with the ability to read any part of the *sefer torah*.

Contemporary serious study of the Bible contrasts sharply with its iconic role. Scholarship sees its goal as "humanizing the iconic book." To make the "iconic book" intelligible, scholars attempt to comprehend the range of meanings that the writings comprising the Bible would have held for the ancient writers and their audiences. Not content with reverence for the Bible, scholars also try to understand it.

There are several reasons that this is not an easy task. First, we lack reliable texts. In contrast to the students of the literature of ancient

Babylonia and Assyria, for example, who regularly have the opportunity to study documents on the original clay tablets on which they were written, biblicists have only copies of copies of copies. Indeed, before the discovery of the Dead Sea scrolls at Qumran in 1947, we lacked texts of the Bible earlier than the tenth century of the Christian era. And even the biblical texts of the first century B.C.E discovered at Qumran among the Dead Sea scrolls are copies separated by centuries from their originals. Second, in translating ancient texts, the larger the surviving body of texts is, the greater the odds are of achieving linguistic precision. Once again, in contrast to the cuneiform literature of Babylonia and Assyria, the Hebrew Bible is a very small corpus. The fact that almost every Hebrew text newly unearthed from the biblical period contains a word or phrase not previously encountered shows that there are huge gaps in our understanding of biblical language. Third, we often cannot gauge the importance or the constituencies of the writers in their own time. That is, the prophet Ezekiel may have been listening to God, but we cannot tell whether anyone was listening to the prophet Ezekiel.

Another difficulty is the sparse documentary record of Israel's earliest period unearthed thus far by Middle Eastern archaeology. The earliest reference outside the Bible to a group called "Israel" comes from an Egyptian source written about 1220 B.C.E We then have to wait another four hundred years until King Omri of northern Israel turns up in a Moabite text and his son Ahab in an Assyrian document. The same ninth century provides us with a pictorial representation of King Jehu paying tribute to an Assyrian king. Thereafter the number of references to Israel, its rulers, and its political history in outside sources begins to get respectable. Of particular value are ancient Hebrew documents from Israel and Judah from the eighth to sixth centuries, as well as the archives of a fifth-century Jewish colony in Egypt. Although the amount of nonliterary material excavated from Israel of the biblical period has grown tremendously since 1967, we have few instances of the "ideal" archaeological situation in which an artifact is accompanied by a clear identification, on the order of "Palace of Solomon, King of Israel, built in his fifteenth year." The reader should be aware that we have no direct evidence of the existence of characters best known to readers of the Bible, including—but not limited to—Abraham, Sarah, Isaac, Jacob, Esau,

Moses, Joshua, Deborah, Gideon, David, Goliath, and Solomon.[2]

But these difficulties pale beside the most formidable obstacle to humanizing the iconic book: the fact that it is sacred Scripture. By treating the biblical books as sacred Scripture, Jews and Christians have distorted the Bible in two ways. First, they have made Scripture "relevant" by imbuing it with their ever-changing beliefs and values rather than concentrating on what a biblical text might have meant when it was written.

Second, they have tended to treat the Bible monolithically, making reference to what "the Bible says" rather than appreciating that biblical writers might differ, first, among themselves and, second, from later religious Jews and Christians. The very first chapter of the Bible provides an excellent example (Gen 1:26):

> Then God said, "Let *us* make a human in *our* image, after *our* likeness."

Generations of Jews were troubled by God's (Hebrew: *elohim*) use of the plural personal pronouns. If there was only one God in existence, to whom was *elohim* speaking when he said "us" and "our?" Jews who read the *Iliad* were not troubled by the grammatical plurality of the Greek gods because they did not expect Homer to be a monotheist. As monotheistic readers of the Bible, however, they expected Genesis to agree with the monotheistic teachings of Judaism. But in fact, if the author of Genesis 1 had wanted to score a point for monotheism, then Genesis 1:26 would have read differently; perhaps something like the following:

> Then God said, "Let me make a human, in my image, after my likeness."

We can say that it "would have read differently" because some of the Bible's authors really were monotheists. The anonymous prophet whom scholars call "Second Isaiah," or "Deutero-Isaiah," makes monotheistic statements all the time. Here for example, is Isaiah 46:9:

> I am Deity and there is no other. I am God and there is none like me.

This same monotheist also disapproved of the notion that humans are fashioned in the divine likeness as claimed by Genesis 1:26. In his own words:

To whom, then, will you liken God or what likeness compare with him? (Isa 40:18)

Over time, the monotheism of Deutero-Isaiah came to predominate in Judaism. Once monotheism had won the day, it seemed natural to read it into nonmonotheistic scriptural passages; somehow Genesis 1 should express the same sentiments as Deutero-Isaiah. But as the Israeli Bible scholar Moshe Weinfeld asserted, it would be difficult to find two more opposed theologies of creation in the Bible than in Deutero-Isaiah and Genesis 1.[3] In addition to their differences over the strictness of monotheism and God's utter incomparability, the two biblical writers differ over God's fundamental character. As anyone even remotely familiar with the Bible will recall, Genesis 1 repeatedly emphasizes that God's creation is completely good. In contrast, Deutero-Isaiah teaches (Isa 45:8) that the creator God is the "maker of good and creator of evil."

Only when we have dated these texts and set them in the historical period of their composition can we begin to understand the reason for the controversy between Genesis 1 and Deutero-Isaiah: The respective biblical writers were attempting to come to grips with the religious currents of their own time. We now know that both Genesis 1 and Deutero-Isaiah were composed during a period in which virtually all world Jewry was governed by the Persian Empire. The primary object of worship in the Zoroastrian religion of the Persian rulers was the divinity Ahuramazda, "the Lord Wisdom," author of the "good creation." In a royal inscription roughly contemporary with Deutero-Isaiah and Genesis 1, King Darius the Great (521–486 B.C.E) praises his god in the following words:[4]

> A great god is Ahuramazda
> Who created this earth
> Who created that heaven
> Who created humanity
> Who created happiness for humanity.

The Persians conceived of Ahuramazda as the one who created happiness for humanity. He was a wholly good god to whom evil or suffering was never attributed. In the dualistic system of Zoroastrianism, all evil comes from Ahuramazda's primeval foe, the archfiend

Angra Mainyu. Genesis 1 and Deutero-Isaiah, each in opposition to the other, provide a Jewish account of the creation in response to the dominant religious currents of their time. The writer of Genesis 1 accepted the Persian notion that the creation was completely good but maintained that its goodness was due to Elohim, the Hebrew divinity. In contrast, Deutero-Isaiah insisted that the Hebrew god was responsible for both good and evil, an ancient Israelite teaching that had always been taken for granted but now needed to be articulated in the most forceful terms, stressing the monism, or unity, of his god in order to counter the influences of Persian dualism on Jewish belief. When we understand the historical circumstances and the intellectual currents of the Persian period, we can begin to appreciate the significance of the controversy between Genesis 1 and Deutero-Isaiah.

The Original Torah is an attempt to appreciate the significance of the Torah by humanizing the icon, to figure out the agenda of the writers against the background of the times in which they wrote. But discovering those times and their agenda is harder for the Torah than for other parts of the Bible, for example, the Prophets or, in Hebrew, Nevi'im.

The narratives that comprise this second section of the Bible in the traditional Jewish sequence are set mostly in the land of Israel. Chronologically, Nevi'im covers a manageable period, from the beginnings of Israel through the demise of the Israelite states Israel and Judah. Many of the events referred to in Nevi'im are corroborated by extrabiblical sources, some of which name, and even describe, biblical locales and personalities. As a result, we are able to translate the chronology of the books in this section into our own terminology and to say, with confidence, that Nevi'im covers events between the late thirteenth century B.C.E and the fifth century. In contrast, the Torah, beginning with the creation, is set long before the rise of the Israelite states and, in the main, outside the land of Israel, in what are now Iraq, Syria, Turkey, Armenia, Egypt, and, especially, Jordan.

When it comes to chronology, our quests for specific detail are constantly frustrated: First, the writers of Torah literature often fail to provide the kind of information necessary for establishing a chronology for not only the Hebrew characters but also their gentile contemporaries. To cite the most notorious examples, we lack the name of the pharaoh whom Joseph served and the names of his successors, the pharaohs of the enslavement and the exodus. Second, we cannot rely on the Torah's internal relative chronology because the life spans attributed to the characters run the gamut from contradictory, through schematic, to fantastic. Nonetheless, we are now in a position unrivaled in the more than two millennia since the completion of the Torah to recover the historical circumstances of much of its composition. Thanks to archaeological and historical research, we can make some very confident statements about when particular traditions of the Torah originated. To illustrate, we cite a simple example from a rarely quoted verse, Numbers 34:25:

> Of the tribe of the Zebulunites a leader, Eli-zaphan, son of Parnach.

This verse is part of a list of tribal leaders designated by the Israelite god Yahweh to assist the successors of Moses in dividing the promised land among the tribes of Israel. The setting of the story is the Israelite encampment in the desert during the lifetime of Moses, who is supposed by some to have been a historical figure in the thirteenth century B.C.E But a more likely time for the composition of the verse is revealed by the name of Eli-zaphan's father. "Parnach" is the well-documented Persian name Farnaka, which would not have been known to the Israelites leaving Egypt and trekking through the desert in the thirteenth century B.C.E.[5] As far as we know, Jews did not come into contact with Persians until the sixth century B.C.E. Therefore, Numbers 34:25 can be dated no earlier. But although the detail reveals that Numbers 34:25 has no historical value for its setting, it does provide valuable information for the period of its composition. First, Numbers 34:25 is an early witness to the Jewish practice of adopting Persian names. Much more important, by using the clue provided by the date of the text, we may find that the chapter in which it is embedded does not have a thirteenth-century agenda but, instead, a sixth-century agenda. In fact, the chapter turns out to be part of a blueprint for Jewish political and religious organization under Persian rule.

The detail "Parnach" is emblematic of how we must approach the Torah if we want to understand it. As we explain in our first chapter, the archaeology of the past three decades demonstrates that the Torah's fundamental claims appear to be unhistorical. Israel was never enslaved in Egypt, so consequently there was no exodus and no trek through the desert. The people "Israel" did not come from outside the land, so there was no conquest. What this means is that the Torah does not have a thirteenth-century agenda, and certainly none that reaches further back into the second millennium. Instead, the stories in the Torah reflect religious-political concerns of the Israelite-Jewish communities between 1100 and 400 B.C.E We suggest in this book that to advance their own platforms, the authors of the Torah set their tales in times and places far removed from their own. In other words, the narratives of the Torah are best described as *allegories*, narratives contrived to signify a second order of meaning from what they present on the surface.

Allegorical interpretation of the Hebrew Bible is not new, of course. From antiquity to modern times, many readers of the Bible have construed the Garden of Eden, Noah's ark, and the Book of Jonah as allegories because these tales seemed incredible. The Song of Songs, in contrast, tended to be read as an allegory of spiritual love between God and the Jews or between Christ and the church because it was all too credible in its sexually explicit descriptions of human eroticism. Christian readers are used to reading the Hebrew Bible in the specialized allegorical form of "typology," so that events and persons in the Old Testament are seen to "prefigure" events and persons depicted in the New Testament. As St. Paul explained in his classic statement in 1 Corinthians 10:11,[6]

> All these things happened to them [the earlier Hebrews] symbolically [Greek: *typikos*] and were recorded as a warning for us.

To be sure, the method of allegorical interpretation applied in the following chapters differs significantly in its fundamental assumptions from those made by most earlier allegorical interpreters. I begin with the premise that the Bible is a completely human document to be studied with the same tools that have been accredited in the study of other ancient human documents. In light of what we now know, it is clear that Paul was wrong in accepting that "all these things happened" in the way his Jewish Bible said they did. Nonetheless, the method I advocate in this study would have been impossible without the work of earlier Jewish and Christian allegorizers.

First, like Philo, who allegorized the rivers of Paradise, I am compelled to read the Torah allegorically because it cannot be read historically. If "historical" means that an event occurred in the time and place in which it is set, then nothing in the Torah is historical. Whether these events are constructed as fantasies about talking snakes and donkeys or, given more naturalistic settings, as a war between King Sihon of Heshbon and an Israel led by Moses is irrelevant. Second, in reading the Torah allegorically to show that stories about such prehistoric figures as Abraham, Joseph, and Moses were written consciously to "prefigure" and allegorize personalities and institutions of the Israelite historical period, I find myself secularizing Paul: The things that supposedly "happened" were "symbolically recorded for us," that is, if we understand "us" to be the earliest and primary audiences of the writers of the Torah.

This book begins with a summary of the Torah's narrative. We then turn to a brief survey of recent research on the Torah's historicity and the early application of allegorical interpretation. The major part of the study is devoted to demonstrating how interpreting the Torah as an allegorical work can humanize this iconic book.

CHAPTER I

It Says in the Torah

I freely acknowledge that the fundamentals of my faith make it impossible for me to conclude that the Torah was not written by Moses, and surely not that it was written after the time of Moses. . . . We are obligated to accept with complete faith that everything written in the Torah is absolute truth.

—Rabbi David Z. Hoffmann (1843–1921)

The holy canonical Scriptures in their original text are the infallible truth and are free from every error. That is to say, in the sacred canonical Scriptures there is no untruth, no deceit, no error, not even a minor one, either in content or words, but each and everything presented to us in Scripture is absolutely true whether it pertains to doctrine, ethics, history, chronology, topography, or onomastics, and no ignorance, no lack of understanding, no forgetfulness or loss of memory can or should be ascribed to the amanuenses of the Holy Spirit in their writing of the Holy Scriptures.

—Johann Quenstadt (1617–1688)

The narrative contents of the first five books of the Bible, the Pentateuch, or the Torah in the Jewish tradition, are easily summarized, because the Torah provides a chronological account running from the creation until the eve of the settlement of ancient Israel in its promised land. This account is completed in the Book of Joshua.

The first book, Genesis, relates how God—known variously in Hebrew as Yahweh and Elohim—creates the heaven and earth and all that they encompass, what we now call *the world*. Dissatisfied with the behavior of his human and animal creatures, this same God obliterates most of them in a great flood, sparing only the righteous Noah and his family among the humans and enough animals to repopulate the earth after allowing for sufficient burned offerings by Noah. In the tenth generation from Noah through the line of Noah's son Shem, Yahweh begins calling on the ancestors of Israel to promise them the land of Canaan to which they have immigrated. In the meantime, however, famine in Canaan causes Israel's ancestors to move to Egypt, where God has thoughtfully brought one of their own to great power.

The second book, Exodus, continues the tale. Having grown to immense numbers in Egypt and become a great nation there, the Israelites are subjugated by the Egyptians for a considerable period, during which they are treated with extreme forms of brutality, including infanticide. God responds to their outcries by sending his plagues on the Egyptians and drowning their army in the sea. Guided by two pillars, one of fire and one of cloud, as well as by the man Moses, the Israelites travel through the desert to Mount Sinai where God descends from heaven and speaks to them. He takes the occasion to enter a covenant with them, which certifies Israel as his people, and to give them ten commandments and all manner of good laws. For their physical needs, God provides bread from heaven and water from stone, and for their religious requirements, he offers detailed instructions on the construction of a portable sanctuary where they may serve him. This same sanctuary also provides for atonement, which is frequently required, considering Israel's tendency to be ungrateful and inconstant, as witnessed in their worship of a golden calf.

In the third book, Leviticus, the Israelites are still in the desert, where they are given the needed instructions about who is to perform the divine service of the sanctuary and how and when to perform it. God's presence in the midst of the Israelites requires him to legislate detailed rules to maintain cultic and ethical purity. With divine foresight Yahweh also prepares them for life in the promised land, where they will need to know about such practical matters as land sales, slave purchase, accurate weights and measures, and the proper treatment of the less fortunate. But God's closeness to Israel also has its disadvantages. Israel is warned in no uncertain terms that its future tenure in the promised land is contingent on avoiding the "way of Egypt and the way of Canaan" and adhering to the divine statutes.

Numbers, the fourth book of the Torah, brings us to the second year of the wilderness journey, when a detailed census is undertaken.

The Israelites are organized into the military units essential to an army on the march. Again they are given numerous laws to govern them in the promised land. To aid Moses and advise the Israelites, God appoints seventy elders to whom he gives divine spirit, qualitatively equal to that of Moses himself. Despite Yahweh's manifold provisions, however, the ungrateful Israelites complain continually about the food and the leaders that they have been given.

The breaking point is reached when a party of twelve Israelite spies returns from a survey of the promised land. Ten members of the group report that Canaan is populated by gigantic warriors living in massively fortified cities, and so the promised land will be impossible to conquer. The Israelites, discouraged by the report and lacking faith in the divine ability to overcome the natives of Canaan, express the wish that they had died in Egypt or the desert. In punishment, God announces that they will get their wish, that the people will wander in the desert for forty years until the entire exodus generation has perished. Only their children will enter the promised land, along with faithful Joshua and Caleb, the two lone dissenters from the majority report. Although Moses and Aaron are not culpable in this matter, they fail to sanctify Yahweh publicly when he commands them to bring water out of a rock. As punishment, they too are barred from the land, sharing the fate of the rest of their generation. Despite these setbacks, God resumes his kindnesses by turning the curses of the seer Balaam into a blessing and by giving the people victory over two powerful Transjordanian rulers, Sihon and Og.

In the final book of the Torah, Deuteronomy, we find Moses on the east bank of the Jordan River (present-day Jordan) within sight of the promised land but barred from it. Moses takes the opportunity offered by his impending death to deliver a farewell programmatic speech, in which he revises many of the narratives and laws contained in the previous four books. God's covenant with Israel is presented elaborately, echoing the wondrous blessings for adherence and the severe penalties for violation found at the end of Leviticus. The book ends with the new generation of Israelites poised to enter the promised land, following the death of Moses, still in his prime at the age of 120.

The Book of Joshua completes the narrative. As Moses' legitimate successor, Joshua leads the Israelites across the Jordan. With God fighting for Israel, many of the formidable city-states of Canaan, including the great-walled Jericho, are destroyed. The land is pacified and distributed among the tribes, and Yahweh's covenant is renewed. According to the Book of Joshua, everything promised to the ancestors in the Torah is given to their descendants. Joshua dies contentedly at the age of 110. This, in brief, is the account from the creation to the Israelite settlement of the promised land as narrated in the traditional sequence of biblical books from Genesis through Joshua.[1]

How much of this narrative may be considered historical, that is, in reasonable agreement with actual events? Nowhere in the Torah, nor in the rest of the Hebrew Bible, is there a claim that the events related actually happened.[2] Nonetheless, for much of Jewish and Christian history, the factual nature of the Bible was not questioned. Such original thinkers as the Dutch Jewish philosopher Baruch Benedict Spinoza, the English political philosopher Thomas Hobbes, and the French thinker Voltaire became notorious for casting doubt on the historical reliability of the Bible, and they were not the first such questioners. Nonetheless, it is safe to say that until the nineteenth century, most Jewish and Christian believers would have agreed with David Hoffmann and Johann Quenstadt, quoted at the beginning of this chapter, that the Torah and the rest of the Bible are factual.

The books of the Torah are also known as the "Five Books of Moses," the biblical figure considered their author in Jewish sources as well as in the writings of the New Testament. Traditions of Mosaic authorship played a significant role in the Torah's credibility because God had, according to the Torah, spoken to Moses. Accordingly, challenges to Mosaic authorship called into question the very reliability of the Torah, even though it does not actually name Moses as its author. Indeed, no Old Testament source goes beyond what we find in Malachi, the book that concludes the prophetic section of the Hebrew Bible:

> Remember the Torah of Moses, my servant, to whom I gave at Horeb laws and statutes for all Israel. (Mal 3:22)

Although "laws and statutes" would accurately characterize much of Exodus through Deuteronomy, that characterization would be inapplicable to Genesis. Nehemiah, chapter 9, which summarizes the narratives of the Torah, including those of Genesis, and is probably our earliest witness to some of those narratives, says only:

> You decreed commands, statutes, and law for them [the Israelites] through Moses, your servant. (v. 14b)

Neither Malachi nor Nehemiah says anything about the Mosaic authorship of the Torah's narratives. Nonetheless, by the first century, Jews took for granted that Moses had written the whole Torah. The historian Josephus devotes books 1–2:9 of his *Antiquities of the Jews* to a paraphrase of Genesis, accompanied by frequent comments in which he repeatedly refers to Moses as the author of Genesis. Similarly, the Alexandrian Jewish philosopher Philo understood Genesis as the necessary introduction to the Mosaic laws:[3]

> Moses . . . introduced his laws with an admirable and most impressive exordium. . . . It consists of an account of the creation of the world implying that the world [*cosmos*] is in harmony with the law [*nomos*] and the law with the world.

Despite such early witnesses, as late as the thirteenth century, Jewish scholars still felt the need to prove the Mosaic authorship of the Torah from the Torah itself. Consider the following "proof" adduced by Moses Nahmanides (1194–1270) from Exodus 24:12:[4]

> He [God] told him: "Come up to me on the mountain and while you are there I will give you the tablets of stone and the Torah and the commandment that I have written to instruct them."—The "tablets of stone" means the ten commandments; "the commandment" means the entirety of positive and negative commandments. Therefore "and the Torah" includes the stories from the beginning of creation. . . . It is the clear and manifest truth that the entire Torah from the beginning of the Book of Genesis until "in the presence of all Israel" [the final verse of Deuteronomy] reached the ear of Moses from the mouth of God.

Nahmanides' "proof" of Mosaic authorship is far from "clear and manifest" and will convince only those who need no proof. The Torah itself claims Mosaic authorship only for some specific sections. Most of the narratives about Moses refer to him in the third person, including those describing the man as uniquely humble (Num 12:3) or dead, buried, and lamented (Deut 34:5–8).

The reason that the claim of the Torah's Mosaic authorship persisted as long as it did may be explained by subsequent religious developments. As we have seen, the author of Nehemiah 9 (fifth-fourth century B.C.E.) attributed all the laws and statutes of the Torah to Moses. Sometime before the first century C.E., the attribution had been imprecisely broadened to include the entire Torah. By the first century C.E., this imprecise attribution had become accepted, so that for such seminal figures as Philo, Josephus, Jesus, Paul, and Rabban Yohanan b. Zakkai, the Mosaic authorship of the Torah was a given, an article of faith to be passed on and defended. Employing this given as a foundation, classical Christianity and rabbinic Judaism constructed massive theological and institutional edifices that, in their different ways, claimed to be the fulfillment of the "Torah of Moses."

As long as these edifices remained intact, so did the notion of the Mosaic authorship of the Torah. By the late nineteenth century, however, historical forces had combined to undermine the solidarity and authority of institutional Christianity and Judaism, so that authorship of the Torah could be viewed as an academic question rather than an article of faith, not just in universities, but even in seminaries. In the earlier dogmatic context, internal contradictions and historical anachronisms had been viewed as challenges to the audience rather than as problems inherent in the Torah proper or in its attribution to the single author Moses.

In the newer academic context, these same contradictions and anachronisms were explained in a manner that attempted to do them justice. Simply put, the origin of the Torah seemed much better explained by the hypothesis that it was not the work of a single author but a compilation of literary "sources" or "documents," which had originated at different times and places, some of them written many centuries later than the events they related. But the documentary hypothesis, although infinitely superior to the earlier theologically grounded attempts to answer what were properly academic questions, raised fundamental issues of historicity. "Moses," personal secretary to God, had been an unimpeachable source for the actions of his remote ancestor Abraham. In contrast, the credibility of the anonymous composers of the reconstructed literary sources J, E, P, D, and R has generated enormous debate over the past century.[5]

Julius Wellhausen, the scholar most closely associated with the "documentary hypothesis," which identifies the hypothetical "sources" or "documents" from which the Torah was composed, insisted that the Pentateuchal narratives had historical value only for the period in which they were composed but not for the period of their setting.[6] In practice, this means that if a story told about Abraham and set (in modern chronology) in the eighteenth century B.C.E. contains an anachronism—the geographic name Chaldees, for example, which did not come into use until a millennium later—then the story can tell us nothing about the period of Abraham. After all, Wellhausen argued, even if a real patriarch named Abraham had existed in the second millennium B.C.E., no genuine record of him or his activities could have been preserved, because literacy had not yet reached Syria-Palestine.

When Wellhausen began writing, the potential of archaeology to contribute to biblical interpretation had barely been glimpsed. Accordingly, in 1878 there was nothing unusual about making an unverified statement about the extent of literacy in the second pre-Christian millennium. Wellhausen's pronouncement about the historicity of the Pentateuch's narratives thus went largely unchallenged for more than half a century and continued to dominate biblical studies even after his death in 1918. As we shall soon see, although Wellhausen was essentially correct in his estimation of the Torah's unhistorical character, the significant fallacies in his methods and working assumptions were exploited by the "biblical archaeology" movement.

Unlike Wellhausen, who reached his central conclusions about the literary "sources" or "documents" by closely reading the Bible and comparing and contrasting the agendas of the various texts, biblical archaeologists argued that the Bible could not be properly interpreted without being read in light of the archaeological data from the Middle East of the second and first millennia B.C.E. In 1888, ten years after the publication of Wellhausen's epochal *Prolegomena to the History of Ancient Israel*, the Amarna letters were unearthed in Egypt. These documents from the fourteenth century B.C.E. proved conclusively that there had been extensive scribal activity in second-millennium Syria-Palestine. Nonetheless, Wellhausen did not retract or modify his assertion about the absence of literacy.

Similarly, Wellhausen maintained that the names of the protagonists in the patriarchal stories were merely backward projections of tribal names from the historical Israelite period, rather than genuine ancient names. This claim, too, was refuted when the name Jacob showed up in an eighteenth-century B.C.E. site uncovered at Chagar Bazar in Iraq and in a fifteenth-century Egyptian list compiled by King Thutmosis III of Egypt. Similarly, the name Ishmael was used in eighteenth-century texts from Mari in Syria, and the personal name Israel was found in thirteenth-century B.C.E. texts from Ugarit, also in Syria. These and other flaws in Wellhausen's reconstruction stemmed from viewing the Bible in isolation from the broader world that ancient Israel had inhabited, an isolation that became increasingly difficult to justify.[7]

Between the two world wars, Middle Eastern archaeology continued to expand, bringing the second pre-Christian millennium into the light of history and nailing the lid on the coffin of Wellhausen's assumptions about literacy. Thousands of written documents from Syria-Palestine provided incontrovertible evidence that ancient traditions could have been written down and preserved, and many of these bore directly on the Bible. To cite a well-known example, scholars had long puzzled over the following passage in Ezekiel:

> If I send a pestilence into that land and pour out my wrath upon it with blood, to cut off humans and animals from it; even if Noah, Daniel, and Job were in it, as I live, says the God Yahweh, they would save neither son nor daughter; they would save only their own lives by their righteousness. (Ezek 14:19–21)

The structure of the passage is clear enough. Ezekiel, the prophet, is attempting to shock his audience into realizing that they can no longer be guided by past precedent. In ancient times, perhaps, out of consideration for their righteous fathers, a punishing god might have spared persons with little merit of their own. But that, says the prophet, is no longer true for his own time. If Noah, Daniel, and Job were alive today, their righteousness would enable them to survive divine wrath, but even they would be unable to save their own children. The inclusion of Noah made sense in this list because the hero of the Great Flood had managed to secure passage for his children on the ark. Similarly, Job's children were restored along with his fortunes in the book's final chapter.

What troubled scholars was the example of Daniel. If Ezekiel was referring to the Daniel of lion's den fame, that hero would have been, according to inner biblical chronology, a younger contemporary of Ezekiel himself, not a figure of the ancient past. In addition, the Book of Daniel says nothing about the hero's family. The solution was provided in 1929 by the accidental discovery of Ugarit, a city in ancient Syria that had lain buried since the time of its destruction in about 1200 B.C.E. One of the significant finds at Ugarit was an epic about a righteous man named Daniel, who resurrected his beloved son after the boy had been unjustly slain by the agent of a vengeful goddess. Clearly, it was this figure Daniel to whom Ezekiel was referring, not the Daniel of the biblical book.[8] The fact that the prophet refers to the tale as a pedagogical example indicates that he expected his audience to be familiar with the story. Although we do not know how the story reached Ezekiel at least seven centuries after the fall of Ugarit, we can be certain that it did.

If an ancient Syrian legend could be known by a prophet and his audience in the sixth century B.C.E., then it was no longer impossible for an Israelite writer in the tenth or ninth century B.C.E. to have known similarly ancient traditions regarding a figure of the second millennium named Abraham. The "biblical archaeology" movement, whose most renowned figures were W. F. Albright and G. E. Wright in the United States and Yigael Yadin in Israel, enthusiastically attempted to synthesize with the Torah's traditions the data concerning the second millennium freshly recovered from the Middle East. In contrast to some scholars who employed polemically the results of archaeology to attack the credibility of the Bible,[9] biblical archaeologists began with a "positive" attitude, giving the historicity and accuracy of biblical tradition the benefit of the doubt. The reader should be aware, however, that the positive attitude, like the negative, was not free of ideological motivation, in light of[10]

> the simple fact that the ancient Near Eastern sources from the 3rd and 2nd millennia B.C. do not contain a single direct reference to any of the features mentioned in the Old Testament narrative. There is not a single reference to Abraham the Patriarch, or to Joseph and his brothers in Egypt, or to Moses and the Exodus, or to the conquest of Canaan.

Second, the biblical archaeologists tended to equate antiquity with historicity. That is, the older a tradition was, the stronger its claims to be historical were. Within this framework, biblical archaeologists used archaeology to provide historical validation for most of the Torah's traditions. Beginning with a patriarchal age in the early second millennium, archaeological validation was sought for the enslavement in Egypt, the Exodus, the desert wanderings, and the conquest period. If the major historical claims of the Bible were demonstrated archaeologically, then inner biblical inconsistencies and contradictions, as well as exaggerated numbers and incredible wonder tales, would become minor annoyances at worst. The following is a characteristic evaluation of Genesis by William Foxwell Albright:[11]

> As a whole the picture in Genesis is historical, and there is no reason to doubt the general accuracy of the biographical details and the sketches of personality which make the patriarchs come alive with a vividness unknown to a single extra biblical character in the whole vast literature of the ancient Near East.

Although the movement never flourished in Europe, biblical archaeology dominated biblical studies in Palestine (later Israel) and the United States from the mid-1930s until the early 1970s, for somewhat different reasons.[12] In Israel, nationalistic pride was a primary motivation. Jewish biblicists of the early twentieth century were mostly secularists, for whom the Bible was a national book. Living in the country where the Bible had its origin, Israeli scholars viewed biblical history as the beginning of Jewish history. Having witnessed the destruction of European Jewry, the Israelis were antipathetic to much of European biblical scholarship. German scholarship, in particular, had tended to combine a late dating for much of Torah literature with gratuitous statements about the degenerate nature of "Jewish" practices advocated or described in late biblical works, and so it could be accurately faulted on the charge of anti-Judaism or, worse, anti-Semitism.[13]

In the United States, in contrast, the enthusiasm for biblical archaeology was often religiously motivated. The movement did not develop roots among fundamentalist Christians and Orthodox Jews because, on one hand, for them the Bible needed no archaeological validation and, on the other hand, "general accuracy" was insufficient. Biblical archaeology held particular sway among religious moderates who could not in good conscience reject either the credibility of the Bible or scientific method, and it seemed for a while that they could have both.

A good example of how biblical archaeology could be practiced successfully is the story of Sennacherib's invasion of Judah. Chapters 18 and 19 of 2 Kings relate that Sennacherib, king of Assyria (704–681 B.C.E.), had besieged Jerusalem but that the city was miraculously delivered:

> That very night the angel of the Lord set out and struck down 185,000 in the camp of the Assyrians; when morning dawned, they were all dead bodies. Then King Sennacherib of Assyria left, went home, and lived at Nineveh. (2Kgs 19:35–36)

Sennacherib's own royal annals describe in great detail the siege of Jerusalem. He tells of the huge amounts of booty he took and the men and women he took captive. He even boasts that he shut up King Hezekiah in Jerusalem like a bird in a cage. What scholars have observed is the absence of one particular detail: The formula "I took that city"—which was always used in the royal Assyrian annals to describe the fall of a city to the Assyrians—is not found in Sennacherib's account of the siege of Jerusalem. Apparently the Assyrian king's grandiose description of triumph deliberately glossed over the failure of the king and his troops to take the city. A comparison of the biblical and Assyrian accounts may be said to confirm the "general accuracy" of 2 Kings 18–19. Perhaps an angel of the Lord did not slay the Assyrian troops (2Kgs 19:35), but "some remarkable deliverance must be assumed,"[14] and the biblical account that Jerusalem was not taken may be characterized as "essentially historical."

The case of the siege of Jerusalem was a clear demonstration of the validity of evaluating biblical claims in light of archaeology. But biblical archaeology made bolder claims for its methods, and it was these that ultimately discredited the movement.[15] When archaeological data contradicted biblical information, some scholars did not shrink from adjusting a detail or two on either the biblical or the archaeological side to maintain the "general accuracy" of the biblical account. For example, Genesis 21:32–34 tells us of dealings between Abraham and the Philistines (see chap. 4):

> When they had made a covenant at Beersheba, Abimelech, with Phicol,

the commander of his army, left and returned to the land of the Philistines. Abraham planted a tamarisk tree in Beersheba and called there on the name of Yahweh, the Everlasting God. And Abraham sojourned many days in the land of the Philistines.

In a recent commentary on Genesis, Nahum Sarna repeats a classic argument from the heyday of biblical archaeology. Sarna first observes that[16]

the earliest historical reference to them [the Philistines] so far comes from the time of Ramses III . . . among a group of . . . "sea peoples" who invaded the Levant from the Cretan-Mycenaean area at the beginning of the twelfth century. . . . Groups of the *peleset* settled at points along the coast of Canaan.

The obvious conclusion from Sarna's observation seems to be that any story about Abraham and Philistines must have been composed after the Philistines reached Canaan, that is, after the time of Ramses III, no earlier than 1100 B.C.E. But that conclusion would undermine the position of the classical school of biblical archaeology, that Abraham lived in the early second millennium B.C.E., a theory to which Sarna still appears to subscribe. Rather than acknowledge the obvious, Sarna draws a different inference:

Accordingly, the "Philistines" of patriarchal times may have belonged to a much earlier, minor wave of Aegean invaders . . . long before the large-scale invasions.

In other words, Sarna's placement of the biblical narrative in the second millennium leads him to conjecture a "minor wave of Aegean invaders," for which there is no warrant other than his commitment to a date for Abraham in the early second millennium.

Even more remarkable are the assertions of some scholars that many of the contradictions and duplications discovered by critics could be traced to the authors of the documentary sources who had faithfully preserved ancient traditions that they themselves no longer understood. The wife-sister tales of Genesis are an example of this last tenet of biblical archaeology. Genesis 12, 20, and 26 offer different versions of the same story: A patriarch traveling abroad with his wife attempts to conceal their marital status by claiming that the woman in question is his sister. In each case, the ruse is only partly successful because the wife is coveted by a foreign king, and the resulting complications call into question the moral and ethical character of the ancestors of Israel. Classical criticism had been content to attribute the repetitions to a compiler who had not bothered to harmonize or edit his original "sources."

E. A. Speiser, an Assyriologist with broad archaeological experience, went further and attempted to recover the original tale behind the repetitious sources. He claimed that the thrice-told tale had originated in the mid-second millennium B.C.E. According to Speiser, contracts found at ancient Nuzi in Iraq documented that a man might marry a woman and simultaneously adopt her as his legal sister. Such wife-sister marriages, Speiser continued, were a perquisite of the upper classes. Being aristocrats concerned about the purity of their lineage, the biblical patriarchs who lived in the second millennium B.C.E. followed the Nuzian practice and took their wives as legal "sisters."

Succeeding generations of Israelites took care to preserve details about these distinguished families from which they had sprung. But as their descendants continued to retell the tales of the patriarchs far from their time and place of origin, the original significance of wife-sister marriage was forgotten. Because no author of the Torah had access to the social setting of the original story, each one attempted to explain it in a different way. And this is why the present Torah offers three accounts of this same story.[17]

Speiser's reading of the wife-sister stories was an ingenious attempt to demonstrate the compatibility of archaeology, source criticism, and biblical veracity. Criticism demonstrated how the sources diverged with respect to detail, and archaeology showed "what really happened." The fact that the writers of the Torah preserved traditions they no longer completely understood was a testimony to their trustworthiness and the "general accuracy" of the preserved traditions. But as scholars later demonstrated, Speiser's analysis, once a parade example of the application of biblical archaeology, was hopelessly misguided.[18]

As it turned out, there was no evidence from the documents cited by Speiser that a woman could be simultaneously a wife and a sister. Instead, what these documents showed was a case in which a woman had been contracted for a marriage. When the marriage failed to materialize, the same woman was adopted as a "sister" by the man who no longer wished to take her as a wife. Especially damaging to Speiser's reading was the discovery that women adopted as sisters came from the lower classes, not from the upper class, as Speiser maintained. By adopting these lower-class women, their "brothers" gained the right to sell them as slaves or to derive financial profit from arranging their marriages to other parties. Thus Speiser had rewritten not only the biblical account but the extrabiblical documents as well. In attempting to interpret the wife-sister stories of Genesis in light of the second-millennium documents, he did justice to neither.[19]

The past two decades have given biblical archaeology a bad reputation in some circles. But in fact, this bad reputation is undeserved. It is not a mistake to apply archaeology to the study of the Bible. Rather, the mistake is in expecting archaeology to verify the biblical accounts. In fact, the examination of the Torah in light of archaeology has performed a far greater service than demonstrating "general accuracy." The systematic excavation of Israel since 1967 has shown that the Torah's account of the period preceding the rise of the first Israelite commonwealth is completely unhistorical. Whereas the Torah devotes more than four books to the proposition that the Israelites came to Canaan after having been subjugated in Egypt for generations, there is no archaeological evidence in Egyptian sources that any elements of later Israel were ever in Egypt. In addition, a prolonged Egyptian stay should have left Egyptian elements in the material culture of the early Israelite settlements in Palestine, but there are none.[20]

As for the desert-wandering tradition, we would expect a large transient group to have left some indication of its desert presence. Instead, extensive exploration of the entire Sinai has found "virtually no Middle Bronze–Late Bronze presence in the central or southern Sinai." Likewise, "the notion of large-scale 13th-12th century Israelite military campaigns in Southern Transjordan, or even of peaceful settlement there, is no longer tenable; the occupational history of the region simply does not fit." What appears most likely from the available archaeological evidence is that the nucleus of Israel was "derived from the local Late Bronze culture of Canaan through relatively normal processes." The continuity of material culture discovered by archaeologists is in complete accord with the linguistic continuity of biblical Hebrew and the Canaanite dialects reflected in the Amarna letters of the fourteenth century B.C.E.[21]

If history is understood as tied to time and place, the only conclusion can be that the Pentateuch is not history. The American scholar Baruch Halpern argues that the biblical writers should be considered historians because they thought they were writing history.[22] With only a few exceptions, however, the Torah is not even historiographical in any way that the term *historiography* may be understood, unless we mean "historiographic appearance," fiction composed to look like history, as in a historical novel. Inasmuch as archaeology has shown that the Pentateuch cannot be characterized as a "historical" document, we must seek a more accurate characterization.[23]

CHAPTER 2

History and Allegory

"Literal" ether historial understondyng techith what thing is don; alle-
gorik techith what we owen for to bileue.

—John Wyclif (1388)

We saw in the previous chapter that the Torah is unhistorical, a finding that has led some scholars to conclude that the work has no historical value. One of the most articulate exponents of this conclusion
is Edmund Leach:[1]

> If we ignore the rather small number of named biblical characters
> whose existence is fully vouched for by independent evidence . . . I re-
> gard *all* [emphasis in original] the personalities of biblical narrative
> both in the Old Testament and in the New as wholly fictional. . . . The
> view that I adopt—that the biblical narrative is a myth, a sacred tale—
> implies that I treat the entire text as synchronic . . . there is no devel-
> opment, only dialectical inversion.

Leach's statement is not without irony. On one hand, as a social
anthropologist, Leach regards all the personalities of both Testaments
as wholly fictional, a sentiment that should horrify many believing
Christians and Jews. At the same time, he shares a fundamental article of faith with the true believer, that the entire text is synchronic,
without development, and thus not subject to the categories of historical analysis. In my opinion, the fact that the Torah is unhistorical
does not mean that it may not be used as a source of significant historical information. It is, rather, a question of how to extract the historical information. As we saw, the primary failure of the biblical archaeology movement was not in the application of archaeology to the

Bible but in the expectation that archaeology would prove the Bible to be "essentially historical."

In this book, I maintain that the most productive method of interpreting the Torah is to regard it as historical and political allegory. By comparing the Torah with other parts of the Bible and by enlisting the data provided by archaeological sources, written and unwritten, I argue that the stories about the wholly fictitious characters Abraham, Jacob, Joseph, Aaron, and Moses allude to characters like Saul, David, and Jeroboam, who are more firmly anchored in history. Similarly, I contend that the theological constructs "Covenant" and "God" are to be understood as allegorical reflections of historical and political realities. Because over the course of two millennia, the Old Testament has often been read allegorically, it is useful to describe some earlier readings and then to illustrate how the present reading is both dependent on and divergent from its predecessors.[2]

The word *allegory* is derived from the Greek *allēgorein*, "to speak so as to imply other than what is said." As applied to a literary work,

> allegory is a narrative in which the agents and the action, and sometimes the setting as well, are contrived not only to make sense in themselves, but also to signify a second correlated order of things, concepts or events.[3]

For clarity, we will use *allegorizing* when we speak of the activity of readers who interpret a work as an allegory without claiming that the work was composed as an allegory; this is what one scholar calls "imposed allegory." We will use *allegoresis* when we describe the activity of readers who claim that a particular literary work was in fact written as an allegory. Both activities are extremely ancient. First applied in ancient Greece to the poems of Homer and Hesiod, allegoresis was essentially of two kinds. *Positive* or *philosophical allegoresis* sought support for philosophical theories in the writings of the venerated poets of antiquity. *Grammatical* or *negative allegoresis* sought to defend the same ancient poets from charges that their work was offensive or unreasonable. By the late fifth century B.C.E., philosophers were systematically finding *hyponoiai*, "hidden meanings," in the great poets.[4]

Despite the antiquity of the allegorical method, the verb itself, *allēgorein*, "to speak allegorically" and "to explain allegorically," is late Greek. Although not found in the Septuagint (the Jewish translation of the Bible into Greek), the word is found in works by three Jewish writers of the first century; Philo of Alexandria (ca. 20 B.C.E.–C.E. 50), Flavius Josephus (37– ca. C.E. 100), and Paul (d. ca. C.E. 64). In a well-known New Testament passage (Gal 4:24), Paul disputes those who wish to be under the law. In Paul's terminology, the Greek *nomos*, which we translate as "law," refers to both the written Torah and the entire body of Jewish law and practice that had evolved by Paul's time:[5]

> It is written there [in the law] that Abraham had two sons, the one by a slave-girl, the other by a free-born woman. The slave-girl's son was born according to flesh but the one of the free woman through God's promise, which things are allegorical utterances [Greek: *allēgoroumena*].

Paul then explains the allegory of the slave girl and the free woman in order to make a theological argument against those Christians who are drawn to the observance of Jewish law:[6]

> The two stand for two covenants, the one from Mount Sinai, which is Hagar, has children born into slavery. Now this Hagar . . . corresponds to the present Jerusalem, for she and her children are in slavery. But the Jerusalem above is the free woman, and she is *our* [emphasis added] mother.

The slave girl, Hagar, stands for the first covenant, the one made at Sinai, which bound Israel to the law. According to that same law, because Hagar (that is, Sinai) is a gentile slave, her children are slaves from birth.[7] The law-observing Jews in the Jerusalem of Paul's day are children of the covenant of Sinai and thus are children of Hagar.[8] As children of Sinai/Hagar, they are in slavery to the law. By implication, the free woman allegorically represents the second covenant, what Paul calls elsewhere (2Cor 3:6) the "new covenant." Those who enter this covenant are free from the law and are justified by faith. As free persons, they are children of the free woman, the "Jerusalem above," an eschatological city, presumably located in the "kingdom of God" (Gal 5:21). Paul then turns to Isaiah 54:3, which is figurative by all accounts, and applies this verse to his allegorical reading of the Genesis narrative about Abraham's family:

> For Scripture says: "Rejoice, O barren woman who never bore a child; break into a shout of joy, you who have never been in labor; for the deserted wife will have more children than she who lives with her husband."

The free woman of Genesis is identified with the barren woman of Isaiah 54:3.[9] Sarah, who had been barren and who was deserted when Abraham left her bed for Hagar the slave girl, "will have more children than she who lives with her husband" (Isa 54:3). From Paul's associative reading of Genesis and Isaiah, Paul's audience may be assured of what will happen in the future: First, Christians, represented by the children of the free woman/deserted wife, will be more populous than Jews, represented by the slave girl/she who lives with her husband. Second, Christians who by faith live in Christ and forsake the Law, will outnumber Jews, who live by the Law and not by faith in Christ. Third, Christians who forsake the Law will outnumber those Christians who insist on living by the Law.

But more is involved than the numerical superiority of those justified by faith over those who keep the law:

> Now we, brothers, like Isaac, are children of the promise. But just as then the one born according to the flesh persecuted the one of the spirit, so also now. But what does Scripture say? "Drive out the slave girl and her son, for the son of the slave girl shall by no means share the inheritance with the son of the free woman."

Allegorically read, Genesis 21 predicts the ultimate expulsion of the Jews and their supersession by the Christians. In Abraham's time, Ishmael, the son born according to flesh, persecuted Isaac, the son born according to the promise of the spirit.[10] In the time of Paul and his audience, Jews persecuted Christians.[11] In the future, the reverse will be true, and Christians will persecute Jews; Genesis 21:10 commands that the slave woman and her son, who will not share in the inheritance with the son of the free woman, are to be driven out.[12] Like the Jews, Christians (whether or not Jews by birth) who follow the law will not share in the inheritance, because in seeking their justification through the law (Gal 5:4), they will have become obligated to all of it and therefore are slaves: (slave) children of the flesh rather than (free) children of the spirit.

Although mentioned specifically in the New Testament only in the preceding passage from Galatians, allegory had significant value to Christian interpreters of the Old Testament. Sometimes the allegorical meaning could coexist with the literal. At other times the allegorical interpretation was required to displace the literal. And sometimes, when crucial doctrines were at stake, one had to be careful not to displace the literal by the allegorical.[13]

Paul and the writers of what would become the canonical gospels taught that Jesus was the messianic savior whose coming had been foretold in the Hebrew Scriptures. This meant that Christians should be able to support their faith in Christ by appealing to the plain sense of scriptural "messianic" texts. Matthew 22:41–46 is a good example:

> Turning to the assembled Pharisees, Jesus asked them, "What is your opinion about the Messiah? Whose son is he?" "The son of David," they replied. "How then is it," he asked, "that David by inspiration calls him 'LORD'? For he says [Ps 110:1], 'The LORD said to my LORD, "Sit at my right hand until I put your enemies under your feet".' If David calls him 'LORD,' how can he be David's son?" Not a man could answer him in reply, and from that day forward no one dared ask him another question.

This selection assumes that Jesus and the Pharisees share a hope in the coming of the Messiah as well as a belief in the divine inspiration of Scripture, in which the Messiah's coming is foretold. Likewise, both Jesus and the Pharisees require David, whom Psalm 110 identifies as its author, to be a historical character. Finally, the author of the pericope assumes that both parties believe that Psalm 110 contains information about the identity of the Messiah. Given these shared premises, the Christian writer can portray his Jesus as besting the Pharisees on their own terms, as follows: Psalm 110 of Scripture was written by David, the inspired king of Israel. David quotes the word of the LORD to David's LORD in which David's LORD is invited by the LORD to sit at his right hand. Whoever David's LORD is, he cannot be David's son, because it would have been unseemly for David to call his own son "LORD."

In a similar vein, Paul needed to use Old Testament "history" to support some of his own theological arguments. If Abraham was the "forefather of us according to flesh" (Rom 4:1) and the paradigm of salvation through faith (Rom 4–5; Gal 3:6–18, 29), then Abraham required fleshly existence. Accordingly, even Paul's allegorical exegesis in Galatians 4 does not deny the historical existence of Hagar, the freeborn wife, or the two sons, for that could lead to the denial of Abraham's historicity.[14]

Yet at the same time that Paul, a Jew by birth and education, required the Hebrew scriptures to demonstrate that salvation lay in faith in the crucified and risen Christ, he also needed to show that the laws found in those selfsame scriptures were no longer binding on Christians. Allegoresis was one effective approach, even when the word *allegory* was not specified:

> Your self-satisfaction ill becomes you. Have you never heard the saying, "A little leaven leavens all the dough?" The old leaven of corruption is working among you. Purge it out and then you will be bread of a new baking. As Christians you are unleavened Passover bread; for indeed our Passover has begun; the sacrifice is offered—Christ himself. So we who observe the festival must not use the old leaven, the leaven of corruption and wickedness, but only the unleavened bread which is sincerity and truth. (1Cor 5:6–8)

This passage follows Paul's denunciation of certain sexual practices among members of the Corinthian church (1Cor 5:1–5) and immediately precedes his condemnation of swindlers, idolaters, slanderers, and drunkards in that same community. In Paul's allegorical reading, the leaven that is to be purged stands for corruption and wickedness. The unleavened bread has two related allegorical meanings; the Christian who has purged himself of corruption and the qualities of sincerity and truth.

Just as the biblical Passover began with the sacrifice of a special Passover offering, so the sacrifice of Christ begins the new festival ("our Passover") or, what Paul calls elsewhere, the "way of life in Christ" (1Cor 4:17). Although Paul's remarks are not directly addressed to the question of whether Christians should eat only unleavened bread on Passover, his allegorical interpretation has the potential to nullify the literal Old Testament prohibition against eating real leaven on Passover.

Among the early church fathers, Origen is especially well known for his allegorical readings. Of particular interest to contemporary readers is Origen's attempt to show that certain scriptural pericopes demand an allegorical, rather than a literal, interpretation. Numbers 12, says Origen, is such a chapter.

Miriam and Aaron spoke against Moses because of the Cushite woman whom he had married, for he had married a Cushite woman; and they said, "Has Yahweh indeed spoken only through Moses? Has he not spoken through us also?" And Yahweh heard it. Now the man Moses was very meek, more than all men that were on the face of the earth.

Origen observes that the narrative opens with Miriam and Aaron defaming Moses for having married a Cushite woman. Rather than pursuing that theme, however, verse 2 immediately shifts to an account of Miriam and Aaron's boast that they, like their brother Moses, have been conduits of the divine word. Origen argues that is impossible to interpret Scripture literally in this instance. If that were the case, verse 2 would have continued the criticism by suggesting that Moses take instead an Israelite wife, preferably a Levite. The fact that verse 2 shifts to an attack on the uniqueness of Moses as a prophet impels the reader to allegoresis. That is, Moses is the "spiritual law" (*spiritalis lex*), and the Cushite woman, the gentile church. Miriam is the superseded Jewish nation and Aaron the priesthood according to the flesh.[15]

Jewish scholars also dealt with the problems raised by allegoresis. An ancient Jewish tradition later adopted by Christians, that the Song of Songs was allegorical, was universally accepted because it appeared more seemly for a book of the Bible to speak metaphorically of God's love for his people than literally and explicitly of human eroticism. But allegoresis could go too far. Moses Maimonides (1135–1204) was accused by his opponents of treating all of Scripture as a philosophical allegory, although he himself avoided that characterization. Other scholars were much more explicit. In his elaboration of a talmudic statement (Babylonian Talmud Baba Batra, 15a) that Job had never existed in reality, Zerahiah of Barcelona (late thirteenth century) argued, as had Origen, that in certain cases, an allegorical reading was demanded because from its opening verse, the text demonstrated that it was not to be taken literally:[16]

There was once a man in the land of *Uz* whose name was *Job*. That man was blameless and upright, one who feared God and turned away from evil.

Zerahiah pointed to the transparency of the name of Job's homeland, Uz-Land, which means "land of counsel." Indeed, the very name Job (Hebrew: *Iyyob*) was obviously related to *'ebah* (the consonantal Hebrew skeleton of both words is *'yb*), "antagonism and hatred," most appropriate to one antagonized by God and treated hatefully by him.[17]

Although readers of the Bible from Paul and Philo onward had sought allegorical meanings in Scripture, most had assumed that the allegorical meaning could coexist with the literal and the historical. Those in the faith communities who had their doubts tended to express them in subdued fashion. In contrast, Zerahiah's critique of the historicity of one biblical book is unique in its articulate character:[18]

> If our stated proofs that Job is an allegory are insufficient for the party of fools, we will continue with a further proof that this book was composed as an allegory. For should you say that Job and his companions did indeed exist, one might come along and ask you how the sequence of respondents was composed. For were you to say that these men all assembled and each one spoke his words and transcribed them in his own idiom; and then afterward Elihu spoke his words and transcribed them, and then God came afterward and spoke them, a questioner might respond and ask further: "Then who incorporated their words in a single volume once they had spoken their words?" And should you say that our master Moses found their words written but disjointed and scattered, and collected them and wrote them down—where did he find God's words, and who collected them from God's mouth and wrote them down?

Zerahiah also provided a modernist argument from the standpoint of style, noting that

> if Job and his companions were . . . not allegorical, individual differences of speech should have appeared among them. . . . Job is stylistically uniform from start to finish.

The implications of Zerahiah's allegoresis of Job were not lost on Joseph ibn Kaspi (1279–1340), who noted that by using the same method, one could read the entire Bible as allegory and deny its historicity:[19]

> I am amazed that both ancient and modern scholars have doubted [the historicity of Job simply because it lacks precise chronological and geographic data]. For what is the difference between "There was a man in the land of Uz etc." [Job 1:1] and "There was a certain man from Haramathaim-Zophim, whose name was Elkanah" [1Sam 1:1] and the

entire story about Eli, Samuel, and others? Note, as well, "It was in the days that the judges judged" [Ruth 1:1]; and of "It was in the days of Ahasuerus?" [Est 1:1]. And note that we have written in the Torah: "These are the generations of Noah . . . Noah had three sons" [Gen 6:9–10] and the entire story of the deluge and the ark. For if we characterize the tale of Job and his companions as an allegory written by a sage to instill wisdom and faith in the hearts of readers, the same might be said of the rest. If so, we have no Torah or Prophets or Sacred Writings of any kind. So what concern is it of ours if some of our blessed predecessors did not know when Job lived or where?

On one hand, Kaspi's antipathy to allegoresis of the Bible is consistent with his dictum that "all the words of the Torah and the remainder of the Bible are, in my opinion, to be accepted in their own meaning, like the books on logic and nature of Aristotle."[20] On the other hand, in his commentary on Maimonides, Kaspi wrote a far more revealing paragraph about his understanding of the Bible:[21]

> In order that the masses should not think that the prophets made up what they said and that these words were not from God, the prophets permitted themselves to lie by saying: "The Lord said to Moses," or "The Lord said to me" and *all such similar phrases* [emphasis added]. As the physicians have said: "It is better to amputate one infected finger than to let the entire body grow ill or die."

The medievalist Leonard Kravitz observes that the second statement is completely consistent with Kaspi's overall philosophy.[22] Kaspi, a thorough rationalist, believed that the people whom the Bible calls "prophets" were, in reality, philosophers. The words of these prophets were true because they expressed the truths of philosophy. These same philosophical words of the prophets were divine in origin because, for Kaspi, God was identical with the Aristotelian Active Intellect. But the biblical prophets did not reveal the true source of their knowledge, that is, philosophy, because the masses could not understand that philosophy was divine knowledge. Instead, the prophets lied and said that God had "spoken" to them, because this was a claim that the masses could accept. For a prophet to lie was like a surgeon amputating an infected finger. The amputation enabled the patient, the body of Israel, to live. Without prophecy, that is, philosophy, the entire body of Israel would have become ill and died. Kaspi's description of prophetic strategy is, in fact, a description of his own philosophical strategy. His statement that "all the words of the Torah are to be accepted in their own meaning" is for "the masses," whom he knows to be incapable of accepting philosophical truth.

The details of Kaspi's critique of Zerahiah demonstrate his concern about the likely reactions of the "masses." Kravitz observes that it was common for medieval scholars to vilify unpopular opinions with which they secretly agreed. By condemning these opinions without refuting their substance, these same scholars could give voice to even more unpopular opinions of their own, and that is just what Kaspi did here. Let us look closely at what Kaspi buried in the core of his criticism of Zerahiah:

> And note that we have written in the Torah: "These are the generations of Noah . . . Noah had three sons" [Gen 6:9–10] and the entire story of the deluge and the ark.

Kaspi's citation of the Noah tale is completely irrelevant to Zerahiah's reading of Job. Unlike Job, which provides minimal chronological data, the Noah tale is extremely precise. We are given Noah's age when the flood began, the stages of the flood, the day and month on which the ark landed in the mountains of Ararat, and how long Noah waited between birds. By referring to "the entire story of the deluge and the ark," Kaspi calls attention to the tale's incredible character and calls into question the historicity of the Torah itself, something that Zerahiah had not done at all.

Whereas Zerahiah showed only why one biblical selection might be unhistorical, Kaspi provided criteria for regarding the entire Bible as unhistorical. Not only was Job to be read as allegory, but because prophets, the authors of Scripture, permitted themselves to lie, all of Scripture might be philosophical allegory.

For all their differences, the Jews Zerahiah and Kaspi agreed with the Christian Origen that allegoresis may be required by the nature of a text. To assert the obvious, all ancient myths require historical allegoresis in order to be understood fully, because the gods who populate the myths never existed. It follows that the events described in myth cannot have happened in precisely the way that the myth describes them.[23]

At the same time—and here we must part company with Leach,

with whom we began—the language in which a myth is related, the institutions and values presented in the myth, and the depictions of the mythical characters inform us about the historical human realities that brought the myth into being. Often a myth informs us about the circles in which it was told and the political and social agenda that it advanced.[24] The same is true of the fairy tale, which allegorizes in much the same way as the myth does. Once we have identified a story as a fairy tale, we abandon certain avenues of historical investigation in favor of others. The tale of the giant living at the top of the beanstalk, who smells the blood of an Englishman and wants to grind his bones to make bread, turns us away from investigating giants' culinary proclivities and beanstalks' weight-bearing capacities and toward Englishmen's perceptions of their enemies. Outside myths and fairy tales, the application of historical-political allegoresis is of obvious value in the study of literary works in which human traits are assigned to nonhumans. Anatole France's *Penguin Island* and George Orwell's *Animal Farm* come readily to mind.

Some stories in the Hebrew Bible immediately invite allegoresis because their unhistorical character is as obvious as Greco-Roman myths and European fairy tales.[25] The story of the Garden of Eden in Genesis 2–3, in which a snake talks and trees confer wisdom or eternal life on those who eat their fruit is an obvious example. With a long history of figurative interpretation behind it, the tale has continued to benefit in recent years from acute and perceptive allegorical readings.[26]

Because the tale cannot be true literally, we are free to pursue the story's internal clues to its historical setting, proceeding from the obvious to the arcane. The language of the Garden story is classical Hebrew of the period around 900–700 B.C.E. The only named divinity in the story is Yahweh-Elohim, a god found thus far only in Israel.[27] Accordingly, although Israel is not one of the several place-names mentioned in the Garden story, the author was almost certainly an Israelite and was aware of the sources of gold, lapis lazuli, and bdellium. Some contact with Mesopotamian culture is presupposed by the word *kerubim*, "cherubs," borrowed from the Akkadian language of ancient Iraq, and by the reference to the Tigris and Euphrates Rivers.[28] More specifically, the reference to Assyria rather than Babylonia suggests an Israel within the Assyrian orbit. Another detail is the collocation of "thorns and thistles." The phrase occurs in the Bible again only in the book of Hosea (Hos 10:8), a document of the early eighth century B.C.E., when Assyria was beginning to dominate Israelite political life and, outside the Bible, in the Assyrian royal annals.[29]

Because allegories often arose out of the need for an author to be indirect and to stay out of harm's way, knowledge of the author's historical circumstances may contribute greatly to our understanding of the allegory.[30] It is remarkable, therefore, how little attention has been given to the historical circumstance of God's act in planting the pleasure garden in Eden. That it is, in fact, a pleasure garden is evident from the place-name Eden, a transparent pun on the word for "abundance" or "pleasure," as well as from God's habit of strolling through it at the breezy time of day (Gen 3:8).[31] In the ancient world, it was common to assign the powers and perquisites enjoyed by human royalty to the great gods who populate the myths. What this means is that Genesis 2–3, which describes Yahweh-Elohim planting a garden, must reflect a period in which human rulers planted gardens.[32] Once again, this indicates an Israel in the shadow of Assyria, as one function of the Assyrian royal garden was to underline the king's "cosmic role in assuring the fertility and fruitfulness of the land."[33]

As early as the twelfth century B.C.E., the Assyrian king Tiglath Pileser I (1115–1077) showed a strong interest in horticulture, but it was not until the ninth century that the royal garden came into its own. It is then that we begin to see the kings of Assyria speaking eloquently of their luxuriant pleasure garden, the *kirimaḫu*.[34] The great eighth-century king, Sargon of Assyria, boasts of his own pleasure garden. He also glories in the destruction of the royal gardens of Urartu, modern-day Armenia, because his action proves that his archrival, the king of Urartu, is no longer fit to rule.[35] The linguistic and cultural evidence from Assyria fits perfectly with the biblical datum that the first named Israelite king to plant a royal garden (1Kgs 21:2) was Ahab, the ninth-century king of northern Israel, who is mentioned in the inscriptions of Shalmaneser III of Assyria.

Within these historic-geographic parameters, the social setting of the Garden of Eden story indicates an audience of small farmers and land tillers who suffered from the curse of the soil.[36] Not included in that curse is any threat that rapacious large landholders would drive the small farmers off the land, a practice that drew the righteous ire of the prophets Amos and Isaiah and ignited the classical prophecy movement. If we accept this argument from silence, we might date the Eden story earlier than the mid-eighth century B.C.E., and any historical allegoresis of the tale must take that dating into account.

One reason that historical allegoresis has not been uniformly applied to the Torah's narratives is that many of them describe events in which the laws of nature are not violated, events that could conceivably be historical.

Unlike the Eden story, the tale of Joseph, an example that we will study later, contains nothing completely unbelievable other than a few exaggerated life spans. In consequence, numerous attempts have been made to find its setting in second-millennium Egypt. But believability and historiographic appearance do not necessarily amount to historicity; they may just as easily indicate allegory. An excellent example is available in a seventeenth-century poem with a biblical theme, John Dryden's "Absalom and Achitophel."

Dryden composed "Absalom and Achitophel" in 1681. The poem purports to recount the circumstances that led Prince Absalom to attempt to seize the throne of his father, David. In the biblical account on which Dryden drew (2Sam 15–18), the succession lines to David's throne were not clarified. Seizing the opportunity, David's son Absalom—aided by David's wise but disloyal counselor Achitophel—took advantage of the popular resentment of David and attempted to take the throne for himself. In the latter half of the seventeenth century, the Bible-reading public was well aware of the numerous parallels between the biblical tale and the current political situation of England.

The Puritan Revolution (1640–1660) ended with the restoration of Charles Stuart as King Charles II of England. But the royal succession had not been settled because Charles had no legitimate children of his own. The fact that Charles had a brother, James, duke of York, who was an avowed Roman Catholic and whose succession to the throne might engender a new religious war, complicated matters even more. The Whigs, led by the earl of Shaftesbury, gathered behind the succession of Charles's handsome illegitimate son, James Scott, duke of Monmouth, who allowed himself to be used against his father. In the manner of the biblical Absalom, Monmouth was sent on a triumphant progress through the country and, like him, was enthusiastically received. But Charles, realizing that the Whigs had overreached themselves, had Shaftesbury imprisoned.

Before Shaftesbury's trial, Dryden wrote "Absalom and Achitophel" in the hopes of influencing the grand jury's verdict. Ostensibly, the poem is set in the reign of David. All the names of the protagonists are taken from the Bible. But as Dryden's audience knew, David stood for Charles, Monmouth for Absalom, Achitophel for Shaftesbury, and so on. They knew this, first of all, because from the pulpit, their preachers had been comparing Monmouth with Absalom even before Dryden wrote the poem. Second, the events in the poem corresponded broadly to the biblical tale but specifically only to the events of Dryden's own time.

When examining the historical narrative traditions of the Pentateuch, it is useful to keep "Absalom and Achitophel" in mind. In the manner of Dryden, the Torah's writers set their tales in a historical period far distant from their own—in the time period between the creation of heaven and earth and the death of Moses—and outside the land of Israel. As we have seen, contemporary archaeological research has revealed that the Torah's settings are as fictional as Dryden's. Consequently, we shall follow the leads of Origen, Zerahiah, and Kaspi, who argued that when a biblical text cannot be taken at face value, it must be read allegorically. Whereas these predecessors employed theological and philosophical allegoresis, we will argue that the Torah is more like "Absalom and Achitophel," namely, that it is a more fitting candidate for historical allegoresis. Specifically, we will subject specific elements of the Torah's narratives to close analysis and show that they are allegories reflecting the historical circumstances and ideological concerns of their respective periods of composition, rather than being reliable witnesses to their alleged settings. Our first topic will be the Egyptian servitude and the Exodus.

CHAPTER 3

The Allegory of Servitude in Egypt and the Exodus

There can really be little doubt that ancestors of Israel had been slaves in Egypt and had escaped in some marvelous way. Almost no one today would question it. . . . Although there is no direct witness in Egyptian records to Israel's presence in Egypt, the Biblical tradition a priori demands belief: it is not the sort of tradition any people would invent.
—John Bright, *A History of Israel*

It is generally acknowledged by scholars that the traditions about Israel's sojourn in Egypt and the Exodus of the Israelites are legendary and epic in nature.
—Niels P. Lemche, *Ancient Israel*

Virtually every American biblicist or seminary graduate of a certain age grew up reading John Bright's *History of Israel*, the source of the first quotation. Bright's book was deservedly popular in circles of religious moderates for its attempt to balance the critical study of Israelite history with respect and reverence for the biblical tradition. But then there was a radical shift in the scholarly consensus in the sixteen years between Bright's *History of Israel* and Lemche's *Ancient Israel*, from which the second quotation is taken, which requires an explanation.[1]

Contemporary literary criticism of the Bible has been one factor in shaping the newer consensus. Until recently, in the world of Bible scholarship, *literary criticism* was synonymous with *source criticism*, that is, the identification of the literary sources or documents from which ancient compilers, redactors, and editors produced our existing Bible. Nowadays, biblical criticism has learned from general literary criticism that it is a mistake to study the Bible without taking into account such aesthetic considerations as narrative, plot, development of theme, and delineation of character. But in the newer context, the "a priori" credibility argument for the servitude traditions falls apart. Viewed as narrative, the servitude traditions find a natural sequel in the triumphalist conquest traditions. A good example is provided in the following passage, in which the humble beginnings of the people Israel serve as a prelude to Yahweh's response to their outcries and to a description of how his saving acts brought about Israel's present happy state:

> My ancestor was a wandering Aramaean who descended to Egypt, so-journing there few in number. But there he became a nation, powerful and numerous. The Egyptians ill treated us, humiliated us, and set hard labor upon us. So we cried out to Yahweh, our ancestral god, who took to heart our humiliation at oppressive labor. Yahweh took us out of Egypt with a hand mighty and an arm outstretched, accompanied by great terror and by signs and wonders. He brought us to this very place. He gave us this land, a land flowing with milk and honey. (Deut 26:5–9)

From a comparative literary perspective, the biblical accounts of Israel's journey from servitude to freedom are an example of the common motif of the hero who rises from humble origins with the aid of divine providence. One such tale from the ancient Near East, written long before the Bible, is the story of Sargon of Agade (ca. 2334–2279 B.C.E.). According to a legend written centuries after his time but still much earlier than the oldest surviving biblical writings, Sargon was the son of an unknown father and a priestess who bore the title Entu, which carried with it an obligation of celibacy. Having violated the rule and fearing detection, Sargon's mother put her son in a basket and abandoned him in the river.[2] But the goddess Ishtar did not abandon Sargon; she provided a rescuer for the infant and continued to watch over him for the rest of his life. Eventually, Sargon founded the first empire in history, called Agade, or Akkad.

Numerous other examples come from the genre that the historian of the ancient Near East Hayim Tadmor calls *autobiographical apology*, literary compositions found in Egypt, among the Hittites, in the smaller Syrian kingdoms, and especially in Assyria and Babylonia.[3] The hero in these "autobiographies" is a king who comes to the throne in an irregular fashion. In the Bible, the group has taken the place of the individual, so the role of the hero-king who rises from obscurity or humble origins is played by the entire people of Israel. That is, the humble origins of Israel in Egypt are a necessary prelude to the greatness brought about by divine favor.[4]

But if the literary approach to the Bible has been significant in reevaluating the historicity of the Egyptian servitude and the Exodus, the evidence from archaeology has been decisive. As we saw in the opening chapter, the traditions of servitude in Egypt, the tales of Israel wandering in the desert, and the stories of the conquest of the promised land appear to be fictitious. To cite a specific example, the locale of Kadesh-Barnea figures prominently in the Torah's traditions about the Exodus. Moses dispatched the spies from there (Num 13) and was himself there barred from the promised land, and it was at Kadesh-Barnea that the prophet Miriam, the sister of Moses, was buried (Num 20). But as observed by the Israeli archaeologist Amihai Mazar,

> Not one Late Bronze or Iron Age I sherd was found in the survey, which combed the oasis of Kadesh Barnea and its vicinity, or in the systematic excavations of the mound.

That lack of discovery and numerous others caused Mazar to conclude:[5]

> There is nothing in the archaeological record to suggest that the settlers came from outside the land of Israel, as stated in the biblical tradition.

What this means is that the biblical traditions are allegories invented deliberately to obscure the fact that the people of Israel were native to their country.[6] But why should Israelite writers have invented traditions of foreignness when these would seem to undercut their claims to the land in which they lived? When were such traditions invented, and by whom?

In an important book, Thomas L. Thompson provided a significant starting point for our investigation by demonstrating that the foreignness traditions could not have arisen later than the end of the sixth century B.C.E., the period often labeled *postexilic*.[7] In his discussion of Israel's origin traditions, Thompson explains Genesis 10–11 as a continuation[8] of the spread of mankind abroad according to their nations and their languages which is the heart of the aetiological narratives in Genesis 10:1–11:9. As all nations spread abroad to take their proper place in the world after Babel, so too did Israel. . . . According to the origin tradition . . . Israel is autochthonous and indigenous to Palestine.

These traditions belong to what Thompson terms "The Toledoth of Terah: The Story of Abraham."[9] It is generally agreed that these traditions concerning how Terah took his offspring (Hebrew: *toledot*), including his son Abraham, from the city of Ur in southern Babylonia on a journey to the land of Canaan are among the latest stories in the Torah. The evidence is that the language of these stories and the geographical and historical references in them indicate that "The Toledoth of Terah" tales originated after 539 B.C.E., when the Persian Empire had granted Jews living abroad the right to return to their ancient homeland. As Thompson points out, the Toledoth convey a strong ideological message, that Israel is not a foreigner in Canaan but is "autochthonous and indigenous." The Jews who returned to their ancestral land were not simply inhabiting a Persian province called Yehud; they were fulfilling a divine plan put in place immediately after Noah's flood. Accordingly, any opposition to Jewish claims to the land was a challenge to the divine plan.

Indeed, the Toledoth traditions share that ideology with other compositions of the postexilic period. As the Israeli biblicists Yairah Amit and Sara Japhet contend, the Exodus tradition in Chronicles, a biblical book composed in the fourth to third century B.C.E., is muted and underplayed to the point of virtual absence, creating the impression that Israel had always been in the land before the exile. In marked contrast to the Babylonian and Egyptian exiles who had maintained the Exodus traditions in the hope that a second Exodus to the promised land was possible, the Jews returning from exile in Babylonia portrayed themselves as coming back to what had always been their homeland.[10] For them, and subsequently for their descendants, exile from the land of Israel had to be presented as an abnormality, an aberration. By ignoring the preexilic traditions of Israel's origin in Egypt, those who "came up from Babylonia" consciously and deliberately devalued the very traditions that had succored the Jews in exile a generation or two earlier.

But if the traditions of Israel's foreignness are much earlier than the postexilic stories claiming that Israel was native to the land, they still are not historical and did not originate at the time the people Israel was formed, the period in which they are set. We can, however, identify the foreignness traditions in indisputably preexilic texts from the eighth century B.C.E. For example, the prophet Micah refers by name to the three primary heroes of the Exodus:

> For I brought you up from the land of Egypt and redeemed you from the house of slavery, and I sent before you Moses, Aaron, and Miriam. (Micah 6:4)

The prophet Amos also knows the Exodus traditions, which he sets in the larger context of migrations. According to Amos, Israel was not the only people whose movements had been directed by God:

> Are you not like the Ethiopians to me, O people of Israel? says Yahweh. Did I not bring Israel up from the land of Egypt and the Philistines from Caphtor and the Arameans from Kir? (Amos 9:7)

The detailed prose account of the Exodus and conquest traditions in Joshua 24, set at the northern sanctuary of Shechem, likewise dates from the eighth century.[11] In contrast to the texts just cited, one of our earliest extant biblical records—a long, premonarchic poem preserved in Deuteronomy 33 and set in the southern region of Israel in the period of the nation's origins—makes no mention whatever of the Exodus from Egypt. References to the Exodus are likewise rather sparse in the account of the eighth-century Judahite prophet Isaiah, son of Amoz.[12]

A quarter century ago, Robert Carroll showed that the obvious explanation of these and similar data is an original "northern tradition of the Exodus," which was virtually unknown in the south. Between 920 and 720 B.C.E., the land of Israel was divided into two separate kingdoms, Judah in the south with its capital at Jerusalem, and Israel in the north with its capital at Samaria.[13] It was in the northern kingdom that the Exodus traditions originated. With the fall of Samaria, many northern Israelites found refuge in Judah, bringing with them their native literature and traditions, among them the traditions of the Exodus, which depicted the people of Israel as foreigners invading from Egypt.

Given that these traditions arose in the north, we must now ask why they arose. What ideology underlies the foreignness traditions, and what historical circumstances before the eighth century encouraged that ideology? We believe that the ideological underpinnings of the foreignness traditions may be classified under two headings: the first "religious" and the second "political." Ultimately, however, "religious" and "political" are only two aspects of a single phenomenon.

First, the religious: The tradition that Israel originated outside Canaan is allegorical for Israelite religious "distinctiveness," the particular notion of distinctiveness that Peter Machinist named "the making of a counter-identity." Machinist, a professor of biblical studies at Harvard, isolated "approximately 433 distinctiveness passages in the Hebrew Bible," held together by a common content:[14]

> All speak of Israel or one of its representative groups or individuals, including its god, as distinct from outsiders, whether humans or gods.

Of course, claims of "distinctiveness" are not unique to Israel. Analogous claims were made in the cultures of Israel's large neighbors, Egypt and Mesopotamia. But precisely in those older and more populous cultures, distinctiveness is closely connected with notions of "autochthonous origins—of a primordial connection between the people and a particular territory." Machinist observes that in contrast, Israel's claim to come from the outside is itself distinct, if not unique. In Egypt and Mesopotamia, "the tendency was to equate national history [and] the origins of particular cities and urban regions, with cosmogony."[15] Myth and ritual articulated the notion that the proper places of the great Egyptian and Mesopotamian cities and their inhabitants had been fixed by the gods at creation.

Machinist accounts for the difference in conception between Israelites, on one hand, and Egyptians and Mesopotamians, on the other, by appealing to history, namely, that the Israelite ideology of foreignness was based, at least in part, on Israel's origins as a people outside its land:[16]

> Admittedly, not all of Israel's components were from the outside . . .
> but even in the most radical of modern theories about Israelite state
> formation in Palestine, the outside component is conceded a crucial
> role.

From the acceptance of Israel's foreignness as at least partly historical, Machinist brilliantly argues that biblical writers employed[17] this very status as newcomer and marginal . . . as the basis for a positive picture. In other words, if newcomer and marginal had meant, say, for the Egyptians, barbarian, immoral and chaotic, in the Bible they became proof of the choice of "the almighty God"—of new freedom, purity, and power.

But as we saw in the previous chapter, no statistically insignificant or culturally identifiable evidence has yet been discovered.[18] We may contrast this situation with that of the Philistines:[19]

The Philistines when they settled, as they did on the coastal plain of Israel, these peoples introduced *by means of material culture, cultic practices, and architecture, a new ethnic element which reflected their origins in the Aegean.*

Because Israelite "material culture, cultic practices, and architecture" do not reflect "a new ethnic element," Israel's claims to foreignness cannot have originated in a historical reality. Instead, Israel's outsider status must be considered an ideological statement. In other words, it was not that Israel elevated foreignness to distinctiveness but, rather, that Israel asserted its distinctiveness by claiming foreignness:[20]

There really is an "us" over against a "them." The more sharply they [the biblical authors] affirm the boundary, the more we can be certain that the reality was muddier and more fragile.

They "affirm the boundary" by depicting "Israel" as a self-conscious entity distinct from its surroundings, its foreignness "proof of the choice of the almighty God." Israel's ideological self-consciousness and religious distinctiveness are expressed by the Torah's repeated denial of Israel's Canaanite heritage. According to the Torah, the priesthood, the sacrificial cult (contrast Amos 5:25), the tabernacle, the festivals, most of the covenant traditions to serve Yahweh exclusively (Joshua 24 is the notable exception), and the laws governing most of life's activities originated outside the promised land. By claiming that Israel's most important religious institutions had originated in the desert—the "no-man's land" (Jer 2:6) where Yahweh found the people (Deut 32:10)—the writers of the Torah strengthen the claims they wish to make for Israelite distinctiveness. Particularly illustrative is Leviticus 18;1–5:

> Yahweh spoke to Moses, saying, "Speak to the Israelite people and say to them: I am Yahweh your god. You shall not emulate the practices of the land of Egypt where you dwelled, nor shall you emulate the practices of the land of Canaan where I am taking you. Not *their* statutes shall you follow but my norms you shall observe and you shall take care to follow *my* statutes. I am Yahweh, your god."

The phrases "practices of Egypt" and "practices of Canaan" are used pejoratively here. Furthermore, "their statutes" are fundamentally different from Israelite practices, which are Yahweh's "statutes" and "norms." The chapters of Leviticus that follow this selection list the "abominations"—sexual, cultic, and moral—allegedly favored by Canaanites. Indeed, Leviticus 18;27–28 asserts that these abominations had polluted Canaan so thoroughly that the land itself revolted and "vomited" out the Canaanites. Not content to let the members of the audience draw the inference themselves, the writer of the chapter informs them that if they, Israel, persist in Canaanite practices, they, too, will be regurgitated.

Only recently has contemporary scholarship begun to retreat from its uncritical acceptance of the biblical depiction of the religions of Israel's neighbors, especially the Canaanites, as cults of lawless lechers who delighted in abominable practices.[21] In a description quite typical of its time, William F. Albright, one of the pioneering students of Canaanite culture and a great admirer of Canaanite literary, artistic, and technological achievements, nonetheless referred to[22]

> the extremely low level of Canaanite religion . . . relatively primitive mythology . . . demoralizing cultic practices . . . brutality of Canaanite mythology.

But Albright's view and biblical perspective aside, we now know that Israel was not unique in its view that a "fear of god," or what we now call "ethics" and "morals," was divinely commanded.[23] The Ugaritians of ancient Syria, whom Albright included in his account of Canaanite culture, praised the legendary King Daniel for "getting justice for the widow, and adjudicating the case of the fatherless." Likewise, Yehimilk of Byblos in Phoenicia, present-day Lebanon, prided himself on being "a king of justice and a king of righteousness before the holy gods." In Egypt, justice was embodied in the great goddess

Ma'at. In Mesopotamia, law was often personified by the gods Kittu, "Justice," and Misharu, "Equity." At other times, the law was viewed as an independent power to which the gods were subject.[24] Kings Lipit-Ishtar and Hammurapi explicitly told their audiences that they had compiled "law codes" because the gods had authorized them to promote law and justice.[25] Shamash, the all-seeing sun god, was hymned as "judge of gods and humans" and as "Lord of Law."[26]

In Israel and elsewhere, ritual law was not divorced from moral law. About the same time that the prophet Amos condemned his people for trampling the heads of the poor into the dust (Amos 2:7)[27] and equally for giving wine to the Nazirites (Amos 2:12), the author of the incantation series, Shurpu, cataloged the Mesopotamian sins, which included cheating on weights and measures, marking boundaries falsely, having intercourse with the wife of a neighbor, omitting the name of a god from an incense offering, disarranging an altar, and eating the taboo food of a city.[28] Similar associations of conduct prevailed in Egypt. The Middle Egyptian work *Going Forth by Day* was a set of instructions that the dead should take with them so that they would know what to tell the divine judges who examined them before they passed into the next life. Buried in tombs, this composition—also known as *The Book of the Dead*—directed its readers to proclaim their innocence of blaspheming the gods, doing violence to a poor man, killing, depriving cattle of fodder, damaging the bread of a god, having sexual relations with a boy, and passing the time of sacrifice.[29]

In other words, the biblical assertion that Israel had access to superior norms and statutes is not a simple factual description but an attempt to foster Israelite religious, social, and political solidarity. Israel is encouraged to maintain its solidarity by asserting its distinctiveness from its neighbors, a distinctiveness that, according to the Torah, was closely related to Israel's foreign origins. As long as Israelites are conscious of their foreignness, they will be able to maintain their alleged religious and moral superiority. As foreigners with no roots in Canaan or Egypt, they will find it easier to heed the admonitions of the authors of the Torah to reject Canaanite and Egyptian practices favoring the ways of Yahweh, which are, it is claimed, fundamentally different.

Just as we questioned whether or not the claim to foreignness was historical, we may ask the same question about the claim of fundamental difference between the Israelites' religion and other religions of the ancient Near East. There can be little doubt that Yahwistic monotheism—the belief that Yahweh was the sole god in existence, which came to characterize late Israelite religion and the forms of Judaism that began to emerge in the late sixth century B.C.E.—was distinctive. Indeed, it was this monotheistic ideology that motivated the later prophets to call for all the peoples of the earth, not just Israelites, to worship Yahweh.[30] Likewise, there can be little doubt that Yahwistic monotheism had not been the dominant stream in Israelite religion before the exile.[31] Nonetheless, the worship of Yahweh in pre-exilic Israel must have differed from the worship by Israel's neighbors of quite similar gods.[32]

Israelite religion contained elements that enabled it to survive and to evolve into Judaism at a time that other cults of eastern Mediterranean gods disappeared with the fall of their national states and the exile of significant elements of their populations.[33] If anything, the fall of Judah—which followed closely on the heels of King Josiah's great religious reform, rooting out the cults of Yahweh's rivals—should have attested to Yahweh's insufficiency.[34] That it did not was due to the particular form of the worship of Yahweh in influential Israelite circles, that is, monolatry.

For all their diversity of opinion, the many writers of the individual compositions that became the Bible agree that it was never legitimate for an Israelite to worship a god other than Yahweh. In other words, although some writers accept the existence of other divinities and others deny it, the consensus demanded of all Israelites is the worship of the god Yahweh to the exclusion of all others. Historians of religion refer to the form of worship in which only one god is served as *monolatry*.

Monolatry was not entirely unknown in the ancient Near East outside Israel. In the fourteenth century B.C.E., Akhenaten, king of Egypt, inaugurated a solar monolatry in which the royal family worshiped the Aten, the disk representing the sun, and prohibited the worship of Egypt's traditional gods.[35] Mesopotamian mythology describes the temporary worship of a single god in an emergency.[36] In addition, ancient Near Eastern prayer literature regularly employed monolatrous language. That is, a worshiper might approach various gods in succession, declaring that each one was the only divinity worthy of worship.[37]

Even though monolatry was not unique to Israel—a fact that makes the biblical demands more credible—monolatry seems to have been much more significant in Israel than elsewhere. Specifically, if Israelite history begins at the time that a segment of the population of Palestine begins to think of itself as Israelite, then we should think of the worship of Yahweh alone as part of the formation of an Israelite identity.[38]

The ancient historian Morton Smith made an important contribution to the discussion by drawing attention to the political aspects of Israelite monolatry. In his provocative book *Palestinian Parties and Politics that Shaped the Old Testament*, Smith portrays Israel's continuing vacillation between periods of "following other gods" and fidelity to Yahweh alone as a struggle between the "Yahweh-alone" party, whose activities, according to Smith, began only in the ninth century, and the syncretists, those who included Yahweh in a larger pantheon with other gods.[39]

By examining the Yahweh-alone religious ideology from a political standpoint, the Smith thesis successfully avoids any appeal to "uniqueness." Thus, what Smith labels the "Yahweh-alone movement" may be compared with such diverse phenomena as the Amarna monolatry of the Aten sun disk in Egypt, the exaltation of Marduk in Babylonia, and the triumph of Catholic trinitarianism in early Christianity.[40] The Yahweh-alone thesis is especially convincing as applied to the constant shifts in royal religious policies. Smith, however, does not account in detail for the origins of the religious ideology advocated by the Yahweh-alone party, nor does he examine the religious dimensions of the views held by the opposing sides. Instead, he contents himself with the following paragraph of conjectures:[41]

> The priests and prophets of Yahweh would not have wished the Israelites to resort to his (and their) competitors; Israelites attached to desert life would have opposed the worship of the gods of Canaan as part of an alien culture; military leaders would have tried to keep their followers distinct from the subjugated population and united by the cult of their particular deity; Israelites who wished to preserve their own segregation as members of a ruling party from the conquered

Canaanites would have demanded that Israelites worship only the Israelite god.

Each of these conjectures is faulty. The first begs the question. After all, most ancient Near Eastern priesthoods were tolerant because there was enough business to go around. Why should Israelite priests have been more intolerant than others? The second conjecture accepts the unhistorical view of the Bible that Israel came out of the desert (Deut 32:10, cf. Jer 2:6).[42] As for the third conjecture, given the ethnically diverse nature of the Israelite armies, their military leaders could hardly have been segregationists.[43] Finally, the picture of conquered Canaanites is, once more, based on biblical ideology rather than history. Our own approach to the problem takes up Smith's hypothesis but attempts, in addition, to account for the religious ideologies of the Yahweh monolaters and their opponents by using Max Weber's notion of "covenant union," a form of association "determined by quite concrete religious-historical and often highly personal circumstances and vicissitudes."[44]

What were the "concrete religious historical circumstances" that coalesced to make the Yahweh-alone ideology so forceful in Israel? We believe that those circumstances may be reconstructed as follows: Current archaeological data lead to a model of "internal conquest" in which dissident elements of a Late Bronze Age society in Canaan colonized new areas in the hinterland. Archaeology has revealed a sharp increase in small unwalled settlements in the central Palestinian hills during the twelfth and eleventh centuries.

As Dever found, residents of the Iron I hill-country villages left in the lowlands clear archaeological indications of their Late Bronze Age background, as peasant farmers whose material culture was mainly Canaanite.[45] As these farmers withdrew from a more stratified social order, which was economically and politically burdensome, they encountered hostility from the older order. This order had been imposed by the Egyptian empire, which claimed Canaan as its own from the eighteenth through twentieth dynasties (ca. 1560–1080 B.C.E.) As shown by the fourteenth-century Amarna letters from Egypt, there was a close "feudal" relation between the pharaoh and his underlings, the rulers of the petty Canaanite city-states, to the extent that reports about uncooperative Canaanite labor forces were sent to Egypt.[46] An extremely revealing letter to the Egyptian court from the loyalist Rib-Addi purports to quote some revolutionary rhetoric directed against the king of Egypt:

> We shall drive the city-state rulers out of the lands so that all the land will become ḫāpiru-land, and so justice will be done in all the lands. [Our] sons and daughters will be undisturbed forever. If then the king [of Egypt] ventures forth, with all the lands in opposition to him, what can he do to us?

The ḫāpiru were a social class whose presence was found all over the Near East throughout the second millennium B.C.E. The word means, roughly, "fugitive" and, in the Amarna letters, has the connotation of "brigand" or "outlaw."[47] Rib-Addi adds: "To this end they have sworn an oath [or "covenant"], among themselves" (El Amarna, 74). Clearly, then, natives of Syria-Palestine resented working for the king of Egypt and his local allies, or collaborators. Expelling the local rulers would lead to throwing off the yoke of Egypt.

Although we do not have literary sources like the Amarna letters for the succeeding centuries, it is clear that Canaan of the thirteenth and twelfth centuries witnessed considerable turmoil as part of the general disruption of the western Mediterranean. One disruptive group, called Israel, is mentioned in a stela dating from the fifth regnal year of Pharaoh Merneptah (ca. 1220 B.C.E.). The relevant text, the only mention of Israel in an Egyptian source, reads:

> Canaan is captive with all woe
> Ashkelon is captured, Gezer seized
> Yanoam made non-existent
> Israel is wasted, bare of seed.

The mention of Israel has given the text the modern name "Israel stela," even though most of it is dedicated to Merneptah's account of his victory over the Libyans. Only the final twelve lines speak of Syria-Palestine, probably to convey the impression that the pharaoh was victorious throughout the countries. The text has been studied by many scholars.[48] Although there remain many points of disagreement, the general consensus is that by the thirteenth century B.C.E., a group designated as Israel had a political identity. Unfortunately, we have a gap of a century or more between the Israel of the stela and any relevant archaeological data on the Israel of the Bible.

Despite the sparse documentation of Israel in Egyptian sources, the biblical figure of 430 years of servitude in Egypt (Exod 12:40) fits remarkably well with the chronology of the eighteenth Egyptian dynasty. The overthrow of the Hyksos by Ahmose (1570–1546) in about 1560 B.C.E. was followed by extensive Egyptian military campaigning in Syria-Palestine, thereby laying the foundations of the Egyptian empire in Asia. Ahmose's successors continued his policy, attempting to expand beyond the Euphrates at the expense of the rival imperialist power Mitanni. At the battle of Megiddo, Thutmose III (1504–1450) won a decisive victory, after which he established an administrative system in Canaan that survived until the end of the Late Bronze Age. It was only with the invasions of the sea peoples that the old order began to break down.[49] By the middle of the twelfth century, Egypt's ruling presence in Canaan had ceased. It is at this point that the presence of Israel in the hill country and the Philistines on the coastal plain becomes increasingly visible in the archaeological record.

Given that the Amarna letters demonstrate local consciousness and strong opposition to the collusion between the Canaanite rulers and Egypt, we must interpret the Hebrew traditions of servitude *in* Egypt as allegories of servitude *to* Egypt. The 430 years of the Bible reflect the duration of Egypt's empire in Asia from a Canaanite perspective. The group that became first-millennium Israel had indeed been subjugated by kings of Egypt, but in its native land. Very little accurate information about that period of subjugation has survived, but there are some precious vestiges. One is in Exodus 1:11:

> Over them they appointed *mas*-overseers in order to humble them with their *sebel*-projects.

The NJV offers a typical translation:

> So they set taskmasters over them to oppress them with forced labor.

Although not inaccurate, the NJV, like most other translations, ignores the technical nuances of *mas* and *sebel*. For *mas*, let us turn to El Amarna letter 365, a report written for the king of Egypt by

Biridiya, ruler of the city of Megiddo, in the north of present-day Israel.[50]

> May the king, my lord, be apprised concerning his servant and concerning his city. Now, I alone am cultivating in Shunem and I alone am bringing *mas*-people. But see! The city rulers who are with me do not do as I. They are not cultivating in Shunem, and they are not bringing *mas*-people. I alone, the only one [of the city rulers] am bringing *mas*-people. From Jaffa they come, from . . . Nuribta. [So] may the king be apprised concerning his city.

Megiddo, a large Canaanite city, is referred to by its ruler, Biridiya, as belonging to the king. Biridiya himself was required by the pharaoh to import corvée workers to cultivate the fields of Shunem.[51] Workers were brought from Nuribta and Jaffa as well as from Megiddo itself. If these *mas*-people were cultivating royal land, they had good reasons for resentment, because they could not work their own fields, which would have required cultivation at the same time. The fact that *mas*-workers could be moved from one area to another would have added to their resentment. Perhaps that is why other city rulers were not as conscientious as Biridiya in assembling workers for the *mas*. It is unlikely that this ancient institution of *mas*-corvée was any more popular in Biridiya's time than it would be four centuries later at the time of Rehoboam, son of Solomon, when a rebellious mob stoned the *mas*-supervisor to death as a prelude to civil war (1Kgs 12).[52]

Like the *mas*, the *sebel*, too, was a highly unpopular ancient institution of forced labor. Note the following extract from a letter of the eighteenth century B.C.E. from Mari in Syria, written by Kibri-Dagan, a royal governor:[53]

> Concerning the *sablu* [that is, *sebel*]-workers from my district, my lord ordered me to assemble male and female minors into the fortress. I sent the inhabitants of Terqa and they assembled the *sablu*-workers of Zurubban, Hishamta, and Hanna here for me. But when I sent to the towns of the Jaminites, the sheik of Dumeti answered me this way, and I quote: "Let the enemy [that is, "you the governor Kibri-Dagan, or the king himself"] come here and pull us out of our towns!" This he answered! And the same thing, at harvest time in the towns of the Jaminites, there is no one to help me.

That male and female minors at Mari were subject to the *sablu/sebel*-corvée was particularly offensive. As with the Amarna *mas*, there was strong resistance to a practice that benefited a central authority at the expense of local populations. In light of the extra-biblical sources, we should translate Exodus 1:11 as follows:

> Over them they appointed corvée-overseers in order to humble them with their forced-labor projects.

The passage does not describe Egyptian institutions of subjugation in Egypt proper but, rather, institutions native to Syria-Palestine that served the needs of the ruling Egyptian empire. Once the group that became Israel had succeeded in withdrawing from the Egyptian system, it began to describe the process as a withdrawal from the land of Egypt itself.

This model of withdrawal from the Egyptian system, primarily associated with the scholars George Mendenhall and Norman Gottwald, has often been called a *peasant revolt*, a term that is much too limited.[54] An analysis of records from the Near East of the thirteenth and twelfth centuries B.C.E. shows that[55]

> the destruction of the Canaanite urban culture and the withdrawal of Egypt from Canaan during the second third of the twelfth century were part of a "worldwide" historical process that extended over the entire eastern Mediterranean region.

Within that process we must reckon with the dislocations caused by ecological calamities, the collapse of the Hittite Empire in Turkey around 1200 B.C.E., the resultant disintegrations of the urban cultures of the Bronze Age, and the influx of the sea peoples. Against this international background of turbulence, we see populations caught in the middle of fighting among rival city-states, traders whose living was being disturbed by unstable conditions, debtors, and peasants who felt themselves overtaxed in both money and kind or overburdened by corvée. We must also reckon with[56]

> the ever present pastoralists who inhabited the steppe between the Levantine coast and the Syrian-Arabian desert, as well as the steppe from Jebel Bishri down the Euphrates.

The Bible, the Amarna letters, and other sources show how different groups of malcontents could be mobilized by talented and opportunistic leaders.[57] In a "long, gradual and complicated process," one such coalition emerged as Israel.[58] Because this new group consisted of locals who no longer had a place in the social order, its members gave themselves a new "national" identity. They began to depict themselves as an invading group from outside the land, a phenomenon for which they had more than one model. Let us look again at the stirring lines of Amos that we quoted earlier, but this time with an eye to their significance as an ideological account of Israel's origins:

> Are you not like the Ethiopians [or Nubians; Hebrew: Cushites] to me,
> O people of Israel? says Yahweh. Did I not bring Israel up from the
> land of Egypt and the Philistines from Caphtor and the Arameans from
> Kir? (Amos 9:7)

This passage shows that Amos's listeners were aware that some of their neighbors were immigrants. The Aramaeans had come to Aram (present-day Syria), from a place called Kir. Closer to home, Israel had the model of the Philistines, who had come to Canaan from Caphtor (either Crete or Cyprus).[59] Originally one of the sea peoples, the Philistines, who had been enemies of Egypt, were settled by Ramses III (1198–1166) to man garrisons in coastal areas in Canaan in order to protect Egypt against newer invaders. This system worked as long as it served the interests of both groups: the Egyptians, who no longer needed to deploy their own native troops on the coast of Canaan, and the Philistine immigrants from the Aegean, who needed a place to live. But once the Egyptian government became too weak to exercise close control, the Philistines broke free of Egyptian rule and were able to organize themselves into a pentapolis of five city-states.

The Israelites had another example in the Sikil, one of the sea peoples mentioned in Egyptian sources. In the manner of the Philistines, the Sikil originated in the Aegean and settled on the Mediterranean coast at Dor, south of Mount Carmel, after being repulsed by the Egyptians.[60] The Aramaeans, the Sikil, and the Philistines were an inspiration for the Israelite ideologues. If these peoples could come from abroad and establish their own polities, why could not the Israelites have done the same?[61]

In sum, the stories of servitude *in* Egypt are allegories of servitude *to* Egypt. The traditions of foreignness are allegories of religious difference. In addition, they serve a specific political agenda: northern Israelite claims in Jordan. The traditions regarding Israel's encounters with Moab after leaving Egypt may serve as a good example.[62]

The tablelands of northern Moab are frequently cited by the biblical writers. The chief city in northern Moab was Medeba, about thirty kilometers south of present-day Amman, Jordan. Among other towns in the area were Heshbon and Elealeh. According to the Moabite stone erected in triumphal celebration by King Mesha of Moab in the mid-ninth century, the Gadites—that is, members of the Israelite tribe Gad—had dwelled in the land of Ataroth in northern Moab "forever" (Moabite: *m'lm*). Mesha observes that the king of Israel had built up the land of Ataroth for them. The king of Israel mentioned by name in this same inscription is Omri, and reference is made to his son as well, providing synchronisms between rulers of Israel and kings of Moab.

It is in light of the Moabite stone that we must read such passages as Numbers 21:21–31:

> Israel now sent messengers to Sihon king of the Amorites. . . . Let me pass through your country . . . we will follow the king's highway. . . . But Sihon would not let Israel pass . . . and went out against Israel in the wilderness. He came to Jahaz and engaged Israel. . . . But Israel put him to the sword and took possession of their land, from the Arnon to the Jabbok. . . . Israel took possession of all those towns . . . of the Amorites, in Heshbon and all its dependencies. Now Heshbon was the city of Sihon, king of the Amorites, who had fought against the first king of Moab and taken all his land from him as far as the Arnon. Therefore the bards recite, "Come to Heshbon . . . Sihon's city. Fire went forth from Heshbon, flame from Sihon's city, consuming Ar of Moab. You are undone people of Chemosh. His sons are made fugitive and his daughters captive by the Amorite king Sihon." So Israel occupied the land of the Amorites.

According to this passage, Israel's holdings in northern Moab had not come at the Moabites' expense. Israel of the Exodus, en route from Egypt, had attempted to pass peacefully through territory held by an Amorite king, Sihon, whose city was Heshbon. From that center, Heshbon, Sihon had made his conquests, taking territory captured in battle from the first Moabite king. Translated into political propaganda, the biblical traditions are vindications of Israelite claims to northern Moab against counterclaims made by the Moabites. First, Moab is not entitled to this land because it did not possess the territory for the reign of even a single Moabite king. Second, Israel never took that land from Moab but from an ancient conqueror, Sihon, an Amorite king who dwelled in Heshbon.

We might be tempted initially to credit the story with some historicity, especially because King Mesha himself says that the Gadites had dwelled in Ataroth "forever." But once again, the archaeological evidence points in another direction. Extensive excavations at Tell Hesban, the site of Heshbon, show that the site was first occupied only in Iron Age I, a couple of centuries too late for a connection with any "thirteenth-century Exodus." The flimsy architectural remains from that period militate strongly against the tradition of Numbers 21 that Heshbon was a royal city in what we now call "the Late Bronze Age." There is, however, evidence for the construction of a nearly two-million-liter-capacity reservoir sometime in the ninth to the eighth century. The archaeologist Lawrence Geraty surmises that the reservoir might have been part of Mesha's attempt to fortify his northern border with Israel.[63]

It appears, then, that the account of Numbers 21 is allegorical. Behind the tale of an Israelite conquest of Amorite territory during the Exodus is a historical military push by King Omri and his son Ahab into Transjordan early in the ninth century.[64] In fact, it was the prophet Amos who first formulated the clear connection between the Exodus and the Transjordanian conquests:

> For I brought you up out of Egypt and led you through the wilderness
> for *forty years* so that you would conquer the land of the Amorites.
> (Amos 2:10)

From this we should hardly be surprised by the following account by Mesha in lines 4 through 9 of the Moabite stone:[65]

> As for Omri, king of Israel, he humbled Moab many days, for [the god] Chemosh was wroth with his land. His [Omri's] son succeeded him. He too said, "I shall humble Moab." In my days said he thus. But I saw [my triumph] over him and his dynasty, and Israel perished utterly and forever. For Omri had taken possession of Madeba-Land and dwelled

there throughout his days and half his son's days, *forty years*. But Chemosh returned it in my days.

According to Amos 2:9, the Amorites were "as tall as cedars and as stout as the oaks." If Yahweh could defeat these legendary Amorites, surely he would aid his people against the historical Moabites.

CHAPTER 4

Yahweh's *Berît* (Covenant):
Which Came First—Sex or Politics?

It is widely believed that among the cultures of the ancient Near East, only Israel believed that its god acted directly in human affairs, in what we now call *history*. Yahweh is supposed to have been qualitatively different from the many gods of the Gentiles, who alternately cooperated and battled with one another, acting primarily in the realm of what we now call *nature*. The supposed practical consequence of this alleged qualitative difference between Yahweh and the other gods was that Israel did not depict Yahweh in myth and its gentile contemporaries did not portray their gods as active in history. But this widespread belief is mistaken. The Bible often depicts Yahweh in mythic terms, and the literature of the ancient Near East often depicts the gods of the nations in historical terms.[1]

The difference between Israel and the Gentiles was in "history's" role in the cult. In contrast to the cults of first millennium B.C.E., Egypt, Mesopotamia, and non-Israelite Syria-Palestine, the worshipers of Yahweh emphasized the acts of salvation that had brought his people political triumph.[2] In Israel, agricultural festivals—Maṣṣot and Sukkot, for example—had their seasonal character subordinated to the themes of exodus and settlement.[3] The offering of the first fruits at the sanctuary (Deut 26:1–11) celebrated Israel's transformation from the offspring of a "wandering Aramaean" into a people with its own land. The Sabbath, whatever its origin, became a reminder of servitude in Egypt.[4] The dedication to Yahweh of the first born of animals and humans (Exod 13:11–16) was related to the punishment of the Egyptians. The covenant of circumcision was related to the promise of the land (Gen 17:7–14).

The contrast between the Israelite and the Canaanite emphasis is clearest when we compare the victories of Yahweh with the victories of the Ugaritic god Baal. Whereas the citizens of ancient Ugarit in Syria celebrated the victory of Baal, the land god, over Yamm, the sea god, the Israelites celebrated the victory of Yahweh over the Egyptian enemies of his people.[5] In other words, Israel drew its religious imagery primarily from what we would now call *politics* or *government*. In one central political image, Israel is depicted allegorically as having made itself subject to Yahweh the king (Judg 8:23; 1Sam 8:7), through *berît*, "pact" or "covenant." From earliest times, Israel saw itself united to Yahweh in a conditional *berît*, which carried rewards for obedience and penalties for disobedience.[6]

According to this allegory, Yahweh and Israel were linked in a conditional covenant under terms requiring Israel to pledge exclusive loyalty to Yahweh and promise not to serve other gods. Through the instrumentality of this covenant with Yahweh, Israel held the land of Canaan. Adherence to the prescriptions of the covenant would ensure Yahweh's continuing support of Israel and its title to the land. Disobedience, however, would provoke Yahweh's wrath and cause him to punish his disloyal subjects by destroying their nation and expelling them from the land.[7] Some of the best-known texts in the Torah allege that the covenant between Yahweh and Israel had been mediated by Moses in the desert, after the Exodus from Egypt:

> So Moses ascended to God [Hebrew: *elohim*], and Yahweh called him from the mountain, saying, "Speak thus to the house of Jacob, and tell the children of Israel [that] you have seen what I did to Egypt, how I carried you on wings of eagles and brought you to me. Now if you heed my voice closely and observe my covenant [Hebrew: *berît*], then you shall be my personal possession more than any other people, for the earth is mine, and you shall be to me a kingdom of priests and a holy nation. These are the words you are to speak to the children of Israel." So Moses came and gathered the elders of the people and set before them all these words [*kol ha-debarim ha-eleh*] that Yahweh commanded him. The people spoke up all together, saying, "Whatever Yahweh has said, we will perform." Moses brought the people's words back to Yahweh. (Exod 19:3–8)

This selection precedes the Ten Commandments, which are identified with the covenant in Exodus 20:1–7. The crucial element of this covenant is expressed in the commandments that Israel serve no other gods than Yahweh and that they make sure not to identify false gods with Yahweh himself:[8]

> God spoke all these words [*kol ha-debarim ha-eleh*], saying, I am Yahweh, your god, who took you out of the land of Egypt—the slave barracks. You shall have no other gods in my presence. You shall not bow before them or serve them, for I, Yahweh, your god, am a jealous god, requiting ancestral sin on children, on the third, and on the fourth generation to my foes but maintaining loyalty [*hesed*] to those who love me and observe my commandments. You shall not pronounce the name "Yahweh," your god, to that which is false [that is, a false god], for Yahweh will not acquit one who pronounces his [Yahweh's] name to that which is false.

Another text in Exodus provides a detailed and graphic account of how Moses mediated a covenant between Yahweh and the people (Exod 24:3–11):[9]

> Moses came and related to the people all the words and norms of Yahweh. Then the people spoke up with one voice, saying, "All the words [*kol ha-debarim*] that Yahweh spoke, we will perform." So Moses wrote down all Yahweh's words. Upon rising in the morning, he built an altar at the bottom of the mountain, as well as twelve stelae for the twelve tribes of Israel. He then sent Israelite lads who offered bulls as whole burned-offerings and as sacrifices of well-being to Yahweh. Moses took half the blood and put it in bowls, and half he dashed on the altar. He took the book of the covenant [*seper ha-berît*] and read it in the people's hearing. They said, "Everything Yahweh has said, we will perform obediently." So Moses took the blood [in the bowls], dashed it on the people, and said, "This is the blood, of the covenant [*dam ha-berît*] that Yahweh concluded with you regarding all these words [*kol ha-debarim ha-eleh*]. Then ascended Moses and Aaron and Nadab and Abihu and seventy of the elders of Israel. They saw the god of Israel, the soles of whose feet were like worked white sapphire, as pure as heaven itself. But he did not harm the representatives of Israel, who saw the god but ate and drank.

Because these selections from the Torah have not been dated with certainty, modern scholars have differed widely in their assessment of the antiquity of the covenant allegory. Julius Wellhausen, the founder of modern biblical criticism, characterized the covenant allegory as a "legalistic" formulation of Israel's relation to its god. In Wellhausen's scheme, early Israelite religion was "natural." Gradually evolving from polytheism to monotheism under the influence of the great literary prophets Amos, Isaiah, and Jeremiah, the religion of Israel became further and further removed from its natural roots. In this scheme, the less "natural" a biblical concept or institution seemed to be, the later it had to be. A closely regulated hierarchical priesthood, for example, was obviously not "natural" and therefore was a late development. By the same criterion, the covenant notion was not "natural" but "legalistic" and, accordingly, a latecomer to Israelite ideology.

Specifically, Wellhausen considered the notion of covenant particularly well suited to the thinking of the postexilic Jewish community, which, in his analysis, had bound itself to the letter of the law by seeking salvation in the punctilious observance of complicated rituals.[10] For Wellhausen, the covenant allegory was the late derivative of the marriage allegory employed by the classical prophets.[11] Hosea, an eighth-century northern prophet, had been the first to depict Israel as the bride of Yahweh. In one striking passage, Hosea is told by Yahweh:

> Go love a woman . . . love her as I, Yahweh, love the Israelites, although they resort to other gods. (Hos 3:1)

To fulfill the command to love the woman as Yahweh loves Israel, Hosea hires a prostitute. And in calling on the people of Israel to chasten the rulers of Israel for faithlessness to Yahweh, Hosea refers allegorically to Yahweh as the wronged husband, to the rulers of Israel as the faithless wife and mother, and to the common people of people of Israel as the children of the union. In Hosea 2, the prophet parodies the imagery of marriage by using the graphic image of an outraged husband accusing his wife of infidelity in the most vulgar language:

> Call your mother to account, for she is not my wife, nor am I her husband. Let her get her whoring out of my sight, along with her adulterous breasts! Or else I shall strip her bare, parade her naked as the day she was born. . . . She has been promiscuous, their mother has. She who bore them has been shameless.

The prophets Jeremiah and Ezekiel, who succeeded Hosea, elaborated the bridal image, which had become increasingly popular as

monotheism evolved in Israelite religion. In the following passage
from Ezekiel 16, Yahweh speaks to Israel:

> I tended you like an evergreen plant growing in the woods; you thrived
> and grew. You came to full womanhood; your breasts became firm and
> your hair grew, but you were still bare and naked. I came by and saw
> that you were ripe for love. I spread the skirt of my robe over you and
> covered your body. I plighted my troth and entered in covenant [*berît*]
> with you, says my Lord Yahweh, and you became mine.

In Wellhausen's analysis, the authors of the Pentateuch—in its final
form, a postexilic work—accepted the prophetic depiction of Yahweh
and Israel as bride and groom but, in keeping with the legalistic thinking of Judaism, chose to emphasize the contractual aspects of marriage. As Yahweh's bride, Israel was legally bound by the stipulations
of its marriage contract. In other words, according to Wellhausen,
covenant was the unromantic legalistic expression of prophetic ethical monotheism. The fact that *berît*, "covenant," is used frequently in
the Pentateuch to refer to the union of Yahweh and Israel, but rarely
in that sense in the preexilic prophets, was proof enough to Wellhausen of the lateness of the conception.

But philological evidence points in the opposite direction. Neither
the (late) Pentateuch nor (the early) Hosea employs *berît* in the context of marriage.[12] According to Wellhausen, however, the word *berît*
should have been found at an early period in the terminology of marriage and only later extended to the sphere of law. It is far more likely
that the extension was in the opposite direction. In undisputed preexilic biblical writings, *berît* is used to describe political and social relations of various kinds, but not the relation of marriage. The only
biblical occurrences of *berît* in connection with marriage are (Ezek
16:8) "I plighted my troth and entered into a covenant [*berît*] with
you" and (Mal 2:14) *'ešet berîteka*, "your covenanted spouse," both
of undisputed exilic or postexilic origin.[13]

Beginning with the Babylonian exile, the Hebrew language was
greatly influenced by Akkadian, the ancient Semitic language of
Mesopotamia. There can be little doubt that postexilic Hebrew
broadened the semantic range of *berît* to include the marriage relation, under the influence of the Akkadian *riksu/rikistu*. Like *berît*, the
Akkadian term *riksu* means "contract" but was used from earliest

times for a full range of contractual agreements, from marriage to international treaties.[14]

The philological evidence is in complete harmony with comparative religious data drawn from the ancient Near East outside Israel. Wellhausen considered Hosea's image of Israel as Yahweh's bride to be an expression of the early prophets' pioneering monotheistic tendencies, but this is hardly the case. In fact, very similar imagery can be found in the myths and rituals of different kinds of sacred marriage involving humans and gods, well known in the polytheistic cultures of the ancient world.[15] As the following passage, translated by the late Sumerologist Thorkild Jacobsen, shows, the ritual imagery of sacred marriage was quite graphic:

> Milady bathes her holy loins in water, bathes them in water for the loins of the king, bathes them in water for the loins of Iddin-Dagan. Holy [goddess] Inanna rubs with soap, sprinkles the floor with cedar perfume. The king goes with lifted head [euphemistic for "erection"] to her holy loins, goes with lifted head to the loins of Inanna, Amaushumgalanna goes to bed with her. In her holy loins he can but truly praise the woman: O my one of holy loins! O my holy Inanna!" After he on the bed, in the holy loins, has made the queen rejoice, after he on the bed, in the holy loins, has made holy Inanna rejoice, she in return soothes the heart for him there on her bed: "Verily, I am the constant prolonger of [King] Iddin-Dagan's days of life."[16]

In other words, we must turn Wellhausen's analysis on its head. Hosea did not originate the marriage allegory because of its alleged monotheistic implications. On the contrary, Hosea used the marriage allegory despite its polytheistic associations, so that "the devil shouldn't have the best tunes." As we now know, the prophet's audience was made up of Israelite adherents of the fertility worship associated with the ancient Syro-Palestinian god Baal. Baal was sexually involved not only with anthropomorphic deities but with beasts as well:[17]

> Baal loved a heifer in the pasture, a cow in the fields by the shore. . . . He lay with her times seventy and seven. She let him mount times eighty and eight.

Hosea himself makes no claim that Yahweh is the sole god in existence, only that Israel as his bride owes him the fidelity that a wife

owes her husband. All that Hosea did was to restate the old monolatrous demand, that Yahweh alone be worshiped, in a metaphor that
had the potential to appeal to his contemporaries.

Additional support for the early provenance of the conditional
covenant between Yahweh and Israel comes from the much-studied
twenty-fourth chapter of the Book of Joshua.[18] The setting of Joshua
24 is Shechem, a city not connected with the conquest traditions elsewhere in Joshua or in the Book of Judges.[19] Joshua has summoned all
of Israel to stand before God. In the presence of all assembled, Joshua
summarizes Israel's "history," beginning with the ancestors, who
lived beyond the river and served other gods. Joshua relates Jacob's
descent into Egypt, the dispatch of Moses and Aaron, the smiting of
Egypt, the drowning of the Egyptian army in the darkness, the sojourn in the wilderness, the conquest of Transjordan, the encounter
with Balaq aided by Balaam the curser, the crossing of the Jordan, the
battle at Jericho, the dispatch of the hornet, and God's gift of the land.

After completing his narration, Joshua turns to the people, ad-
monishing them to remove the "foreign gods" and to serve Yahweh
exclusively (Jos 24:14–15):

> And now, fear Yahweh and serve him fully and faithfully. Remove the
> gods your ancestors served on the other side of the river [Euphrates]
> and in Egypt, and serve Yahweh. But if it displeases you to serve Yah-
> weh, choose now whom you will serve, either the gods your ancestors
> served on the other side of the river or the gods of the Amorite in whose
> land you dwell. But I and my household shall serve Yahweh.

The people then affirm that they too will serve Yahweh. Joshua
warns them that Yahweh's service is "impossible":

> You will not be able to serve Yahweh, for he is [a veritable pantheon
> of] holy gods. He is a jealous god. He will not bear rebellious sinful-
> ness. If you abandon Yahweh and serve foreign gods after the good he
> did for you, he will turn and harm you and destroy you.

The people protest that they are prepared to serve Yahweh and to
bear their own witness to their choice. Once the people have agreed
to abandon all the "foreign gods," Joshua makes a covenant in their
behalf. There, at Shechem, he provides them with a fixed rule. He sets
down all these matters in writing in a document of God's teaching
(*seper torat elohim*). Finally, Joshua sets up a large stone under the

oak in Yahweh's sanctuary. The stone is designated as witness to Yahweh's word to the people.

Joshua 24 cannot be contemporary with the events it describes. For one thing, the chapter accepts the historicity of the Exodus from Egypt and the successful conquest of both sides of the Jordan by a united army of Israelite invaders. For another, the fall of Jericho to the Israelites, although described differently in this chapter and in Joshua 6, nonetheless has no archaeological support. But we can fix the date of the chapter with a good deal of confidence. As we have shown elsewhere, the language of the chapter points to the ninth to eighth century.[20] The audience addressed live in peace and comfort, and there is no reference to external enemies or looming exile. In all likelihood, Joshua 24 dates from a period early in the long and prosperous reign of Jeroboam II (786–746).

Fixing the date of Joshua 24 enables us to clarify the chapter's agenda. Let us supplement what is known from literary and critical study of the chapter with extrabiblical data: Shechem was an important city with ancient religious traditions reaching well back into the second millennium.[21] Numerous scholars have observed a connection between Joshua 24 and Judges 8–9.[22] Those chapters in the narrative refer to a divinity variously known as El Berît, "El of the Covenant/ God of the Covenant" (Judg 9:46), and Baal Berît, "Baal of the Covenant/Lord of the Covenant" (Judg 9:4), to whose worship a temple in Shechem was devoted.

The writer of Judges 8:33–34 clearly distinguishes this divinity from Yahweh. The authenticity of the Judges tradition is demonstrated by the attestation of the divine name *il brt* (that is, El Berît) in a document from the late second millennium.[23] Early in the first millennium, the people of Israel's northern kingdom reinterpreted Shechem's traditions in light of their own historical, mythical, and cultic traditions. Whatever the original significance of the name of the non-Israelite god El Berît, he fit nicely into the Israelite allegory of the god Yahweh, who had made a covenant with his people.[24] Israelites came to speak of Shechem as the holy place where an ancient worthy had brought the whole people to obligate themselves voluntarily to the sole worship of Yahweh and to bear responsibility for failing to live up to the terms of that obligation.

The covenant allegory of Joshua 24 was not an Israelite invention out of whole cloth. As George Mendenhall contends, the writer adapted the language of international treaties to his theological ends. Indeed, there were significant parallels between the biblical accounts of *berît* and the international Hittite "suzerainty treaties" of the latter half of the second millennium B.C.E.[25] The treaties to which Mendenhall refers are essentially elaborate fidelity oaths with two fundamental components: obligations to the great king that must be met and divine punishment for failing to meet the obligations. Only the inferior king is bound by the stipulations of the treaty, and only he takes an oath of obedience.

In the biblical scheme, Yahweh is the great king and Israel plays the part assigned in the political treaties to the minor king. Like the minor king, Israel will be blessed and maintain its land and well-being if it fulfills detailed obligations and serves the great king (Yahweh) exclusively. Should Israel turn to gods other than Yahweh, it will suffer the same accursed fate as the minor king who fails to live up to his detailed obligations but instead serves kings other than the great one to whom he is allied by treaty.

Mendenhall believed that the formal similarities of the political treaties to their biblical reflexes justified assigning the underlying traditions of the Decalogue and Joshua 24 to the period when Israel first arose as a political entity:

> This covenant type is even more important as a starting point for the study of Israelite traditions because it cannot be proven to have survived the downfall of the great empires of the late second millennium B.C. When empires arose again, notably Assyria, the structure of the covenant by which they bound their vassals is entirely different.[26]

More recent studies by such scholars as Delbert Hillers, Rintje Frankena, Dennis McCarthy, and Moshe Weinfeld indicate that Mendenhall overstated his case.[27] That is, there was much more formal continuity between the political treaties of the second and first millennium than Mendenhall originally allowed. Nonetheless, he was essentially correct to stress some significant differences between second- and first-millennium forms and to show that Joshua 24 and the Decalogue contain genuine archaic elements.[28] In contrast, the attempts to return to Wellhausen's position, most notably by Lothar Perlit in his *Bundestheologie*, which maintain that the covenant be-

tween Yahweh and Israel was a theological creation of the Deuteronomic movement of the seventh century B.C.E. formulated in response
to the Assyrian crisis, have no basis.[29]

Paradoxically, the most significant argument in favor of the early
date of the national conditional covenant has been overlooked by
most of the advocates of its early date: The Decalogue, the conditional "Mosaic" covenants in the Pentateuch, and Joshua 24 insist
that the Israelites worship Yahweh alone but make no claims that
Yahweh alone is god. These texts demand that Israelites practice
monolatry, "the worship of one god where others may be presumed
to exist." In contrast to later monotheistic passages in the Bible, the
texts in question do not claim that Yahweh is the sole god in existence
and so make no corollary demand that Gentiles, too, must worship
Yahweh. Mendenhall, however, viewed the covenant notion as
monotheistic:[30]

> The population of the twelve tribes were predominantly native Pales-
> tinians who had *converted to monotheism* [emphasis added] under the
> covenant with Yahweh.

In a similar fashion, Weinfeld claimed that the covenant was a
"perfect metaphor" for loyalty in a monotheistic religion and that the
notion of divine-human covenant was unique to Israel.[31] It may not
be possible, first of all, to expect uniqueness in religious imagery.[32]
Second, the biblical writers themselves conceded the possibility of
covenants with gods other than Yahweh. Thus the early passage in
Exodus 23:22 contains the following prohibition:[33]

> You shall not make a covenant with them [the inhabitants of the land]
> or with their gods.

Apparently there was no more uniqueness in making covenants
with gods than with other humans.

Other extrabiblical sources likewise undermine the claim that a divine-human covenant was a notion unique to Israelite thinking.[34]
One of the Phoenician inscriptions from Arslan Tash guarantees protection from demonic stranglers, claiming, "They made eternal
covenants with us. Asshur made them with us as did every divinity
and great one—the council of all our holy beings."[35] Needless to say,

this same text vitiates the assertion of those scholars who insist that the notion of covenant with divinity is necessarily monotheistic.

Akkadian evidence points to a similar conclusion. The verb *salāmu* is used regularly in Akkadian to describe covenants and political alliances. Forms of the same word are commonly found in Akkadian prayer literature to describe the reconciliation of a god with a worshiper.[36] That both senses of *salāmu* could be simultaneously suggested to an Akkadian speaker is demonstrated by a twelfth-century prophecy attributed to the god Marduk: *rubû šû mātāti kalîšina ibêl u anakūma ilū kalâma ittišu salmāku Elamta iḫeppe*, "that prince shall rule all the countries, for I alone, all you gods, have a covenant with him. He shall destroy Elam." Similarly, another Akkadian text reads: *ilū EN salīmīšu*, "the gods will be his allies."[37]

It is at the monolatrous stage that the allegory of covenant modeled on the international treaty form makes the most sense. The great kings bound the lesser kings by treaty because they acknowledged the very real possibility that the lesser king could serve another master. Both the Decalogue and Joshua 24 acknowledge the possibility that Israelites could serve other gods. This is why it was necessary for Yahweh to bind them by covenant. It is striking that in the exilic and postexilic periods, when the Israelite religion became consistently monotheistic, the concept of a conditional national covenant between Yahweh and the people of Israel became a dead letter.[38]

The allegory of a covenant modeled on international treaties also makes the most sense at the earliest stages of Israel's political development. If we may borrow a leaf from Wellhausen, the political allegory of Israel's covenant with Yahweh was more "natural" in Israel's formative stages than was the marriage allegory.[39] As we have seen, contemporary scholarship is virtually unanimous in viewing Israel as an ethnically diverse group that arose within Canaan. Against this background, we may view the covenant allegory as reflecting the institutional reality described by Max Weber in *Ancient Judaism*. Weber characterized Israel as an "oath-bound confederation" with two main purposes: cultic unity and military unity.

The covenant with Yahweh was the religious expression of the mundane cultic and military union of the different groups that had merged to form the people of Israel. A covenant with Yahweh was the allegorical statement of the emergent national unity. Yahweh, who was viewed as the force responsible for the emergence of the new group, thus became a partner in the confederation and, accordingly, the guarantor of the Israelite social order and its material prosperity. Joshua 24, for all its elaboration, retains formative traditions of the "oath-bound confederation." Among others, the memory of the original diversity of the different groups is preserved in allusions to the gods beyond the river and the gods of the Amorites. In contrast, the marriage allegory, as enunciated by Hosea, preserves no memories of aboriginal diversity among the ancestors of Israel.[40]

Given the early appearance of the covenant allegory in Israel, we may ask why the eighth-century prophets seldom use this notion. The answer is not difficult to find. In Judah, the allegory of the people's conditional covenant with Yahweh was superseded by the royal notion of Yahweh's unconditional *berît*, "covenant," with the king.[41] The teachings of the literary prophets likewise tended to undermine the covenant notion. For one thing, the national covenant was sealed by sacrifices, or cultic procedures that resembled sacrifices, and the eighth-century prophets minimized the importance of the priesthood and the sacrificial system.[42]

It is not that the literary prophets were unaware of the covenant allegory.[43] On the contrary, they ignored or criticized *berît* when they considered the popular perception to be misguided. This may be seen clearly in Hosea 6:6–7, a famous passage whose full significance has not always been appreciated:[44]

> For I delight in loyalty [*ḥesed*], not sacrifice [*zebaḥ*], acknowledgment of God rather than holocausts [animals]. But they at Adam violated the covenant. It was there that they betrayed me.

This passage must be read in the light of Psalms 50:5:

> Gather to me my loyalists [*ḥasiday*]. Those who make a covenant with me by sacrifice [*zebaḥ*].

The Psalms passage demonstrates that sacrifice was a means by which one covenanted with the god of Israel. The covenant between Yahweh and Israel was supposed to establish a relationship of loyalty between the parties. Hosea asserts, however, that his audience had participated in the ritual of covenant making (the sacrifice) but had shown their disloyalty by violating the covenant itself. Yahweh, proclaims Hosea, delights not in the ritual of covenant but in the loyalty in which the relationship of covenant is supposed to be expressed.

The preceding passage is one indication of why the allegory of covenant fell into relative unimportance in the eighth-century prophets' thinking. But the allegory of covenant became popular again in the succeeding two centuries, which witnessed a widespread nostalgia for an old world that was ending, a nostalgia visible all over the Near East during the latter part of the first millennium B.C.E.[45]

The revival of covenant in Israel cannot be separated from analogous phenomena. In Babylonia, for example, at the very time that the ancient native Akkadian language was being heavily Aramaicized, the Neo-Babylonian kings—themselves more at home in Aramaic than in Akkadian—were sponsoring searches for ancient inscriptions and attempting to revive the revered Old Babylonian script. The royal inscriptions of these same Neo-Babylonian kings ignored the proper grammatical case endings but regularly used archaisms of the "yea-verily" kind. In Egypt, the Saite dynasty encouraged a cult of antiquity, which included the restoration to prominence of forgotten divinities and the reuse of Old and Middle Kingdom titles. In keeping with the *Zeitgeist*, the seventh-century book of Deuteronomy revived the ancient allegory of covenant and gave the conditional *berît* an expansive treatment befitting an idea whose time had come and would soon be gone.[46] Beginning in late preexilic times and continuing through the exile and return, Yahweh's unconditional covenant with the Davidic dynasty—kings descended from David—was replaced by Yahweh's unconditional covenant with Israel.[47]

If the comparative method has taught us anything about the realities of "the biblical period," it is that ancient Israel was not fundamentally innovative, if by "innovation" we mean creation *ex nihilo*, out of nothing. The genius of the Israelites' innovation was their remarkable ability to draw out the creative potential of concepts and institutions that Israel shared with its neighbors and to achieve new syntheses. The Hebrews borrowed their earliest script from the Phoenicians and their later script from the Arameans. They borrowed poetic forms from the larger Syro-Palestinian culture and laws from Mesopotamia. They borrowed the story of the great flood from Mesopotamia and the figure of Balaam from Transjordan. We should not be surprised, therefore, to learn that a covenant between divinities and human beings was also not an Israelite invention.[48] Although the allegory of divine-human covenant was not unique to the Bible, the covenant assumed far greater significance in biblical writings than in other extant ancient Near Eastern literatures, because the allegory of covenant expressed the demands of Israelite monolatry, the notion that Israel must serve Yahweh and no other gods.

Put a bit differently, the religion of the new Israelite group was fundamentally political. If Yahweh embodied Israelite nationhood, it made perfect sense for Yahweh's representatives to claim for him total allegiance, and this required that he alone be worshiped. The language that they used for this total allegiance was allegorical imagery drawn from the political language of *berît*, or "covenant."

CHAPTER 5

Abraham

What then are we to say about Abraham, our forefather according to the flesh?

—Romans 4:1

Only through the faith that Abraham had in the Lord, did he come to inherit this world and the next.

—Mekilta D'Rabbi Ismael (Beshallah 6)

For more than a century, modern Bible scholars have argued about the historicity of the patriarchs. Through the first two decades of the twentieth century, most nonfundamentalists denied that the women and men around whom the tales of Genesis revolve were real historical characters. Indeed, there was a widespread current of opinion that the mothers and fathers of Israel had originated as divinities in prebiblical times, that only in the course of time had they been "humanized."

According to this analysis, the tombs of Abraham, Sarah, Isaac, Rebecca, Jacob, and Leah in Hebron originated as cult sites of Canaanite gods and goddesses. Abraham was a particularly good subject for mythic interpretation because biblical traditions associated him with Ur in Iraq and Harran in Syria, both known to have been centers of the ancient Mesopotamian moon cult.[1] In addition, his father's name, Terah, could be related to Yerah, the moon. Abraham even had a relative named Laban, "the white one," a transparent reference to the moon.

By the end of World War I, however, the mythological interpretation of the patriarchal tales had all but disappeared. As we noted earlier, the continuing archaeological discoveries of vast quantities of literary and nonliterary data appeared to supply corroborative "parallels" to the patriarchal stories against the background of the second millennium B.C.E. Moreover, by 1974 the scholarly consensus in favor of historicity had become so overwhelming that Thomas L. Thompson could safely write the following:[2]

> Even literary critical studies of individual traditions within Genesis now accept the basic historicity of Abraham, Isaac and Jacob.

But shortly thereafter, this consensus collapsed. The detailed studies by Thompson and the independent research by John van Seters (especially his *Abraham*) and other scholars combined to demonstrate that many of the "parallels" assembled over a half century to show that the biblical stories of the patriarchs fit the history and institutions of the second millennium B.C.E. could not sustain close examination.

We have seen how one celebrated example—the institution of the wife who, like the biblical Sarah, was simultaneously a wife and a "sister" of the same man—turned out to be based on faulty interpretations of legal documents. Other institutions reflected in the tales of the patriarchs, such as the proper custody of the household gods or the rights and obligations of surrogate mothers were shown to be irrelevant to dating because they were not restricted to the second millennium.[3] The same was true of the names that had been adduced as evidence of remote antiquity. The fact that some of the names of characters in the patriarchal narratives corresponded to names found in second-millennium sources proved only that certain names were tenacious.

Without these props, attention returned to the numerous first-millennium elements, which had been explained by "biblical archaeology" as late additions to much older stories. It became clear that references to "Arameans" had to mean the first-millennium inhabitants of Syria and not the second-millennium "Amorites"; "Philistines" were indeed the Aegean immigrants who first appeared in the eastern Mediterranean at the end of the thirteenth century B.C.E. References to "the city of Beersheba" (Gen 26:33) were to the actual city built under the Israelite kingdom and not a "redactional note." And stories about "camels," which had not been domesticated in Syria-Palestine in the second millennium, did not originally refer to the "donkeys" of an "older," or "original," tradition.[4] Most important, scholars once again had to confront the one fact that could never be explained away: With the veneer of "essential historicity" removed, "the Bible is largely a tissue of miracle stories."[5]

Not all scholars were happy with these developments. The conservative British semiticist A. R. Millard, writing in 1992, argued that a date for a historical Abraham at the beginning of the second millennium B.C.E. was advantageous because the possibility[6]

> that Abraham was a real person is . . . important for all who take biblical teaching about faith seriously. . . . Without Abraham, a major block in the foundations of both Christianity and Judaism is lost; a fictional Abraham might incorporate and illustrate communal beliefs, but could supply no rational evidence. Inasmuch as the Bible claims uniqueness, and the absolute of divine revelation, the Abraham narratives deserve a positive, respectful approach.

In other words, Abraham has to be a historical figure because "biblical teaching about faith" requires a historical figure. Needless to say, this is hardly a historical argument.

When studying the Bible for historical information, we must bear in mind that the writers regularly attempted to explain phenomena that were well known to their audiences (if not to us) but whose origins were remote or obscure. Some of these explanations are less credible than others. Consider, for example, Genesis 4:22:

> Zillah . . . bore Tubal-Cain, the father of all who forge implements of bronze and iron.

The passage cannot be dated earlier than 1200 B.C.E., which is about when Syria-Palestine entered the Iron Age. Indeed, the implication of Genesis 4:22 is that specialized metalwork is well known to the author's audience, who would want to know the name of the inventor, or "father," of the necessary technology. For this ancient audience, the name Tubal-Cain was an obvious choice, because Tubal means "metalworker" and Cain means "smith."[7] Needless to say, a historian of technology would not accept this explanation and would look elsewhere. And this is precisely what we must do with regard to the name Abraham.

Genesis 17:3–5 states that the first Hebrew patriarch was known as Abram until Yahweh changed his name:

God continued speaking, "As for me, this is my covenant with you. You shall be the father of a multitude of nations. And you shall no longer be called Abram, but your name shall be Abraham."

Here, too, it is obvious that the name Abraham was known to the audience of the author, who explains that the name was given by Yahweh. Although the claim that a divinity was responsible surely served the ancient audience, this explanation is, by definition, not historical, and so we, the contemporary audience, must look elsewhere.

Years ago, Hermann Gunkel, a German scholar who emphasized the need to recover the particular situations, or "life-settings," that produced the different forms of biblical literature, suggested one productive avenue of inquiry:

> We are not putting a new meaning into the legends which treat of such race-individuals, when we regard their heroes, Ishmael, Jacob, Esau, and others, as tribes and try to interpret the stories about them as tribal events; we are simply getting at their meaning as it was understood in primitive times in Israel.[8]

The figure of Abraham probably originated in such a "tribal event," in this case, one that we may be able to recover. Early in the thirteenth century B.C.E., Seti I, king of Egypt, set up a victory monument at Beth-Shean, near the present-day border between Israel and Jordan. The stela relates that both a coalition of 'Apiru from a locale named Yarmut and a tribe called Tayar/lu attacked a group by the name of Raham.[9] The aggressors against the Raham group were defeated by the Egyptians. At the present time, we have no further information about the subsequent fortunes of the Raham group. If the Rahamites became part of the new coalition Israel, it would have been natural for a Hebrew writer to provide them with an ancestor, just as was done for all the other Israelite tribes, as well as for the Ammonites and Moabites. The name Ab-Raham would then mean "father of the Raham tribe." Over time, this original sense would have been forgotten and the name reinterpreted as "father of a multitude of nations" (Gen 17:4–5).[10]

We cannot be as certain as Gunkel is about "the meaning as it was understood in primitive times." We may be certain, though, that once invented, characters who originated as the embodiments of tribes acquired more sharply defined human characteristics.[11] Because the biblical characters belonged to the larger community, accounts of their lives were circumscribed by both communal needs and political and social realities. Nonetheless, authorial creativity and the need to entertain audiences must also be reckoned with. Against this background, we may best comprehend the biblical Abraham as a shifting allegory, sometimes symbolizing events both real and imagined in the life of the entire people and at other times standing for historical characters of different periods.[12] Let us turn now to some specific examples.

In Genesis 12:10, Abram, accompanied by his wife Sarai, moves to Egypt to reside there temporarily because of the severe famine in Canaan. Approaching the Egyptian border, he fears that Sarai's great beauty will tempt the Egyptians to kill him and abduct his wife. Both to exploit the situation and to save his life, Abram asks Sarai to say she is his sister. His fears as well as his foresight prove to be well founded. First "the (unspecified) Egyptians" and then Pharaoh's princes remark on Sarai's beauty, and she is taken into Pharaoh's palace to be his wife.[13] As the brother of the bride, it goes well with Abram, who "acquired sheep, oxen, asses, male and female slaves, she-asses, and camels." But as punishment for marrying Sarai (v. 19), who was already Abram's wife, Yahweh afflicts Pharaoh and his household with great plagues.[14] Pharaoh then summons Abram and rebukes him for having misrepresented Sarai's marital status. He then sends Abram and Sarai out of Egypt, who take with them large amounts of cattle, silver, and gold.

On the level of narrative, the story is about the (mis)adventures of Abram and Sarai in Egypt, but the fact that the story also operates at a second level was not lost on the rabbis of late antiquity:[15]

R. Phineas in the name of R. Hoshaya: "The Holy, be he blessed, said to Abraham our father, 'Go pave the way for your children.' So you find that everything written of Abraham our father, is written of his children. Of Abraham is written, 'There was famine in the land.' Of Israel is written, 'For these two years, famine' [Gen 45:6]. Of Abraham is written, 'Abraham went down to Egypt.' Of Israel is written, 'Our ancestors went down to Egypt' [Num 20:15]. Of Abraham is written, 'to sojourn there.' Of Israel is written, 'to sojourn in the land we came' [Gen 47:6]. Of Abraham is written, 'For the famine was severe in the land.' Of Israel is written, 'For the famine was severe in the land' [Gen

43:1]. Of Abraham is written, 'They will kill me but keep you alive.'
Of Israel is written, 'Every male born you shall cast in the Nile but keep
every female alive' [Exod 1:22]. Of Abraham is written, 'Abram was
rich, in cattle, silver and gold.' Of Israel is written, 'He brought them
out with silver and gold' [Ps 105:37]. Of Abraham is written, 'Pharaoh
put men in charge of him and sent him off.' Of Israel is written, 'The
Egyptians pressed the people to send them off quickly.'" [Exod 12:33]

For the rabbis, the story was a typology, a symbolic prefiguration
of what would later happen in Egypt to the descendants of Abram
and Sarai. R. Phineas and R. Hoshaya express no doubt that both the
earlier and the later events had actually transpired. Because God was
the cause of all events, he could shape the contours of an early event
to symbolize and prefigure a later event, of which he was also the
cause. On this point, R. Phineas and R. Hoshaya were in full agreement with Paul, who some two centuries earlier had observed the following of his biblical ancestors:

All these things happened to them as symbolic types [typikos] but were
written for us as warning. (1Cor 10:11)

To understand the critical point of the pericope of Abram/Sarai
and Pharaoh, we need only substitute R. Phineas's typological reading with an allegorical reading. That is, Abram's descent into Egypt is
an allegory of Israel's descent into Egypt. Yahweh's plagues on
Pharaoh and his household are allegories of the plagues that Yahweh
inflicted on Pharaoh and Egypt. The language of Pharaoh's expulsion
of Abraham in Genesis 12 is precisely the language of expulsion of the
Israelites in Exodus 13. That Abraham leaves with riches of silver and
gold is paralleled not only by the verse cited by R. Phineas but also by
Exodus 12:35–36:

The Israelites had asked the Egyptians for silver and gold jewelry. . . .
Because Yahweh had made the Egyptians well disposed toward them,
they let Israelites have whatever they asked.

What R. Phineas did not observe is that because the tradition of Israelite servitude in Egypt seems itself allegorical, the episode involving Abram, Sarai, and Pharaoh is an allegory of an allegory.

In other tales, Abraham/Abram is an allegorical representative of
specific Israelite leaders of the historical period. Genesis 14 is an excellent example.

One of the most debated chapters in contemporary scholarship, Genesis 14 has been assigned dates ranging over a thousand years.[16] The opening phrase, "It was in the days of Chedorlaomer," sets the events of the story in remote antiquity, that is, at a time remote from the author. Because Genesis 14 provides names for eight different kings who reigned simultaneously, some scholars view the chapter as a precious historical record from the second pre-Christian millennium. If some of the kings could be identified with certainty, then a date might be confidently assigned for the historical Abraham. Other scholars have interpreted this chapter as a kind of midrash written in the Persian period between the sixth and fourth centuries B.C.E. or, even later, in the Hasmonean period between the second and first century B.C.E.

The first eleven verses of the story make no mention of Abram or his family. Instead, this section describes a war between two sets of allies: four kings from outside the area of Canaan against their five rebellious tributaries in Canaan, the latter of whom mustered their forces at the Valley of the Dead Sea, known in ancient times as the Valley of Siddim.[17] The four kings invaded along the north-south road east of the Jordan River (in present-day Jordan), defeating the various peoples along the way until they reached El-paran, possibly near present-day Eilat. They turned northwest to Kadesh (ancient En Mishpat and modern Ein Qudeirat), subduing Amalekite territory. Then they continued northeast to Hazazon-tamar (Ein Husb), defeating its Amorite inhabitants and finally encountering and defeating their primary opponents at the Valley of Siddim. Among these opponents was the king of Sodom, and it is at this juncture that the events become relevant to Abram:

> Now the Valley of Siddim was full of bitumen pits, and as the kings of Sodom and Gomorrah fled, some fell into them, and the rest fled to the mountain. So the enemy took all the goods of Sodom and Gomorrah and all their provisions and went their way; they also took Lot, the son of Abram's brother, who dwelled in Sodom, and his goods and departed with Chedorlaomer, king of Elam; Tidal, king of Goyim; Amraphel, king of Shinar; and Arioch, king of Ellasar—four kings against five.

We readers are informed in verses 12–13 that Lot, Abraham's nephew who dwelled in Sodom, has been taken captive by the invaders, along with all his possessions. A refugee from the front brings the bad news to "Abram the Hebrew," who, we learn, is allied to three Amorite brothers. Abram thus has a personal and military obligation to enter the war, even though this puts him on the same side militarily as the kings of the wicked cities of Sodom, Gomorrah, Admah, and Zeboiim. Mustering his 318 troops, Abram pursues the foe as far as Dan, defeating them and following their retreating forces as far as Hobah, north of Damascus. He brings back all the captured possessions as well as Lot and all his possessions and the captive women and the rest of the people. Upon his victory, the king of Sodom comes to meet Abram at the Valley of Shaveh, identical with the Valley of the King.[18] The king of Sodom asks Abram to give him the people he has taken but to keep the possessions for himself. Abram responds:

> I swear to Yahweh [the divine name Yahweh does not occur in the Septuagint to this verse]—El-Elyon, Creator of Heaven and Earth, that I will not partake of anything belonging to you, so much as a thread or a sandal strap. For your part, you will not say, "It was I enriched Abram." Not I—only what the fighters consumed. As for the share of the men who went with me—Aner, Eshkol, and Mamre—let them take their share.

For any number of reasons, this tale cannot be historical. Spinoza already noted the geographic anachronism "Dan" in verse 14.[19] Of the five local kingdoms, four are the legendary "wicked cities" that were overturned by God. The fifth was spared only because of Lot's plea (Gen 19:20–21). The names of the kings of Sodom and Gomorrah—Bera, "In-Evil," and Birsha, "In-Wickedness"—would not be out of place in a morality play. In contrast, although the names of the invaders have a more authentic ring, those that can be identified were not contemporaneous. Needless to say, an international alliance of this scope would almost certainly have left more evidence than simply this chapter. About what and about whom, then, is the story?

Over the centuries, scholars have pointed out parallels between this chapter and the tales of David. The medieval French Jewish scholar Joseph Bekhor Shor compared Melchizedek's provision of bread and wine with the actions of David's supporters during Absalom's rebellion (2Sam 17:27–28).[20] More recently, Benjamin Mazar,

Moshe Weinfeld, and others noted that the story justifies Israel's possession of the land on both sides of the Jordan in the Davidic period. The geographic items deserve particular notice because they would have served to elicit some response from the audience. We may observe that according to the last verse of Genesis 13, immediately preceding the account of the battle, Abram dwelled in Hebron, the city that, as every Israelite knew, had served as David's capital for seven years.

Note also that whereas "Dan" is an anachronism for the time of the patriarch "Abram," this locale served as the northern border of David's Israelite kingdom.[21] In a similar vein, the narrative specifies a campaign stop at Tamar, which, according to 1 Kings 9:18, was built during the Solomonic period. Another stop on the campaign was Kadesh, located at Ein Qudeirat near the junction of a road leading from Suez to Beersheba/Hebron. The site shows three superimposed fortresses, the earliest dating from the tenth century B.C.E., that is, from the time of King Solomon.[22]

In short, we have strong intimations that Genesis 14 was composed for the aggrandizement of David and Solomon. Perhaps the most significant indication of a Davidic background for the story is the manner in which it accentuates the heroic character of "Abram the Hebrew." The biblical scholar Yohanan Muffs showed that in Genesis 14, Abraham is depicted as a paradigmatic noble warrior:[23]

> Each element of Genesis 14 has its exact counterpart in the laws of war and in the etiquette of booty restoration found sporadically in the international treaties of Boghazköi and Ugarit. The Israelite narrator brings together all these ancient laws of war and peace in his depiction of Abraham as the most noble of warriors.

Specifically, Muffs demonstrates that Genesis 14 corresponds very closely to 1 Samuel 30. In that story, the city of Ziklag held by David is attacked when David and his warriors are away. David's wives and the families of his soldiers are taken captive, and David's troops, embittered by their loss of family and property, threaten to stone their leader (v. 6). But by recapturing what had been taken, David turns a disaster into a spectacular triumph:

> David rescued all that the Amalekites had taken away; He rescued his two wives. Nothing of all of theirs was missing, young or old, large or

small, sons or daughters or possessions, whatever had been taken all of
it David brought back. (1Sam 30:18–19)

Instead of keeping the booty, however, David makes gifts of it to
towns that had suffered from the Amalekites' depredations.[24] Plainly,
Genesis 14 is an allegory of the Davidic period. Abraham the noble
warrior represents David the noble warrior. The allegory is a piece of
political propaganda composed in the reign of Solomon, David's son
and successor, to answer criticisms of the monarchy which, in its earliest days, had made radical changes in Israelite society.[25] One of the
most radical of David's policies was military expansionism, which
brought glory and wealth to the throne but at the same time risked
unacceptable losses to the Israelite populace:

> When David and his men came to the city, they found it burned down
> and their wives and sons and daughters taken captive. Then David and
> the people who were with him raised their voices and wept until they
> had no more strength to weep. . . . David was in great danger, for the
> people spoke of stoning him, because all the people were bitter in spirit
> for their sons and daughters. But David strengthened himself in Yah-
> weh his God. (1Sam 30:1–6)

Another interesting detail is provided by Genesis 14:15, which relates how Abram the noble warrior engaged in battle "north of Damascus." That point would hardly have been lost on an audience with
access to the information provided in 2 Samuel 8:5–8:

> When the Arameans of Damascus came to help King Hadadezer of
> Zobah, David killed 22,000 men of the Arameans. Then David put
> garrisons among the Arameans of Damascus, and the Arameans be-
> came servants to David and brought tribute. Yahweh gave victory to
> David wherever he went. David took the gold shields that were carried
> by the servants of Hadadezer and brought them to Jerusalem. From
> Betah and from Berothai, towns of Hadadezer, King David took a great
> amount of bronze.

Like David, Abram fought the enemy far from home, and like
David, Abram was brought reluctantly into the hostilities at Damascus. Neither man entered the lists for personal gain or glory.

But we may go even further in elucidating the Davidic background
of Abraham's nobility. In Genesis 14, Abraham's heroism and nobility overcome the embarrassing fact of the company he keeps. Abra-

ham is on the same side as the wicked kings, the kings of the cities that were justly destroyed by God because of their unmitigated wickedness. His other allies (*ba'ale berît*) are Amorites, one of the indigenous peoples of the land often vilified in the Bible. Because the term "Amorite" is not always used in the Bible for the same specific ethnic group, it is highly instructive to read 1 Samuel 7:16:[26]

> The cities that the Philistines had taken from Israel returned to Israel ... these cities Israel got back from the Philistines, there being a pact [*šalom*] between Israel and these Amorites.

The obvious sense of this verse is that "Amorite" could mean "Philistines" in a text relating events of the time of David, that Abram's Amorite allies reflect David's rapprochement with the Philistines. Surely if Abram could be allied with Amorites, so could David, so long as it was required by realpolitik. After all, had not Abram actually fought on the same side as Sodom when given no other choice? Yet just as he had kept his distance from Sodom, refusing to profit personally, so could David.

Davidic realpolitik of a religious nature underlies the Melchi-zedek episode in Genesis 14:18–20. These verses precede the dialogue between Abram and the king of Sodom, which we discussed earlier:[27]

> Melchi-zedek, king of Salem, brought out bread and wine. He was a priest of [the god] El-Elyon. He blessed him, saying, "Blessed be Abram to El-Elyon, Creator of Heaven and Earth. And blessed be El-Elyon, who delivered your foes into your power." Then [Abram] gave him a tithe of all.

Although the episode is meaningless against a second-millennium background, several scholars have shown that the passage did serve the needs of the Davidic monarchy.[28] Melchi-zedek is designated as the king of Salem, and inasmuch as Salem is identified with Zion in Psalms 76:3, Salem is none other than a nickname for Jerusalem. According to traditions preserved primarily in 2 Samuel and 1 Kings, David and Solomon had turned a foreign city, Jerusalem, into a cult center of Israel's god. David had even appointed sons of his own as priests (2Sam 8:18).

Biblical sources indicate that there was significant opposition to these religious innovations. Significantly, Nathan, a prophet of Yahweh, opposed David's construction of a temple (2Sam 7), and Israelites living in the north soon rejected Jerusalem's monarchy, calendar, and priesthood. There can be little doubt that elements of the native Israelite priesthood(s) were threatened by competition from the local Jerusalem priesthood, elements of which remained in power.

The German scholar Ernest A. Knauf went even further in his assertions about the character of the early cult of Jerusalem:[29]

> Solomon did not build the temple of Jerusalem or any other temple that is presently known, but, he introduced the Israelite and Judaean tribal god Yahweh into the main temple of Canaanite Jerusalem, where Yahweh joined El . . . and Asherah as a lesser god.

Even though Knauf overstepped the limits of the available evidence, he is surely on the right track. For many Israelites, the cultic associations of Jerusalem must have been largely unfavorable. With that in mind, we can see that Genesis 14 has a religious-political objective: to justify the actions of David and Solomon. What the allegory about Abram and his dealings with Melchi-zedek claims is that the relocation of the cult center of the Israelites to Jerusalem, originally a non-Israelite city, was not an innovation. The site of Jerusalem had always been holy. Abram himself recognized the sacred character of Jerusalem's ancient priesthood by offering Melchi-zedek a tithe of all his spoils of war. The kings of the line of David were actually reviving an ancient practice that could be traced back to a revered ancestor.

The second element of Melchi-zedek is the same as that of Adoni-Zedek, a king of Jerusalem contemporary with Joshua.[30] We cannot doubt that the ancient audience would have connected the name Melchi-zedek with the name Zadok, which shares the consonantal root structure ZDK. Zadok was a priest at the shrine of Jerusalem during the reign of David and the sole priest at that same site during the reign of Solomon.[31]

As our final example, we observe that Abraham serves as an allegory of David's relations with the Philistines in the episode related in Genesis 21;22–33:[32]

> At that time, Abimelech and Phicol, chief of his troops, said to Abraham, "God is with you in all you do. Now swear to me by these gods that you will not betray me or my future descendants but that you will be as loyal to me and to the land where you have sojourned as I have

been to you." Abraham responded, "I will swear." Then Abraham raised with Abimelech the issue of the well of water that the servants of Abimelech had seized. Then Abimelech responded, "I don't know who did this thing; you certainly did not tell me, nor have I ever heard of it other than now!" Then Abraham took sheep and oxen and gave them to Abimelech, and the two of them made a pact. Then Abraham specifically set apart seven ewes of the flock. So Abimelech said to Abraham, "What meaning do these seven ewes have that you have set apart?" He replied, "You are to accept these seven ewes from me to attest that I dug this well." This is why that place was named Beersheba, for there the two of them swore an oath. Once they had made the pact at Beersheba, Abimelech and Phicol, chief of his troops, departed and returned to Philistine country. Then [Abraham] planted a tamarisk at Beersheba and invoked there the name Yahweh—God Everlasting.

Just what is behind this story? Sarna suggests a literary motive:[33]

Abraham's encounter with Abimelech is reported with such an economy of detail that the background is obscure. Clearly it is not told for its own sake but for other reasons. It projects a fresh image of the patriarch. . . . He possesses a new sense of confidence.

But this will hardly do. The character who is portrayed as defeating the kings in Genesis 14 and as challenging divine justice in Genesis 18 has demonstrated confidence enough.

For Gunkel, Abimelech and the Hebrew patriarch personify conflicts among larger constituencies:[34]

Once in ancient times, so we may assume, there were conflicts over wells between the citizens of Gerar and the neighboring bedouins, ending in a compromise at Beer-sheba. The legend depicts these affairs as a war and a treaty between Abimelech, king of Gerar, and the patriarchs called in the legend Abraham or Isaac.

Let us first consider the story on its own terms. Abimelech, king of Gerar, initiates the proceedings, averring that God supports all of Abraham's actions. He then asks him to swear an oath. The oath, which is couched in treaty terminology, specifies that Abraham will demonstrate continuing loyalty (ḥesed) to Abimelech, just as Abimelech had done to Abraham. This is appropriate in this context because the two parties are preparing to conclude a covenant (berît). As is the case in treaties of the first millennium, which bind the descendants of the original parties as well as the parties themselves, Abraham is not to be disloyal to Abimelech himself or to his child or grandchild or to the land in which he has lived.[35]

Legally, Abraham is to commit himself by oath to be loyal to Abimelech's land throughout the dynastic succession and perhaps even beyond that. Abraham agrees to swear but first needs to resolve a condition precedent.[36] He raises the issue of the well that had been stolen by Abimelech's underlings.[37] Abimelech does not dispute the claim that his servants had misappropriated Abraham's well. Rather, he offers a threefold exculpation of his own actions: He does not know who the responsible parties are, as Abraham himself never told him. Indeed, this is the first time he has heard about the problem. Abraham accepts this formal denial and concludes the pact. To make certain that the present well will not be subject to a dispute, Abraham sets aside seven ewes as a gift to Abimelech, who accepts them on Abraham's terms. After concluding the pact, Abimelech and Phicol return home. With the jurisdiction over the well no longer in dispute, Abraham is able to consecrate Beersheba by planting a tamarisk and invoking the name Yahweh—God Everlasting.

To understand the historical circumstances underlying the story, we must be more specific about Gunkel's "ancient times." Our starting point is Abraham's treaty with the Philistine king. As we observed earlier, the earliest reference to the Philistines comes from Pharaoh Ramses III (ca. 1198–1166 B.C.E.), who identified them among a group of "sea peoples" who came originally from the area of the Aegean Sea to the Levant in the twelfth century B.C.E. Thus any biblical tale involving Philistines in Canaan cannot have originated earlier than the twelfth century.

As for Beersheba, stratum IX of Tell es-Seba', biblical Beersheba, shows a ceramic collection including shards of Philistine pottery, implying to the excavators a date at the end of the twelfth century or the beginning of the eleventh.[38] Evidence for substantial building increases in stratum VIII from the mid to late eleventh century B.C.E. Stratum VII shows evidence of an organized site plan and should be dated in the late eleventh or early tenth century B.C.E. Inasmuch as the digging of the well is central to the biblical story, establishing the date of its construction would be relevant. Indeed, a deep well found at the eastern edge of the mound was dated by Aharoni to Iron Age I (stratum VII), but because the stratigraphy of the well area had already been disrupted in antiquity, Amihai Mazar remains uncertain about its date.[39]

Against the background of the archaeological data, however, a tenth-century date for this Abraham tale fits perfectly with the events of David's life. The key is the closing verse (Gen 21:34): "Abraham resided in the land of the Philistines a long time." According to the narrative of 1 Samuel 27, David fled from Saul, who suspected him of designs on the throne, and sought shelter in Gath, a Philistine city. He lived for a considerable time in Philistine territory as a military ally of King Achish.[40]

As readers of the Bible have always sensed, the descriptions of David's cooperation with the Philistines are designed to put the best face on an embarrassing situation. The Philistines had been Israel's dedicated opponents throughout Saul's reign (1Sam 14:52). Saul and three of his sons, including Jonathan, allegedly David's closest friend, died in battle with the Philistines at the very time that David and his followers were serving in the Philistine ranks. In fact, according to 1 Samuel 28–29, David's contingent avoided direct battle with Saul on the Philistine side only because some of the Philistine princes questioned David's loyalty, which he himself protested.[41] After David's ascent to the throne, there are some notices of hostility with the Philistines (2Sam 5:17–25; 8:1; 21:15–22). On the whole, though, peace with the Philistines seems to have prevailed during David's reign. As king, David had Philistine detachments in his army (2Sam 8:18; 15:18), and his descendants continued to hold the city of Ziklag, which David had first received in return for his services to Achish (1Sam 27:6).[42]

Considering the allegorical connection between David and Abraham in Genesis 14, the story of Abraham's covenant with Abimelech should also be read as a political allegory, one that serves as an apology for David's pact with the Philistines. If Abraham, the great hero of the past, could cooperate with the Philistines, there was no reason that David could not. That the setting of Genesis 21 is military is indicated by the presence of the chief of the Philistine troops.

The covenant is initiated by Abimelech, who opens the conversation with "God is with you in all you do."[43] That the Philistine king acknowledges that God is with "Abraham" would have been a signal to Israelite audience. That the Lord was "with" David was first noted by an attendant of Saul's (1Sam 16:8), by Saul himself (1Sam 17:37; 18:29), and by the narrator (1Sam 18:14; cf. 2Sam 8:7). That God is "with" Abraham in "everything" indicates allegorically that God approves of *all* of David's actions, including the continuation of good relations with the Philistines in whose land David had dwelled. At the same time, however, the Israelite audience is informed that Abraham/David will stand up to the Philistines when it is necessary to defend the precious right to water. Also note that Beersheba, the scene of the pact between Abraham and Abimelech, is regularly identified as the southern limit of David's kingdom.[44]

CHAPTER 6

Jacob, Jeroboam, and Joseph

The tales we examined in the previous chapter were allegories of the southern hero David. As we might expect, the northerners also told stories about their champions, which they, too, formulated as allegories about legendary worthies of the past. On one level, the task of recovering the historical background of these biblical stories is simpler than for the southern legends because the northern kingdom had a briefer existence. Founded by Jeroboam I in 922 B.C.E., the northern kingdom fell to Assyria in 720. What complicates matters is that the northern traditions that survived the fall of Samaria were brought to Judah and often reworked by southern writers, some of whom considered the entire northern kingdom to have been a sinful aberration. As a result, some northern heroes lost their regional distinctiveness.

For example, in the final form of the book named for him, Joshua is portrayed as the great leader who led a unified Israel forward in the conquest of the promised land. But as scholars have found by combining the results of archaeology with the geographic data from the Book of Joshua, the man Joshua was, in all likelihood, originally a local champion from the tribe of Ephraim. Only in the literature of the seventh century B.C.E. and later was he transformed into the leader of all Israel in its conquest of the land.[1] In other instances, northern personalities and institutions were distorted and vilified to demonstrate that the sinfulness of the northerners had brought about the fall of their state. Consequently, any serious modern reading of the Bible must allow for the editorial process that northern documents underwent in Judah and later in the postexilic Jewish communities. This is especially true of the traditions concerning Jacob, father of the twelve sons from whom the tribes of Israel took their name, and the traditions concerning Joseph, his favorite son.

The name Jacob was very common in the ancient Near East among western Semites, speakers of languages closely akin to biblical Hebrew. Inasmuch as forms of Jacob are found from Old Babylonian to early post-Christian times, the name has no implications for dating the biblical sections in which it appears.[2] More transparently than Abraham, the name Jacob serves as an eponym, the name of a person believed to be the source of the name of a place, people, or the like.[3] In the books of the Pentateuch that follow Genesis, and in other books of the Bible, "Jacob," "House of Jacob," and "Assembly of Jacob" refer to the people "Israel."[4] Genesis itself depicts Jacob as the physical progenitor of the eponyms of individual Israelite tribes and confers on him the alternative name Israel. But if the origin of Jacob was as an eponymous ancestor, his allegorical role extended to the religious-political realm. We illustrate this by turning to the best-known episode in the Jacob tales, his wrestling match in Genesis 32:23–33:[5]

> That same night he rose, and taking his two wives, his two secondary wives, and his eleven sons, he crossed the ford of Jabbok. After taking them across the stream, he brought across all his possessions. Jacob was left alone. And a man wrestled with him until the rising of the morning star. When he saw that he had not prevailed against him, he wrenched his hip at the socket, so that the socket of Jacob's hip was strained as he wrestled with him. Then he said, "Release me, for the morning star has risen." But he answered, "I will not release you unless you bless me." So he said to him, "What is your name?" [He answered,] "Jacob." He replied, "Your name shall no longer be spoken Jacob, but Israel [Hebrew: Yisrael = God's striver], for you have striven with divinities and with humans and have prevailed." Jacob asked, "Pray speak your name." But he said, "Why do you ask my name?" But he blessed him there. So Jacob named the place Peniel [God's face], "for [said he], I have seen a divinity face to face, yet my life has been saved." The sun rose upon him as he passed Penuel, limping on his hip. That is why the children of Israel to this day will not eat the thigh muscle that is on the socket of the hip, since he wounded Jacob's hip socket at the thigh muscle.

This story has deservedly received attention from folklorists, comparative religionists, and, more recently, proponents of the academic study of the "Bible as literature." The most significant observation for understanding the pericope was made by the American Bible scholar Stanley Gevirtz, who wrote in 1976: "The entire incident was fraught with geo-political significance." Gevirtz pointed out that the incident is set in the Gilead region, the area just east of the Jordan River, at the ford of the Jabbok River, one of the Jordan's major tributaries, now known as the Zerqa (Blue) River in modern Jordan. The locales in the area—Mahanaim, Succoth, and Peniel—are "each etymologized in the course of the pericope, and each receives its name from Jacob."[6]

Jacob was surely not a historical figure. Entire peoples do not spring from the loins of historical figures. Historical figures do not wrestle with divinities, nor do they live to be 147 years of age. It is necessary, therefore, to find a historical figure associated with the "geo-political significance" of the locales that Gevirtz observed. Although we cannot point to the historical figure(s) who built Mahanaim and Sukkot, the Bible is more forthcoming about Peniel/Penuel. According to Judges 8:17, in the premonarchic period (twelfth to eleventh century B.C.E.) the tower at Penuel was smashed by Gideon when he slaughtered the inhabitants of the city for failing to provision his troops in the war against Midian.[7] According to 1 Kings 12:25, it was Jeroboam I who "built" Penuel after rebelling against Rehoboam, son of Solomon, and founding the northern kingdom:[8]

> Jeroboam built Shechem in the hill country of Ephraim and took up residence there; from there he went out and built Penuel.

We do not know why Jeroboam forsook Shechem in the heart of the Ephraimite hill country and chose a city across the Jordan as his capital. It has been speculated that he needed an area more secure from his Judahite rival or from Pharaoh Shoshenq I, initially a supporter of Jeroboam but later an enemy of the northern kingdom.[9]

In any case, we can hardly separate the construction of the Penuel of history from the tale of Jacob. Jacob serves here as an allegory of Jeroboam. Although the Judahite writer of 1 Kings 12 does not directly offer a negative judgment of the building activity at Penuel, his account—placed in the narrative immediately before the tale of Jeroboam's cultic misfeasance to be discussed later—has the effect of tainting whatever was done at Penuel. In contrast, Genesis 32 views the foundation of Penuel as a blessed event. Jacob had shown super-human strength in his battle with a divine being. Although wounded in the struggle, Jacob would not release the divinity until he had blessed him. The hero's deed was later recalled by the dietary practices of his descendants. More important, after the blessing, Penuel received a name that memorializes the heroism and special fortune of the name giver.

But there is additional geopolitical significance in the details of Genesis 32. After the struggle, the divinity in the story gives Jacob a new permanent name, Israel. That is precisely what is described in 1 Kings 11:29–37:[10]

> At the time when Jeroboam, clad in a new cloak, was leaving Jerusalem, Ahijah of Shiloh, the prophet, came upon him on the road. The two of them were alone in the field, and Ahijah pulled the new cloak off him and ripped it into twelve pieces. He said to Jeroboam, "Take ten fragments for yourself, for thus says Yahweh, the god of Israel; I am ripping the kingdom from Solomon and giving you the ten tribes . . . for I have taken you to rule over all your heart desires, for you shall be king over *Israel*."

Ahijah of Shiloh promises Jeroboam in Yahweh's name: "You shall rule over *Israel*." This is affirmed by the words put in the mouth of a "man of God" addressed to Rehoboam, son of Solomon, in 1 Kings 12:23–24.

> But the word of God came to Shemaiah, the man of God: Say to King Rehoboam of Judah, son of Solomon, and to all the house of Judah and Benjamin and to the rest of the people, ["Thus, says Yahweh, you shall not go up or fight against your kindred the people of Israel. Let everyone go home, for this thing is from me."] So they heeded the word of Yahweh and went home again, according to the word of Yahweh.

In these verses, the man of God, Shemaiah, warns Rehoboam not to wage war against Jeroboam. He refers to Rehoboam's domain as the "house of Judah" but affirms Jeroboam's claim to "Israel," the official name of the northern kingdom. The change of name from Jacob to Israel declared by the divinity reflects the new political reality of the kingdom established by Jeroboam I. The Bible provides us with a twice-told tale: 1 Kings relates realistically the tale about Jeroboam, and Genesis 32 in the Torah relates allegorically the events about Jacob.

The allegorical identification of Jacob with Jeroboam is evident as well in what is arguably the second most popular story of Jacob, Genesis 28:10–22, which describes the dream Jacob had on his way to Harran in Syria:

When he arrived at the holy place, he stopped for the night, for the sun had set.[11] Taking stones from the holy place, he set them at his head and lay down to sleep in that holy place and had a dream. There was a stairway resting on the ground, with its top reaching to heaven and angels of God ascending and descending it. There was Yahweh standing atop it. He said, "I, Yahweh—the god of Abraham, your father, and the god of Isaac—will give you and your descendants this earth on which you sleep. Your offspring will be as numerous as the dust of the earth, so that you will break out west and east and north and south. And all the families of the land will bless themselves through you and your offspring. Remember it is I who am with you, who will protect you wherever you go and bring you back to this land. For I shall not leave you until I have done what I promised you." Then Jacob awoke from his sleep and said, "Truly there is Yahweh in this holy place, but I did not know." In awe he said, "How awesome is this holy place. This is none other than a god's house, for this is the gate of heaven!" When Jacob bestirred himself in the morning, he took the stone that he had placed at his head and set it up as a sacred pillar, pouring oil over the top of it. He named that holy place Bethel [House of God], but the earlier name of the town there was Luz. Jacob then made a vow, saying, "If God will be with me—if he has protected me on the road I travel and given me food to eat and a garment to wear—once I have returned home in health to my father's house, Yahweh will be my god. And this stone, which I have set up as sacred pillar, will become a god's house [that is, a temple], and everything you give me I shall tithe to you."

Once again, geography is crucial. It is a commonplace of modern scholarship that the story provides a number of etiologies, among them how Bethel got its name and who named it. More important, though, the tale legitimates—indeed commends—cultic activity at Bethel, activity that Jacob himself initiates, according to Genesis 35:7, when he erects an altar at Bethel. The last point would have been very significant to an audience of the tenth century B.C.E. That much is obvious from 1 Kings 12:26–13:11, which describes what Jeroboam did to secure his secession from the united kingdom ruled by his rival Rehoboam:[12]

Jeroboam said to himself [Hebrew: *belibbo*], "My kingdom will return to the Davidic ruler if the people go up to sacrifice in the Yahweh temple in Jerusalem. For the heart of this people will return to their lord, to Rehoboam, king of Judah. Then they will kill me and return to Rehoboam, king of Judah." So taking counsel, the king made two golden calves. He said to them [the people], "It is too far for you to go up to Jerusalem. O Israel, the gods [Hebrew: *elohim*] who brought you up out of Egypt are right here." One of these he set up at Bethel, and the other he placed at Dan. . . . This matter led to sin. . . . He made a platform[?]-enclosure and made priests from all segments of the people who were not descendants of Levi. He made a festival in the eighth month on the fifteenth day of the month, like the festival that is in Judah, and ascended the altar. He ascended the altar thus made in Bethel, to sacrifice to the calves he had made. And he set up in Bethel the platform[?]-priests he had made. He ascended the altar he had made in Bethel on the fifteenth day of the eighth month, in that month in which he himself had invented a festival for Israel. He ascended the altar to offer incense.

This writer's pro-Judahite orientation is clear. He knows Jeroboam's innermost fears: Jeroboam's "Israelites" would be swayed by their cultic loyalties to the Jerusalem temple to return to the service of Rehoboam of Judah. To expose Jeroboam's insincerity, the writer has him inwardly acknowledge Rehoboam as the "lord" of the people. Outwardly, however, Jeroboam presents his actions as motivated by concern for the hardship that his people endure in making long pilgrimages. The use of *elohim* also appears deliberate. Although the term is frequently used as a synonym of Yahweh or an alternative to it, depending on the context, *elohim* can also refer to a "false" god, an angel, or even a ghost. Complicating matters but extremely useful to our author is the fact that *elohim* is grammatically plural.[13] In this context, the audience is encouraged to interpret *elohim* as a reference to the calves and, accordingly, to identify Jeroboam as a maker of calf gods.

Another device the author employs to vilify Jeroboam is his repeated use of the verb *make* (Hebrew: *'aśah*), which often has the connotation of "make something up." Jeroboam not only "makes" the calves and the platform(?)-enclosure, where the verb is appropriate; he also "makes [up]" priests and "makes [up]" a festival to rival the one in Judah. Lest this technique prove too subtle, the writer concludes the section by informing the audience that the festival was "invented" by Jeroboam.

A similar negative evaluation of the cult at Bethel is found in the Book of Hosea, in which the prophet offers his version of how Bethel became a shrine:[14]

> In the womb, he [Jacob] cheated his brother. Grown to manhood, he strove with a divinity; he strove with an angel and triumphed; the other did weep and implore him. It was at Bethel that he met him, so there he invokes him by name! But Yahweh, the god of the hosts, cannot be invoked but as Yahweh! (Hos 12:4–6)

H. L. Ginsberg demonstrated the extent to which Hosea employs the figure of Jacob as a negative typology of the northern kingdom. Hosea attacks the cult at Bethel by condemning its devotees as cheats and fools. Hosea's accusation that Jacob "cheated" his brother in the womb is more extreme than Esau's.[15] In the Torah (Gen 27:36), Esau complains that his brother cheated him twice in adulthood. Hosea says that Jacob was a cheat even before he was born. But Jacob, the cheater, is himself a deluded fool. His shrine should not be called Bethel, "House of God," says Hosea, but Beth-Aven, or "Delusionville."[16] It is really not a shrine to Yahweh but to some lesser divinity named Bethel. According to Hosea, Jacob had wrestled with a "divinity" (singular: *elohim*) or "angel" (*mal'ak*) at Bethel (not Penuel) and overpowered him.

Not found in the Torah's account are Hosea's two additional details. First, the divinity whom Jacob defeated was named Bethel. Second, Jacob had actually brought his divine opponent Bethel to tears. Yet in his stupidity, Jacob worships that same divinity Bethel at the sanctuary named for him, invoking Bethel by name rather than calling on Yahweh.[17]

In contrast to Hosea, Genesis 28 extols all religious practices observed at Bethel. Yahweh himself had been seen there. It was where he promised that the land would be Israelite and that the people would be multitudinous. The sacred pillar at Bethel and the shrine at Bethel where tithes were offered to Yahweh had been established by Jacob. The religious practices of Jeroboam were not to be separated from those of Jacob, and Jacob himself was neither a fool nor a knave but a hero of incredible strength and bravery.[18]

The career of Jeroboam I also provides the background of the novella of Joseph, to which thirteen chapters of the book of Genesis are devoted. In the Bible, Joseph, son of Jacob, is the eponymous ancestor of the northern kingdom, which, among its other names, was known as the House of Joseph or, simply, Joseph.[19] Modern scholarship of a generation ago attempted to seek a historical background for the story of Joseph in the Hyksos period. "Hyksos" is based on an Egyptian phrase meaning "rulers of foreign lands," that is, rulers of alien origin, who reigned over portions of lower Egypt as the fifteenth dynasty in the first half of the second millennium B.C.E. Most of the Hyksos names appear to be linguistically close to Hebrew, including one that contains the element *Y'kb*, "Jacob."[20] Inasmuch as Jacob was a good Hyksos name, it appeared plausible that the biblical Joseph's rise to power had been facilitated by friendly relatives. Indeed, in 1963 the prominent Egyptologist John Wilson wrote: "It is possible that Joseph served a Hyksos pharaoh in the seventeenth century."[21]

Contemporary scholarship has abandoned that avenue for a number of reasons, not the least of which is that a Hyksos background completely negates the fundamental premise of the story, that Joseph and his brothers are foreigners whose "Hebrew" origin visibly distinguishes them from their native Egyptian hosts. They differ not only in language but also in dietary customs and permissible occupations. In addition, the Egyptian names in the story are not found together in the same historical period before the twenty-first dynasty (ca. 1069–945 B.C.E.). At the other chronological extreme, there are no compelling linguistic or historical reasons to date the story later than the ninth to eighth century of the first millennium B.C.E.[22] The tradition of Joseph in Egypt was known to the writer of the early northern Psalm 82. In addition, the story of Joseph is the necessary bridge to the traditions of descent into Egypt and subsequent exodus, which originally were northern Israelite traditions (see chap. 3, n. 7).It is of great interest, therefore, to compare the central elements of the Joseph story with the narrative about Jeroboam.

In Genesis 37, Joseph dreams that the sheaves of his brothers bow down to his sheaf. The brothers' reaction is

> Will you rule over us as king? Will you have complete dominion over us?

As a result of this dream and one that follows, his brothers plot to kill Joseph. He finds sanctuary in Egypt, where he is protected and elevated by Pharaoh.[23] According to 1 Kings 11, Jeroboam, "corvée master of the House of Joseph," was told by the prophet Ahijah that he would be "king over Israel." As a result of this prophecy, Solomon attempted to kill Jeroboam:

> When Solomon sought to kill Jeroboam, he arose and fled to Egypt, to Shishak, king of Egypt. (1Kgs 11:40)

Scholars are unanimous in identifying Shishak, the earliest-named pharaoh in the Bible, with Shoshenq I, the Libyan who founded the twenty-second Egyptian dynasty. In keeping with his policy of undermining strong rulers in Asia, Shoshenq provides a haven for Jeroboam.[24] Thanks to the pharaoh's sponsorship, Ahijah's prophecy is fulfilled and Jeroboam establishes the independent northern kingdom.

What we have in the Joseph story is a thinly veiled allegory. The prophecy that Jeroboam receives corresponds to Joseph's dream, and Shishak corresponds to Joseph's anonymous pharaoh. The development of the allegory of Joseph may now be confidently reconstructed. By the tenth century, the allegory of Israel in Egypt already existed; likewise available were entertaining tales about the rejected brother who rises to power outside his homeland and then returns in triumph. In the Bible, the story of Jephthah comes to mind. Outside the Bible, there is the story of King Idrimi of Alalakh in Syria, rediscovered a quarter century ago. Written no later than the thirteenth century B.C.E., the text purports to be autobiographical.[25] Idrimi begins by explaining that of his brothers, "none had the plans I had." Idrimi goes off on his own, rises to great power, and is reconciled with his brothers, to whom he gives positions of authority. The propagandists of Jeroboam I did not have to create new motifs when they introduced the figure of Joseph—the eponymous ancestor of the group from which Jeroboam I claimed ancestry—into the exodus traditions. As "Joseph," Jeroboam I had been protected by Pharaoh and risen to great power under the ultimate protection of Yahweh.

But there is another stage in the story that must be noted. In Genesis 44, Judah, the older brother, humbles himself before Joseph:

> Please my lord, let your slave appeal to my lord, and do not be impatient with your slave, you who are the equal of Pharaoh. . . . Let your slave remain as a slave to my lord. (vv. 18, 33)

The Joseph story was apparently known to the prophet Ezekiel, who read the reconciliation of Joseph and Judah typologically.[26] But in a figure of his own creation, Ezekiel reversed the terms of the reconciliation:

> The word of Yahweh came to me: "Mortal, take a stick and write on it: 'For Judah and the children of Israel associated with him.' Then take another stick and write on it: 'For Joseph and all the house of Israel associated with him' and join them together into one stick, so that they may become one in your hand. And when your people say to you, 'Will you not tell us what you mean by these?' say to them, 'Thus says my Lord Yahweh: Behold I am about to take the stick of Joseph and the tribes of Israel associated with him and I will join it with the stick of Judah.'" (Ezek 37:15–20)

The prophet immediately interprets the symbolism of his actions:

> When the sticks on which you write are in your hand before their eyes, then say to them, "Thus says my Lord Yahweh: 'Behold, I will take the children of Israel from the nations among which they have gone . . . and make them one nation in the land on the mountains of Israel, and one king shall be king over them all, and they shall be no longer two nations, And no longer be divided in two kingdoms. . . . My servant David shall be king over them.'" (Ezek 37:20–24)

Drawing on the Joseph story, Ezekiel foretells the ultimate reconciliation of Judah and Joseph, by which he means the divided kingdoms. In this reconciliation, the Judahites will have the advantage, in that "David"—that is, a descendant of David the Judahite—would rule over the united monarchy. By the time of Ezekiel, the sixth century B.C.E., the northern Israelite monarchy and the state itself had already been gone for almost two centuries. Judah, however, had only recently fallen, and members of the Davidic dynasty were alive and treated with some respect by the conquerors.[27] Accordingly, it was at least a visionary possibility that Judah's fortunes might soon rise and that an Israelite state under Judahite leadership might reemerge.

Ezekiel's reading contrasts sharply with the denouement provided in the Joseph story itself. As we have seen, in Genesis 44, Judah the older brother humbles himself before Joseph the younger brother. Judah refers to himself as "slave," at the same time comparing Joseph with Pharaoh. If we decode this allegory politically, here is what we get:

The newer kingdom, the northern house of Joseph, will lord it over the older southern kingdom, the house of Judah. Perhaps Jeroboam I had in mind a grand design like that, but it is nowhere documented in our sources. Interestingly, the grand design neatly fits the political situation in the reign of Jeroboam II.

According to 2 Kings 14:23–29, Jeroboam II reigned for forty-one years (789–748 B.C.E.).

> It was he who restored the boundaries of Israel from Lebo-Hamath to the sea of the Arabah, in accordance with the word of Yahweh, the god of Israel. (14:25)

This passage gains in credibility because it is embedded in a context hostile to its subject. Verse 24, immediately preceding, informs us that Jeroboam "did evil in the sight of Yahweh," not abandoning the sins of his namesake. Yet the same writer admits that Jeroboam's victories reestablished the territorial limits of Solomon's reign. The description of the "boundaries of Israel," which leaves no room for Judah, is completely consistent with the biblical description of events immediately before the ascent of Jeroboam II to the throne of his father Jehoash (2Kgs 14:8–14):

> Then Amaziah [king of Judah] sent messengers to Jehoash, son of Jehoahaz, son of Jehu, king of Israel: "Come, let us meet in combat face to face." Jehoash, king of Israel, responded, . . . "Now, why provoke trouble in which you and Judah will fall?" But Amaziah did not listen. So Jehoash, king of Israel, set out, and they met in combat face to face, he and Amaziah, king of Judah, at Beth-Shemesh in Judah. Judah was defeated by Israel, and everyone fled to his tent. But Jehoash, king of Israel, captured Amaziah, king of Judah, at Beth-Shemesh. Then he marched to Jerusalem and breached the walls of Jerusalem. . . . He carried off all the gold and the silver and all the vessels to be found in the temple of Yahweh and the royal treasuries, and hostages as well. He then returned to Samaria.

The capture of the king, the breaching of the walls of the capital city, and the taking of hostages—probably from the royal family and the nobility—indicate that Judah was reduced to the status of a client of Israel during the reign of the father of Jeroboam II. The territorial descriptions of Jeroboam's reign indicate that Judah's client status did not improve for a generation. Against this historical background, it appears that the Joseph story originated as an allegory regarding Jeroboam I.[28] Expelled by his brothers, Jeroboam was exalted by the king of Egypt and rose to great power. But "Joseph" did not rise immediately to the heights predicted by the dream. That had to wait until the reign of the second "Joseph," Jeroboam II, in whose court the story was further elaborated.

CHAPTER 7

Aaron

Be of the disciples of Aaron.

—Mishnah Abot 1:9

For every high priest chosen among men is appointed to act on behalf of men in relation to God, to offer gifts and sacrifices for sins. . . . And one does not take the honor upon himself but is called by God, just as Aaron was.

—Hebrews 5:1–4

According to the priestly source in the Torah, Aaron is the son of Amram and Jochebed and the brother of Miriam and Moses. According to this same source, Aaron is also the founding father, or eponym, of the "sons of Aaron," the only legitimate priestly line. In classical rabbinic sources as well as modern scholarship, Aaron has often been described as a paradigm of the Israelite priesthood, so that regulations pertaining to "Aaron" apply to any priest. But "paradigm" does not adequately describe the varied images of Aaron presented in the Torah. As scholars have often observed, there is sometimes a strong positive image of Aaron as Yahweh's chosen priest, as in Numbers 16–17. At other times, Aaron is vilified or tainted, as in the story of the golden calf (Exod 32), in which he appears at worst as the sculptor of the calf and at best as a spineless collaborator with the sinful Israelites.[1] In Numbers 12, there is again a somewhat negative portrayal of Aaron, who participates with Miriam in gossip about the marriage of Moses to a Cushite woman and about the superior prophetic status of Moses, which Miriam and Aaron consider to be unwarranted (see chap. 8).

The earliest biblical references to Aaron that most scholars have dated with confidence come from the eighth century B.C.E. These do not associate him with the priesthood or with priestly functions. In Joshua 24:5, Aaron is named following Moses as one of two men whom Yahweh "sent" (Hebrew: *šālaḥ*) to "smite" the Egyptians. In Micah 5:4, Aaron is again named after Moses, and before Miriam, as one of three people "sent" (Hebrew: *šālaḥ*) before Israel to bring them up out of Egypt. In neither of these verses is there an indication that Aaron is related to either Moses or Miriam. In the plague tales in the Book of Exodus, Aaron is a wonder worker along with Moses. Yahweh speaks directly to Aaron (Exod 4:27), just as he does to Moses. When Moses and Aaron first meet with the Israelite elders, it is Aaron who relates the divine word given by Yahweh to Moses, and it is he who performs the confirmatory signs given by Yahweh to Moses (Exod 4:29–30). When Yahweh designates Moses as "god" (*elohim*) to Pharaoh, he names Aaron as the prophet (*nabi*) of Moses:[2]

> Yahweh said to Moses: "Observe, I have designated you as god to Pharaoh, and Aaron, your brother, shall be your prophet. You shall speak [to Aaron] whatever I command you. Then Aaron, your brother, will speak to Pharaoh that he send the children of Israel from his land."

In their first audience with Pharaoh, both Moses and Aaron speak, and Pharaoh speaks to the two of them (Exod 5:1, 3, 4). It is Aaron's rod that turns into a crocodile (Hebrew: *tannin*; 7:10), swallows the crocodiles of Pharaoh's lector priests (7:12), turns the Nile into blood (7:19), causes the plague of frogs (8:1), and brings the gnats (8:16–17). Here again, we have Aaron as wonder worker or as prophet but not as priest.

To trace the evolution of the figure of Aaron the priest in Israelite tradition, we begin with episode of the golden calf, which has been the subject of study for two millennia.[3] We saw in the previous chapter how the sanctuary at Bethel, where the calf stood, was extolled by the writer of Genesis 28. Now we shall see how the same sanctuary and its cultic activities were condemned, once in a realistic setting in 1 Kings 12, which we briefly considered in the previous chapter, and then in an allegorical setting in the Torah. First, the realistic setting:

Jeroboam said to himself [Hebrew: *belibbo*], "My kingdom will return to the Davidic ruler if the people go up to sacrifice in the Yahweh temple in Jerusalem. For the heart of this people will return to their lord, to Rehoboam, king of Judah. Then they will kill me and return tô Rehoboam, king of Judah." So taking counsel, the king made two golden calves. He said to them [the people], "It is too far for you to go up to Jerusalem. O Israel, right here are the gods who brought you up out of Egypt." One of these he set up at Bethel, and the other he placed at Dan. . . . This matter led to sin. . . . He made a platform[?]-enclosure and made priests from all segments of the people who were not descendants of Levi. He made a festival in the eighth month on the fifteenth day of the month, like the festival that is in Judah, and ascended the altar. He ascended the altar thus made in Bethel, to sacrifice to the calves he had made. And he set up in Bethel the platform[?]-priests he had made. He ascended the altar he had made in Bethel on the fifteenth day of the eighth month, in that month in which he himself had invented a festival for Israel. He ascended the altar to offer incense. (1Kgs 12:26–33)

With this passage, we must compare the Torah's account of the golden calf.

When he [God] had finished speaking with him at Mount Sinai, he gave Moses two tablets of the pact, stone tablets written with the finger of God [*elohim*]. When the people observed that Moses was so late in coming down from the mountain, they mobbed Aaron and said to him, "Come, make us gods [*elohim*] who shall go [plural] at our head, for this Moses—the man who took us up out of Egypt—we don't know what has become of him." (Exod 31:18–32:1)

As is true of all the Torah's narratives, the golden calf story is set in the period before the rise of the Israelite states in Canaan. But the text provides linguistic and historical clues to its actual date and circumstances of composition. Moses is given *šenē luḥot hāʿedut*, "two tablets of the pact." The material of the tablets is specified; they are made of stone.[4] As for the Hebrew *ʿedut*, "pact," the vocable is a reflex of the Akkadian *adê* and the Aramaic *ʿiddaya*, "pact," "treaty," "covenant." Indeed, the entire Hebrew expression for "tablets of the pact" (*luḥot hāʿedut*) finds its precise semantic counterpart in the Akkadian *ṭuppī adê*, "tablets of the pact." Although scholars continue to debate the precise etymological connections among the Hebrew,

Aramaic, and Akkadian terms, there is no question that around the
middle of the eighth century B.C.E., the word *adê* became common in
Akkadian sources for pacts, treaties, covenants, and loyalty oaths.[5]

Significant as well is that the text of two tablets of the "covenant"
or "pact" given to Moses was etched in stone. Although treaty texts
are known as far back as the early second millennium B.C.E., none of
these has thus far been discovered in stone. But from the middle of the
eighth century B.C.E., we have three texts of treaties found at Sefire, a
small town in the vicinity of Aleppo in Syria. These texts—which describe their contents as *'iddaya*, "pacts," between a local Syrian ruler,
Matiel of Arpad, and a powerful Mesopotamian overlord, Shamshi-
ilu—were written on stone. From a slightly earlier period, we have the
only surviving treaty between Assyria and Babylonia. Concluded between Marduk-Zakir-Shumi I of Babylonia and Shamshi-Adad V of
Assyria and written in, or shortly after, 821 B.C.E., the document is
the only known Mesopotamian treaty written on stone.[6] Admittedly,
we are arguing from a small amount of evidence. Nonetheless, given
the present state of that evidence, if we wish to fix a plausible date for
the biblical image of a pact said to be written in stone, we should look
to the ninth or eighth century B.C.E.

Well within the same chronological setting, the people's request for
"the gods to go before us" is entirely in keeping with the function of
Near Eastern gods as guides and forerunners.[7] One motif that runs
through ancient Near Eastern literature is divine guidance in military
campaigns. In a royal inscription of Adad-Nerari II, the king of Assyria in the tenth century, he refers to the goddess Ishtar as *ālikat
panât ummanātiya rapšāti*, "the one who goes at the head of my extensive army." Because the Torah regularly depicts the Israelites as an
army on the march, we should not be surprised to find in Exodus 32:1
a very close parallel to the king's religious-military imagery. The
Akkadian phrase *ālikat panât*, "who goes at the head," said of the
goddess Ishtar, is etymologically and semantically equivalent to the
Hebrew *yelĕku lĕpanenu*, said of the divine leadership requested by
the Israelites.[8]

The tale continues:

> Aaron said to them, "Break off the gold rings that are in the ears of
> your wives, your sons, and your daughters, and bring them to me."
> Then all the people broke off the gold rings that were in their ears and

brought them to Aaron. What he took from them he tied in a bag, and then made into a molten calf. They declared, "These are your gods, O Israel, who brought you up out of the land of Egypt." When Aaron saw this, he built an altar before it. He then proclaimed as follows: "Tomorrow is a festival to Yahweh."

The people bestirred themselves in the morning and offered holocausts [animals] and brought sacrifices of greeting. They sat down to eat and drink and then rose to make merry.

Aaron's construction of the calf fits well with the use of bovine symbolism and zoomorphic imagery all over the ancient Near East.[9] The bull, a symbol of strength and potency, was a natural choice to represent significant aspects of divinity. In Ugarit, the god El was referred to as "Bull-El," and there are clear indications that Baal—the ancient god of rain, storms, and fertility who was worshiped all over Syria-Palestine—had bovine aspects. Material remains relevant to the golden calf episode come from the northern Samaritan hills, which yielded an open cult site from Iron Age I:[10]

A unique find from this site is a bronze bull figurine, evidently the work of a highly skilled craftsman. It must have been the central cult at the site and is reminiscent of the golden calves described in the exodus and the shrines erected by Jeroboam at Bethel and Dan.

In other words, the archaeological find from northern Israel fits perfectly with the realistic setting of 1 Kings 12. Let us return to the golden calf episode in the allegorical setting of Exodus 32. In 1967, Moses Aberbach and Leivy Smolar adduced "thirteen points of identity or contact" between the Torah's tale of the golden calf and 1 Kings 12.[11] The more significant points are the following: (1) Both Aaron and Jeroboam have golden calves made. (2) The calves are introduced with virtually identical declarations. Whereas Exodus 32:4 reads, "These are your gods, O Israel, who brought you up out of Egypt," 1 Kings 12:28 has, "Here are your gods, O Israel, who brought you up out of Egypt." (3) Both Jeroboam and Aaron build altars. (4) Both Aaron and Jeroboam proclaim festivals. (5) Both men function in a sacerdotal capacity. (6) In both accounts, the calves made by Aaron and Jeroboam are considered the national sin par excellence.[12] (7) The two eldest sons of Aaron, Nadab and Abihu, and the two sons of Jeroboam, Nadab and Abijah, have virtually identical names.[13] (8) Both Aaron and Jeroboam are the objects of severe divine displeasure, but both survive to fill out long terms of office.

It is to point 6 that we must direct our attention. Why was the golden calf considered "the national sin par excellence"? At first, the question appears naive. Stephen's famous speech in the New Testament (Acts 7:41) refers to the calf as an "idol" (Greek: *eidōlon*),[14] and generations of readers have concurred with Stephen's assessment. But the later consensus to characterize the calf as an idol fails to explain the fact that the popularity of the bull as a divine image extended well beyond circles that the biblical writers characterized as "idolatrous." The eighth-century prophet Isaiah (1:24) speaks of Yahweh as "the bull of Israel." His sixth-century successor, Deutero-Isaiah, the Bible's most militant monotheist, speaks of Yahweh as the "bull of Jacob" (Isa 49:26). Although Deutero-Isaiah's reference might be dismissed as verbal imagery, numerous scholars have observed that the cherubs (*kerubim*), which the Torah required in the tabernacle, are related to the *kāribu*, bovine colossi that guarded Mesopotamian temples. Indeed, according to 1 Kings 7:29, Solomon commissioned a ritual laver for the Jerusalem temple in the form of a molten sea that stood on three oxen. If the bull image connected with Yahweh was not inherently idolatrous, why was the construction of the calf viewed as a "great sin"?

The answer is not hard to find. The construction of the calf is viewed as a "great sin" because religious rites and cultic objects are usually not evaluated on their own. The merits or demerits of a particular rite depend on its performer, the group with which the performer is associated, the author of the text in which the action is described, and the audiences to which the text is directed. Exodus 32 allegorizes the events narrated in 1 Kings 12, and Aaron is an allegory of Jeroboam. From the perspective of the Judahite narrator, all of Jeroboam's cultic actions must be sinful because he is a sinner, and no opportunity to document his sinfulness should be ignored. In 1 Kings 12:31, the accusation against Jeroboam descends into absurdity when we read that he

> made priests from all segments of the people who were not descendants of Levi. (1Kgs 12:31)

As we saw in the previous chapter, this statement is embedded in a context describing how Jeroboam selfishly made golden calves so that the northerners would not forsake his rule for that of the southern king, Rehoboam. First, Jeroboam is depicted as hypocrite who tells the people one thing—that he is acting out of concern for them— while he tells himself the truth, that he is acting out of self-interest alone. Then we are given his declaration:

> Here are your gods, O Israel, who brought you up out of the land of Egypt.

The declaration is a an obvious parody of the opening line of the Decalogue:

> I am Yahweh, your god, who took you out of the land of Egypt.

The Judahite writer parodies the Decalogue in order to compound Jeroboam's sin. Having just learned that Jeroboam was a hypocrite, we are encouraged to believe that he was an idolater as well. In the Decalogue (Exod 20, Deut 5), the declaration that Yahweh took the people out of Egypt serves to justify Yahweh's demand that he alone be worshiped as Israel's god. By placing the virtually identical phrase in the mouth of Jeroboam, the writer permits the audience to infer that the king abolished the cult of Yahweh and substituted for it the exclusive worship of the divine calves. Inasmuch as Jeroboam has been shown to be a hypocritical apostate, the writer is able to fault him with an accusation that makes no sense, that he appointed non-Levites to the priesthood. If the calves were indeed idols, would it have been more meritorious to appoint Levite priests to their service? In sum, the writer delegitimates the calves of 1 Kings 12 as part of his larger program to delegitimate Jeroboam.

A close examination reveals that our Bible contains several allegories concerning Jeroboam and the calves that originated in the north. We saw earlier that northerners had represented Jeroboam allegorically as Jacob and Joseph. Another of the writer's allegorical reflexes was Aaron, the good priest, likewise a northern creation. As part of the process of vilification, southern writers distorted traditions favorable to Jeroboam, both realistic and allegorical. It devolves on the contemporary reader to extract the original favorable stories from the present polemical contexts in which they are embedded. If we retain the details of 1 Kings 12 but ignore the southern polemic, the realistic version may be paraphrased approximately as follows:

> As king of united Judah and Israel, Rehoboam, grandson of the Judahite David, overly favored the Judahites. He ignored the northerners by celebrating the great harvest festival in the seventh month, in keeping with the Judahite agricultural calendar. His royal sanctuary in Jerusalem was convenient for Judahite pilgrims but not for the northerners. In response, a former officer of Solomon's, Jeroboam, inspired by Ahijah of Shiloh, a prophet of Yahweh, successfully led the north in its secession from the Davidic monarchy.[15] As a champion of his people, Jeroboam provided for their religious needs and restored their traditions. He established sanctuaries at the northern and southern extremes of his kingdom so that his people would not have to undertake long pilgrimages. At these locations, he celebrated the harvest festival in the eighth month, in keeping with the cooler climate of the north where the autumn crops ripen later.[16] As part of his cult, he incorporated the ancient symbolism of Yahweh, that of the bull calf. To be sure, some northerners, the prophet Hosea, for example, opposed the bovine imagery related to Yahweh. But that was in the eighth century, and there is no reason to believe that Hosea's viewpoint was widespread in the north in his own time, and certainly not in the time of Jeroboam.[17]

A similar result emerges from the allegory in Exodus 32, whose original form may be reconstructed as follows:

> While Moses was on the mountain receiving the tablets from Yahweh, the people wondered what had happened to their leader. Clearly, their faith in a mere mortal had been misplaced. (That is the sense of "this *man* Moses—we don't know what has happened to him.") What they required instead was some lasting manifestation of the divinity that had taken them up out of Egypt. Needing that god to go at their head, they appealed to Aaron, who asked them to donate their personal gold jewelry, which the entire people—men, women, and children—did with unrestrained enthusiasm.

Here is the continuation of the tale with the antinorthern polemic removed:

> What he took from them he tied in a bag [Hebrew: *ḥeret*; others: "he cast in a mold"] and then made into a molten calf. . . . When Aaron saw this, he built an altar before it. He then proclaimed as follows: "Tomorrow is a festival to Yahweh."

> The people bestirred themselves in the morning. They offered holocausts and brought sacrifices of greeting.

At first glance, the events described in this selection are unclear. The verse "when Aaron saw this, he built an altar before it" has troubled exegetes for almost two thousand years. Just what did Aaron see that led him to construct the altar? Aaron's rejoinder to Moses provides the answer:

> I said to them, "Whoever has gold, break it off of you." They gave it to me, I threw it in the fire, and out came this calf.

Most modern scholarship has ridiculed Aaron's statement as a weak attempt at an alibi: He was not really responsible for the construction of the calf, which emerged from the fire fully formed. But the "alibi" interpretation is based on the inaccurate rendition of 32:4 as "he cast in a mold." As the American biblical scholar Stanley Gevirtz pointed out, the Hebrew word *ḥereṭ* does not refer to a mold or to any tool that Aaron used in making a calf.[18] What *ḥereṭ* denotes is the bag in which the precious metal was collected. Consequently, there seems no escape from the conclusion of the Israeli scholar Samuel Loewenstamm:[19]

> Neither the author nor Moses stigmatizes Aaron's statement as a lie. On the contrary, the context proves that the author believed in Aaron's words.

Instead, Loewenstamm shows that our pericope reflects a widespread motif portraying the wondrous production of cultic objects without the benefit of workmanship, a motif already employed in the myth of the construction of Baal's house, that is, his temple. In thirteenth-century B.C.E. texts from Ugarit, Baal, the god of storms and fertility, brings silver and gold for the construction of his house. Then a fire soon consumes the gold and silver for six days, after which the house is described as having spontaneously been completed. The Ugaritic belief finds an analogue in the rabbinic Midrash Exodus Rabbah 5:2:

> The holy spirit alighted on him [Moses], and he erected the tabernacle. You must not say that it was Moses who erected it. But miracles were performed through him, and it rose on its own accord.

The midrash goes on to make similar comments about the construction of Solomon's temple.

In other words, in keeping with an ancient mythical motif, Aaron was not actively involved in constructing the calf. After collecting the precious metals, he bound them in a bag. Once the fire was sufficiently hot, Aaron the cast the metal in the flame. He then "saw" the golden calf spontaneously emerging from the flames, a clear indication that the image represented the divine presence. This is why Aaron built an altar before it. In the original unaltered allegory, the calf was a legitimate representative of Yahweh's presence, which could be credited with leading the people out of Egypt. Its inauguration would more than justify a "festival to Yahweh." In the allegory, Aaron officiated at the altar he had built on a festival day. In reality, the northern festival was celebrated in the eighth month by King Jeroboam, when he himself officiated at the altar. Aaron the high priest was a northern creation, whose positive image was distorted by the southern writers in the golden calf story.

Let us now turn to a story in which the image of Aaron the high priest is positive: the tale of Korah and his "community." In the Korah story, the lower Levite clergy, headed by Korah, oppose the divinely designated priesthood of Aaron. In the extant text of Numbers 16–17, the story of Korah has been "braided" together with a tale of tribal opposition to the concentrated political power of Moses.[20] The translation, which follows, attempts to untangle the braids in order to concentrate on the internal struggle within the clergy.

> Korah, son of Izhar, son of Kohath, son of Levi, . . . became impudent.
> . . . He led a mob against Moses, and Aaron and said to them, "You have too much! For the entire community is holy [plural, Hebrew: qedošim], Yahweh being in their midst. Why then do you exalt yourselves over Yahweh's congregation?" When Moses heard this, he fell prostrate. He then addressed Korah and his community as follows: "On the morrow, let Yahweh make known who is his holy one [singular with definite article, ha-qādoš] by bringing him close to him. The one he chooses he will bring close to him. Do this: Provide yourselves with fire pans, Korah and his entire community. Then place hot coals in them and incense over them, in the presence of Yahweh on the morrow. What will happen is that the one whom Yahweh chooses is his holy one. It is you who have too much, sons of Levi!"

Korah challenges Aaron's authority, which is undergirded by Moses on the vulnerable issue of hierarchy. If every Israelite is qādoš, "holy," how can the priesthood be restricted to a specific line? The answer given by Moses is that there may be many *qedošim*, many who are imbued with holiness, but only one *ha-qādoš*, "*the* holy one," with the definite article.

> Then Moses said to Korah: "Pay attention now, you sons of Levi! Is it of so little importance to you that the god of Israel has set you apart from the community of Israel by bringing you close to him to perform the sanctuary's labor, to stand before the community to serve them? He brought you close to him—you and your fellow Levites with you. Have you now sought the priesthood, too? Truly, it is against Yahweh that you and your community are making common cause. As for Aaron, who is he that you lodge complaint against him?" . . .
>
> Then Moses said to Korah, "You and your entire community be present before Yahweh, you and they and Aaron on the morrow. Let each one take his fire pan and place incense in all of them and offer it, each one of you with his fire pan in the presence of Yahweh, 250 fire pans, and you and Aaron, each one his fire pan. Then every one took his fire pan. They placed hot coals in them and incense over them. Then they stood at the entrance to the tent of meeting, as did Moses and Aaron. Korah then rallied his whole community against them by the entrance to the tent of meeting.
>
> Then the physical presence [Hebrew: *kābod*] of Yahweh appeared to the entire community. . . . Then Moses said, "By this you shall know that it is Yahweh who has sent me to carry out these actions, that they are not of my own devising. If these people die the death of every mortal, if the fate of mortals is theirs, then it is not Yahweh who sent me. But if Yahweh fashions something entirely new, so that the earth opens its mouth and swallows them up, along with everything they possess, so that they descend live into the underworld [Sheol], then you will know for yourselves that these persons have rejected Yahweh.

The condition set by Moses is fulfilled:

> Just as he finished speaking all these words, the earth split open beneath them. The earth opened its mouth and swallowed them up, along with their families, all the people belonging to Korah, and all the property. They and everything belonging to them descended live into the underworld. The earth covered them over so that they vanished from the congregation. All the Israelites in their proximity fled at the sound of their cries, for they said, "The earth may swallow us, too." A fire issued forth from Yahweh and consumed the 250 men, the offerers of the incense.

That "the earth covered them over so that they vanished" is a particularly nice touch. Korah left no descendants or any physical reminder of his presence on earth.[21] He died without leaving a trace. At Yahweh's behest, Moses commands Eleazar, Aaron's son, to collect the fire pans and hammer them into plating for the altar:

> This was a reminder to the Israelites to ensure that no outsider, that is, one not of the legitimate seed of Aaron, would ever come close to Yahweh's presence to offer incense and become like Korah and his community.

The death of Korah and his supporters left the priesthood in Aaron's hands. But rather than content themselves with an Aaronic victory by default, the writers add two wonder tales to show that Aaron truly merited his office. First, an angry Yahweh afflicts Israel with a plague:

> Yahweh spoke to Moses as follows: "Withdraw from the midst of the community, and I will instantly annihilate them." They fell prostrate. Thereupon Moses commanded Aaron, "Take your fire pan and put hot coals from the altar in it and add incense. Quickly carry it over to the community and perform an expiation over them, for the foaming rage has issued from the face of Yahweh, the plague has begun!" Aaron took what Moses had told him to. He ran into the midst of the congregation, where, indeed, the plague had begun. He put on the incense and performed the expiation over the people. He stood between the dead and the living, and the plague was contained. (Num 17:10–15)

Whereas the fire pans filled with incense had brought about the death of those unqualified for the priesthood, Aaron's fire pan saved most of the congregation from annihilation. This event was followed immediately by another sign of Aaron's unique qualifications for the priesthood to the exclusion of all pretenders:

> Yahweh spoke to Moses as follows: "Speak to the Israelites. Then take from them one rod apiece from each ancestral house, from all the chieftains, for their ancestral houses, twelve staffs in all. Write the name of each person on his staff. And Aaron's name you shall write on the staff of Levi, for there is to be one staff for the head of their ancestral house. Place them inside the tent of meeting, in front of the ark of the covenant, where I meet you. The man whom I select—his staff will sprout, and then I will be relieved of the complaints of the Israelites that they incite against you." Moses then spoke to the Israelites, and all their chieftains delivered to him one staff for each chieftain, for the ancestral houses, twelve staffs in all. The staff of Aaron was among

their staffs. Moses deposited the staffs in the presence of Yahweh, inside the tent of the covenant.

It was on the morrow when Moses entered the tent of covenant that, lo and behold, the staff of Aaron of the house of Levi had sprouted. It gave forth a sprout, produced blossoms, and bore almonds. Out from the presence of Yahweh, Moses brought the staffs to the Israelites. Each person identified his own staff and retrieved it. Yahweh then said to Moses: "Replace Aaron's rod in front of the [ark of] the covenant for safekeeping, as a warning to rebellious persons, so that their complaints against me cease and they do not die." Moses did as Yahweh commanded him, so he did. (Num 17:16–26)

That these traditions are no earlier than the sixth century B.C.E. and belong to latest stratum of the Torah is evident from the Bible itself, as well as from archaeology. Let us begin with the inner biblical evidence. According to the Torah, Aaron and his descendants were first chosen for the priesthood in the wilderness when Moses was given the following instruction:

> Go personally and bring near to you Aaron, your brother, and his sons with him from the midst of the Israelites to officiate for me as priests. (Exod 28:1)

To establish the date behind this allegorical designation of the Aaronides as priests, we must compare Exodus 28:1, which has a fictitious setting, with texts whose date is more firmly anchored in historical periods. As scholars have long observed, Aaron is never identified as a priest in the prophetic literature of the preexilic period. Jeremiah, a prophet of priestly lineage who died sometime after 586 B.C.E., knows nothing about Aaron the priest.

More significant than the silence of Jeremiah, however, is the eloquence of Ezekiel, both a priest and a prophet of the sixth century B.C.E. The Book of Ezekiel devotes a good deal of space to questions of priestly conduct and ritual. Ezekiel confers legitimacy on the sons of Zadok (Ezek 44:15–16), but not on the sons of Aaron. It is only with the Books of Ezra, Nehemiah, and Chronicles, composed during the Persian period, that the Aaronide priesthood is depicted as the only legitimate line.[22] Ezra himself belongs to the seventeenth generation of priests descended from Aaron. From Ezra onward, all claimants to the priesthood of Israel must base that claim on descent from Aaron.

The inner biblical evidence that the requirement for all priests to be descended from Aaron originated later than the sixth century B.C.E. is confirmed by archaeology. Exodus 28 describes in detail what the new priesthood is to wear and concludes with the following:

> You shall also make for them linen trousers to cover their nakedness; they shall extend from the hips to the thighs. They shall be worn by Aaron and his sons when they enter the tent of meeting or when they approach the altar to officiate in the sanctuary, so that they do not incur punishment and die. It shall be a law for all time for him and for his offspring to come. (Exod 28:42–43)

In the ancient Near East, both men and women regularly wore kilts or skirtlike garments. The preceding passage requires the new priesthood to wear trousers at the altar to avoid any inadvertent exposure of nakedness in the divine presence. But this requirement can be dated only after trousers were invented. As art historians have documented, breeches and trousers were Iranian inventions, first found in the Persian reliefs of the sixth century B.C.E., precisely when Jews began coming into contact with Iranians.[23] This means that the story in the Torah crediting the institution of the Aaronide priesthood to Moses in Exodus 28 cannot be any earlier than the sixth century B.C.E.

The tale of Korah comes from the same priestly source and, apparently, from the same time period as Exodus 28. This means that the Korah story is several centuries later than the earliest version of the golden calf tale. The development of the traditions concerning Aaron may be summarized in light of Israelite history as follows:

In the earliest traditions regarding Aaron, he was a hero of the Exodus, with no connection to the priesthood. But this changed with the accession of Jeroboam I, when Aaron came to stand allegorically for the king who also served as priest. In that role, the allegory of Aaron the priest served to legitimate the northern cult of Yahweh, in which the calves played a prominent role. With the fall of the northern kingdom in 720 B.C.E., the figure of Aaron the high priest migrated southward. At first, the northern Aaron/calf tradition was distorted by the southern writers of 1 Kings 12–13. The story was rewritten to create the impression that Jeroboam had been an idolater and that the northern kingdom had never recovered from the original sin of its foundation. We can date the southern distortion almost within a decade, thanks to the continuation of the calf story in 1 Kings 13:1–2:

> While Jeroboam was standing by the altar to offer incense, a man of God came out of Judah by the word of Yahweh to Bethel and proclaimed against the altar by the word of Yahweh. He said, ["O altar, altar, thus says Yahweh: 'A son shall be born to the house of David, Josiah by name, and he shall sacrifice on you the priests of the high places who offer incense on you, and human bones shall be burned on you.'"]

We find a "prophecy" in 1 Kings 13:2 concerning the ultimate fate of the altar at Bethel, a prophecy that is fulfilled in 2 Kings 23:15–16:

> As Josiah turned, he saw the tombs there on the mount, and he sent and took the bones out of the tombs and burned them on the altar and defiled it, according to the word of Yahweh that the man of God proclaimed [or "who prophesied this word"] when Jeroboam stood by the altar at the festival; he turned and looked up at the tomb of the man of God who had predicted these things. Then he asked, ["What is that monument that I see?"] The people of the city told him, ["It is the tomb of the man of God who came from Judah and predicted these things that you have done against the altar at Bethel."]

From a historical point of view, the "prophecy" and its fulfillment date from the same period, the reign of King Josiah.[24] Josiah, who began his religious reform about 622 B.C.E., was assassinated by Pharaoh Necho at Megiddo in 609 B.C.E. This means that the story that distorts Jeroboam's actions in inaugurating the calves and predicts their destruction by Josiah must be dated between 622 and 609 B.C.E. The final distorted form of the story of the golden calf as found in the Torah must come from the same era, the nadir of Aaron's career as an allegorical figure.

About two centuries after the death of Josiah, in the former Judah, in what had become Yehud, a Jewish province of the Persian Empire, Aaron the high priest was rehabilitated. His positive image was restored once he was made to serve the religious agenda of certain elements of the second temple priesthood. This agenda is made very clear in the tale of Korah, in which Aaron serves as an allegory of the legitimate priesthood triumphing over the competition. But the alle-

gory must not be allowed to obscure a fact that has been demonstrated only in the past thirty years: the Korahites were historical figures, and Aaron was not.

In 1962 the Israeli archaeologists Ruth Amiran and Yohanan Aharoni began excavations at Arad, a town in the southern Negeb of
Judah. The Arad expedition discovered more than one hundred Hebrew inscriptions in strata of the Iron Age. From the temple compound of the eighth century B.C.E. came an inscription referring to the
bny qrḥ, the "sons of Korah," or "Korahites," as cultic personnel. It
is to these *bny qrḥ* that many biblical Psalms are ascribed. Several
other inscriptions from the same time and place provide names
known from accounts of aspects of cultic life, which the Torah allegorically situates in the desert in the time of Moses and Aaron.[25]

In other words, the "Korahites," if not Korah himself, were real
historical cultic personnel of the preexilic period. What emerges from
studying the biblical texts in light of the inscriptional and nonliterary
archaeological evidence is that during the first half of the first millennium B.C.E., there was a good deal of diversity in the priesthood. Ancient Israel's division into two distinct states with numerous shrines
had not allowed any single priesthood to control all the cultic offices.
The first attempt to centralize the priesthood was not made until
more than a century after the fall of northern Israel, when King Josiah
tried it. But Josiah's reform had been in effect for barely a decade
when the king met his death in 609 B.C.E. The reform probably did
not survive his death, and surely not the fall of Judah in 587/586
B.C.E. In any event, even the account of Josiah's reform in 2 Kings
22–23 does not mention the Aaronide priests.

The temple of Jerusalem was destroyed when Judah fell. When the
temple was rebuilt in the late sixth century B.C.E., it was the only
sanctuary devoted to Yahweh in Yehud, the Persian administrative
district that preserved the ancient name Judah. This meant that only
a small number of contenders for the priestly office could actually become priests. The restriction of the office to the "sons of Aaron" must
have resulted from compromise among many competing factions. But
not every faction was happy with the compromise, among these the
"sons of Korah," and the reason for their unhappiness is clear:

> Then Moses said to Korah, "Pay attention now, you sons of Levi! Is it
> of so little importance to you that the god of Israel has set you apart

from the community of Israel by bringing you close to him to perform the sanctuary's labor, to stand before the community to serve them? He brought you close to him, you and your fellow Levites with you. Have you now sought priesthood, too? Truly, it is against Yahweh that you and your community are making common cause.

Very simply, the Korahites had been demoted to the status of "sons of Levi," that is, those who "perform the sanctuary's labor." They were supposed to be content with that status because it had been divinely ordained. The Torah's story of their unsuccessful challenge to Aaron, which resulted in their horrifying death, was meant to illustrate the fate of all who would challenge the new order:

This was a reminder to the Israelites to ensure that no outsider, that is, one not of the legitimate seed of Aaron, would ever come close to Yahweh's presence to offer incense and become like Korah and his community.

To become "like Korah and his community" meant suffering a fate worse than death.

CHAPTER 8

Moses

The events of exodus and Sinai require a great personality behind
them. And a faith as unique as Israel's demands a founder as surely as
does Christianity—or Islam for that matter. To deny that role to Moses
would force us to posit another person of the same name.
—John Bright, *A History of Israel*

Since large blocks of the Old Testament pass over Moses in silence, sus-
picion is raised about the historicity of this mighty figure. . . . Perhaps
his dominant position [in the Pentateuch] results from the piety of later
generations of Israelites. If they have not actually created the figure of
the nation's founder, perhaps they have magnified his importance and
pictured him in such a way as to derive sanction for their own practices
and values.
—Robert F. Johnson, *IDB*

In its time, the argument offered by John Bright for the historicity of
Moses would have been compelling to most scholars. The second edi-
tion of Bright's *History* was published in 1972 and had been some
years in preparation. Although Johnson's hesitation a decade earlier
was not unique, 1972 was still too early to dismiss the historicity of
the traditions of the Exodus and the traditions of the sojourn in Sinai
with which they are often linked in the Torah. If there really was an
Israelite Exodus from Egypt, someone must have led it. Inasmuch as
tradition supplied that leader with a name, and a good Egyptian name
at that, why not accept it? But as we have seen, the very basis of that
argument has been removed, or at the very least seriously called into
doubt, by the archaeological evidence that Israel arose in Canaan, so
that the Exodus and the consequent tales of Israel at Sinai and wan-

dering through the desert would appear to be unhistorical. In other words, it seems most likely that the writers of the Torah, in Johnson's words, "actually created the figure of the nation's founder."

If Moses was not a historical figure but an allegory from which later Israel could "derive sanctions and values," we must attempt to find the model, or models, for the allegory. There is one thread that runs through all the different Moses traditions: Moses is the prophet who unites the people of Israel under the banner of the god Yahweh. He is also a royal or quasi-royal figure who stands above every Israelite institution. This means that Moses is an allegorical representation of the royal historical figure who united Israel under the banner of Yahweh and who claimed sovereignty over all competing institutions. The prime candidate for the figure who stands behind the creation of the allegorical figure Moses is Saul, the first king of Israel.

I am indebted to the Dutch scholar Karel van der Toorn for two recent studies that provide the background that led me to the conclusions outlined here. First, van der Toorn argues that Saul was responsible for Yahweh's becoming Israel's official god:[1]

> The changes occurring under Saul were first of all political. The founder of a territorial state, Saul put in place an administrative apparatus and a standing military force. By a system of grants and other privileges he succeeded in maintaining the support of several groups in which power was traditionally vested. In its religious politics too, however Saul's rule was an innovation. The god of the head of state was promoted to the rank of national god; . . . [The] priesthood, sworn to loyalty, was expected to serve the king's best interests. They became the civil servants of state religion.

The links between the career of the historical Saul and that of the allegorical "Moses" are striking. First, numerous Bible scholars have called attention to the linguistic resemblance between Yahweh's words to the prophet Samuel about Saul and Yahweh's first address to Moses:

> Tomorrow about this time I will send to you a man from the land of Benjamin, and you shall anoint him to be prince over my people Israel. He shall save my people from the hand of the Philistines, for I have seen the affliction of my people because their cry has come to me. (1Sam 9:16)

Just as Yahweh designated Saul to save his people because he had heard their cry and attended to their sufferings, so did he designate Moses:

> Then Yahweh said, "I have observed the misery of my people who are in Egypt; I have heard their cry on account of their taskmasters. Indeed, I know their sufferings. (Exod 3:7)

In like manner, both heroes were called on to destroy Amalek, an ancient enemy of Israel. Just as Yahweh designated Saul to wipe out Amalek in 1 Samuel 15, so Moses was called on to eradicate Amalek in Exodus 17 and Deuteronomy 25. Both Saul and Moses acted as prophets, and both men presided over the Yahweh cult.

But in these last three areas—Amalek, prophecy, and cult—all of which indicate the original identity of Saul with the "Moses" of allegory, the similarities between Saul and Moses have been obscured by the biblical writers. To recover the underlying traditions, we must proceed as we did earlier with regard to Jeroboam, and for much the same reason: the traditions were transmitted within circles largely unsympathetic to their subject.

As the biblical scholar Joseph Blenkinsopp wrote, when it comes to Saul, "the modern historian finds himself . . . working against the grain of the sources."[2] Saul and three of his sons died in battle against the Philistines. The assassination of his surviving son left the field to Saul's enemy David, who came to the throne and established a dynasty that ruled Judah for more than four hundred years. Because the writers of the Bible favored David, most of the traditions in the Books of Samuel regarding Saul are unfavorable. Positive traditions concerning Saul have been relegated to the margins, embedded in negative contexts, or recast in negative terms. The embedded and marginal positive traditions have a strong claim to veracity because the writers and compilers who transmitted these traditions had no reason to invent them. Most likely, anything positive about Saul was passed on only because it was too well known to be ignored. We deal first with some of the prominent negative traditions, subjecting their point of view to examination before proceeding to the positive traditions.

The Book of Samuel contains two stories explaining the origin of the proverb "Is Saul too among the prophets?" In the first story,

Samuel tells Saul that Yahweh has designated him to be Israel's ruler:

> And you shall go down to Gilgal ahead of me; then I will come down
> to you to present burned offerings and offer sacrifices of well-being.
> Seven days you shall wait, until I come to you and show you what you
> shall do." As he turned away to leave Samuel, God [Hebrew: *elohim*]
> gave him another heart, and all these signs were fulfilled that day.
> When they were going from there [or "they came there"] to Gibeah [or
> "the hill"], a band of prophets met him, and the spirit of God possessed
> him, and he fell into a prophetic frenzy along with them. When all who
> had known him before saw how he prophesied with the prophets, the
> people said to one another, "What has come over the son of Kish? Is
> Saul also among the prophets?" A man of the place answered, "And
> who is their father?" Therefore it became a proverb, "Is Saul also
> among the prophets?" (1Sam 10:8–12)

In this pericope, Saul's prophetic activity is thoroughly positive.
His inclusion among the prophets is a sign that God has given him
"another heart"; he has been changed from an ordinary human being
into someone divinely chosen to lead Israel. The parallel account in 1
Samuel 19 recontextualizes the story, setting the events in a period
after Yahweh has forsaken Saul in favor of David. In the new setting,
Saul tries to have David assassinated at home. After this attempt fails,
Saul tries to hunt David down elsewhere:

> Saul was told, "David is at Naioth in Ramah." Then Saul sent mes-
> sengers to take David. When they saw the company of the prophets in
> a frenzy, with Samuel standing in charge of them, the spirit of God
> came upon the messengers of Saul, and they also fell into a prophetic
> frenzy. When Saul was told, he sent other messengers, and they also fell
> into a frenzy. Saul sent messengers again the third time, and they also
> fell into a frenzy. Then he himself went to Ramah. He came to the great
> well that is in Secu; he asked, "Where are Samuel and David?" And
> someone said, "They are at Naioth in Ramah." He went there, toward
> Naioth in Ramah, and the spirit of God came upon him. As he was
> going, he fell into a prophetic frenzy, until he came to Naioth in
> Ramah. He too stripped off his clothes, and he too fell into a frenzy be-
> fore Samuel. He lay naked all that day and all that night. Therefore, it
> is asked, "Is Saul also among the prophets?"

In this version, the king is found on the ground naked, "in a frenzy
before Samuel." The medieval French Jewish scholar Joseph Kara ap-
provingly cites Targum's rendition of "naked" as *biršan*, "out of his

mind." Despite the general esteem in which prophets are held in the Bible, in some instances prophets are associated with madmen, and this is one of them.[3] Saul's inclusion among the prophets here means that Saul is mad. The fact that he is "naked" also is significant. When biblical writers wish to speak positively about the human anatomy they refer to comely form or to specific beautiful parts of the body. The word translated as "naked" (Hebrew: *'ārum*) is found only in contexts of "fear," "humiliation," "defeat," and sexual activity of which the writer disapproves.[4] The writer of this pericope thus disfigured the tradition of Saul's inclusion among the prophets so that it now connotes Saul's utter unfitness for royal office.

The writers similarly disfigured the biblical traditions that describe Saul's presiding over the cult of Yahweh. Let us turn to 1 Samuel 13:8–14, an episode designed to show why after having told the prophet Samuel to anoint Saul as king, Yahweh later changed his divine mind.

> He [Saul] waited seven days, the time appointed by Samuel, but Samuel did not come to Gilgal, and the people began to scatter away from him. So Saul said, "Bring the holocaust (that is, animal) here to me, and the offerings of well-being." He offered the holocaust, but as soon as he had finished offering it, Samuel arrived. Saul went out to meet him and greet him. Samuel asked, "What have you done?" Saul replied, "When I saw that the people were scattering away from me and that you did not come within the days appointed and that the Philistines were mustering at Michmash, I said, 'Now the Philistines will come down on me at Gilgal, and I have not entreated the favor of Yahweh'; so I composed myself and offered the holocaust."

The word *scatter* (Hebrew: *wayyāpeṣ*), elsewhere used to describe the aimless movement of sheep and goats who have lost their shepherd, foreshadows Saul's downfall. The people are out of Saul's control, and the writer has Saul admit as much by putting the same verb in his mouth (v. 11). In the same fashion, the verb that Saul uses in the phrase "I composed myself" (Hebrew: *wā'et'apaq*) is also used in the Joseph story (Gen 43:31) to describe Joseph's attempt to recover from an unexpected outburst of tears. Although the detail is charming in the Joseph story, it denotes inappropriate royal behavior in Saul's circumstances. As king, he should not have been so upset in the first place. The pericope continues:

Samuel said to Saul, "You have done foolishly; had you kept the commandment of Yahweh, your God, which he commanded you, Yahweh would have established your kingdom over Israel forever, but now your kingdom will not continue. Yahweh has sought out a man after his own heart, and Yahweh has appointed him to be ruler over his people because you have not kept what Yahweh commanded you."

It is not entirely clear what Saul did wrong. One explanation is that he should have been patient. He should not have disobeyed "the commandment of Yahweh," namely, the word of Samuel, who had told him to wait to offer the sacrifice until his arrival; never mind that Samuel was late. Another possibility has to do with the offering itself. Like many other ancient (and modern) warriors, the Israelites preferred to have divine sanction before going into battle.

In Israel's sacrificial system, the 'olah, a whole burned offering or "holocaust," was considered the most efficacious because it was selfless. The burned fat and smoke were a pleasing aroma to Yahweh, but no meat was left for human consumption. By offering this special sacrifice, Saul may have usurped a cultic function that, in the writer's opinion, belonged properly to priests or to prophets like Samuel, but not to kings. In either case, this sin cost Saul the chance at a dynasty. The pericope surely does not date from Saul's time. From the anachronism that Yahweh has already sought out Saul's successor, we learn that the tradition originated no earlier than the reign of David.

As if this were not enough, there is a second account of how a cultic violation by Saul cost him the dynasty in 1 Samuel 15:1–19:

Samuel said to Saul, "Yahweh sent me to anoint you king over his people Israel; now, therefore, listen to the words of Yahweh. Thus says Yahweh-of-Hosts, 'I will punish the Amalekites for what they did in opposing the Israelites when they came up out of Egypt. Now go and attack Amalek, and utterly destroy all that they have; do not spare them, but kill man and woman, child and infant, ox and sheep, camel and donkey.'"

So Saul summoned the people and numbered them in Telaim, 200,000 foot soldiers, and 10,000 soldiers of Judah. Saul came to the city of the Amalekites and lay in wait in the valley. Saul said to the Kenites, "Go! Leave! Withdraw from among the Amalekites, or I will destroy you with them, for you showed kindness to all the people of Israel when they came up out of Egypt." So the Kenites withdrew from the Amalekites. Saul defeated the Amalekites, who dwelled from Havilah to Shur, which is east of Egypt. He took King Agag of the Amalekites alive but utterly destroyed all his people with the edge of the sword. Saul and his people showed pity to Agag and the best of the sheep, the cattle, the fatlings, and the lambs and all that was valuable. These they refused to destroy utterly; whatever was despicable and worthless, they utterly destroyed.

The word translated here as "utterly destroyed" is *heherim*, literally, "subject to the practice of *herem*." When an enemy was put to the *herem*, the victorious soldiers did not share in the booty, as was usually the case. Instead, as we know from the Bible and from a ninth-century B.C.E. Moabite source in which Israel was a victim of the *herem*, the spoils of war were required to be consecrated to the victorious deity by being destroyed.[5] The writer sardonically describes how Saul and the people "showed pity" to the Amalekite king and to the valuable cattle and utterly destroyed only what was not worth keeping. As a result of this violation of the *herem*,

the word of Yahweh came to Samuel: "I regret that I made Saul king, for he has turned back from following me and has not carried out my commands." Samuel was angry, and he cried out to Yahweh all night. Samuel rose early in the morning to meet Saul, and Samuel was told, "Saul went to Carmel, where he set up a monument for himself, and on returning, he passed on down to Gilgal."

That the king "set up a monument to himself" verifies Yahweh's evaluation of Saul; that is, Saul cares more for his monument than for the divine command:

When Samuel came to Saul, Saul said to him, "May you be blessed by Yahweh, I have carried out the command of Yahweh." But Samuel asked, "What, then, is this bleating of sheep in my ears and the lowing of cattle that I hear?" Saul said, "They have brought them from the Amalekites, for the people showed pity for the best sheep and cattle, to sacrifice to Yahweh, your God, but the rest we have utterly destroyed." Then Samuel said to Saul, "Stop! I will tell you what Yahweh said to me last night." He replied, "Speak." Samuel said, "Perhaps you are little in your own eyes (a reference to 1 Samuel 9:21, in which Saul modestly refers to his humble origins), but are you not head of the tribes of Israel? Yahweh anointed you king over Israel. And Yahweh sent you on a mission, saying, 'Go, utterly destroy the sinners, the Amalekites, and fight against them until their final annihilation.' Why, then, did you not obey the voice of Yahweh? Why did you swoop down on the spoil and do what was evil in the sight of Yahweh?"

Saul is here portrayed as weak and ineffectual at best. His claim to have "carried out the command of Yahweh" is belied by the bleating of animals. His reference to "Yahweh, your god" rather than "my god" amounts to self-incrimination rather than the intended exculpation. Worst of all, by blaming the people for his failure to carry out the *ḥerem*, he shows himself unqualified to be "head of the tribes of Israel."

As scholars have shown, the traditional story that Saul failed to annihilate the Amalekites is based on Deuteronomy 25:17–19, a seventh-century B.C.E. text. In other words, the *ḥerem* story is an attempt several centuries after the fact to account for Saul's displacement by David.[6] Once again, a positive tradition concerning the first king of Israel, in which the historical destroyer of Amalek, Saul, originally stood behind Moses, the allegorical scourge of Amalek, was distorted by writers sympathetic to David and his dynasty.

More significant historically are the positive traditions regarding Saul that are likely to come from his own time. The claim made by van der Toorn, that Saul as head of state made Yahweh into the national god is fully supported by the Book of Samuel, in which Saul's zeal for Yahweh is well documented. Despite the ignominy heaped on Saul in the late negative stories that we have just read, he is never accused of the one sin attributed to all the "bad" kings of Israel: he never deserts Yahweh for other gods. In fact, he is credited with wiping out forms of divination that the cult of Yahweh considered illicit:

> The woman said to him, "Surely you know what Saul has done, how he has cut off the mediums and the wizards from the land. Why, then, are you laying a snare for my life to bring about my death?" (1Sam 28:9; cf. Deut 18:11)

Saul's piety to Yahweh is also reflected in the name of his oldest son, Jonathan (Hebrew: Yeho-natan, "Yahweh-has-given"). Saul was chosen by Yahweh, for there was none like him in the entire people (1Sam 10:24). He credits Yahweh with his victory over the Ammonites (1Sam 11:13), as does his son Jonathan for victory over the Philistines (1Sam 14:12). Saul is Yahweh's "anointed" (Hebrew:

māšiaḥ). In the traditions of Saul's role in the Yahweh cult, the following notice is of particular interest:

> They struck down the Philistines that day from Michmash to Ayalon. And the people were famished; the people lit upon the spoil and took sheep and oxen and calves and slew them on the ground and the people ate them with the blood. Then Saul was told, "The people are sinning against Yahweh, by eating with the blood." He said, "You have dealt treacherously; roll a great stone to me here. Then Saul said, "Disperse yourselves among the people, and say to them, 'Let every one bring his ox or his sheep and slay them here and eat. Do not sin against Yahweh by eating with the blood.'" So every one of the people brought his ox with him that night and slew them there. Then Saul built an altar to Yahweh; he was the first to build an altar to Yahweh. (1Sam 14:31–35)

This tale must be understood against the background of biblical views of blood.[7] Because blood was identified with the life force, biblical legislation allotted the blood to Yahweh alone, who was popularly believed to consume it.[8] All humans, including non-Israelites, were forbidden to eat blood, but Israelites had an additional obligation. They were required to abstain from eating the flesh of a slaughtered animal with the blood still in it.[9] Precisely because of blood's potency as a life force, its consumption appealed to famished soldiers who would need to revitalize themselves for battle. But in Saul's eyes, the consumption of blood was a "sin against Yahweh." By insisting that the animals be slaughtered ceremonially at the great stone, Saul made sure that the blood would be poured out and that the flesh would not be eaten "with the blood."

The last verse in this "marginal" tale, in which Saul is depicted as a hero, is particularly instructive. It reads:

'oto heḥel libnot mizbeaḥ l-YHWH

I translated this as "He was the first to build an altar to Yahweh." In contrast, most of the ancient and modern translations are similar to the NRSV:

> And Saul built an altar to the LORD; it was the first altar that he built to the LORD.

But in fact, the correct understanding of the verse was known to Jewish scholars of late antiquity and the medieval period. What follows is drawn from a homily found in the Palestinian Jewish Midrash, Leviticus Rabbah:[10]

> It is written: *wayyiben ša'ul mizbeaḥ l-YHWH 'oto heḥel libnot mizbeaḥ l-YHWH*—So many altars were built by the ancients—Noah, Abraham, Isaac, Jacob, Moses, and Joshua, and you [the verse] say *'oto heḥel*—"he was the first?" The rabbis say: *'oto heḥel* means "he was the first of the kings." But Rabbi Yudan said: Because he was prepared to give his life for this matter, Scripture assigned him as much credit as if he himself had been the first to build an altar to the Lord.

Notice that the midrashic pericope has three speakers: an anonymous questioner, one anonymous respondent—"the rabbis"—and a named respondent—Rabbi Yudan. All the speakers agree that 1 Samuel 14:35 asserts that Saul was the first to build an altar to Yahweh. For the midrashists, the assertion is problematic because it contradicts other biblical traditions set in the premonarchic period, which claim that "so many altars were built by the ancients." The rabbis resolve the contradiction by imposing a larger context: Saul, the first of the kings, set the royal precedent of building altars to Yahweh. In contrast, Rabbi Yudan resolves the problem by treating the scriptural claim as hyperbole: We are not to accept the plain sense of the verse. Saul was not chronologically the first to build an altar to Yahweh, but because of the courage he showed in building it, he might as well have been the first.

Among the medievals, some of whom cite the preceding midrash, Levi b. Gershon, David Kimhi, Joseph Kara, and Isaiah of Trani understood the verse correctly, despite their discomfort with its implications. Here is Kara's comment:

> This would imply that he was the first in the world to build an altar, but that cannot be correct, for after all, many altars had earlier been built. Therefore what is written *'oto heḥel libnot mizbeaḥ* must be understood as if it read *'oto mizbeaḥ heḥel libnot*; that is, "this was the first altar he built."

Kara's problem is that the text cannot mean what it says. Therefore, "it must be understood as if it read" something other than it does.[11] But the problem shared by Kara and his successors is not inherent in 1 Samuel 14:35. Rather, the problem comes from accepting the historicity of the tales about Noah, Abraham, Isaac, Jacob, Moses, and Joshua. Once we accept, as we must, the fact that the stories of the presettlement period have no historical value for the period of their setting, then we are free to consider seriously the tradition that Saul was the first to build an altar to Yahweh. Such a story would have been told in circles favorable to Saul and those who shared his zeal for the worship of Yahweh.

Where would this zeal have originated? The story of Saul and Amalek mentions Saul's connection with a group known as the Kenites. Despite the generally unhistorical character of the pericope, its introduction contains extremely valuable information linking Saul to Moses as the founder of Israelite Yahwism. Let us turn to that introduction once more:

> Saul came to the city of the Amalekites and lay in wait in the valley. Saul said to the Kenites, "Go! Leave! Withdraw from among the Amalekites, or I will destroy you with them, for you showed kindness to all the people of Israel when they came up out of Egypt." So the Kenites withdrew from the Amalekites. (1Sam 15:6)

If we wish to pursue the allegory of Moses and its origin in Saul, we must ask where the Kenites withdrew to? According to Judges 1:16,

> the descendants of Hobab the *Kenite*, Moses' father-in-law, went up from Jericho . . . and lived with the people.

These notices belong to a persistent inner biblical tradition that the Kenites had not been part of the groups that coalesced as "Israel." In fact, according to Genesis 15:17–20, they were one of the peoples whom Israel was supposed to dispossess:

> When the sun had gone down and it was dark, a smoking fire pot and a flaming torch passed between these pieces. On that day, Yahweh made a covenant with Abram, saying, "To your descendants I give this land, from the river of Egypt to the great river, the river Euphrates, *the land of the Kenites*, the Kadmonites, the Hittites, the Perizzites, and the Rephaim."

According to Judges 4:11, one element of the Kenites had broken away from the larger body:

Now Heber the Kenite had separated from the other Kenites, that is, the descendants of Hobab, the father-in-law of Moses, and had encamped as far away as Elon-bezaanannim, which is near Kedesh.

According to the same chapter, the Kenites had once been federated with the Canaanites, so that a defeated Canaanite general might think to find refuge among the Kenites:

Now Sisera had fled away on foot to the tent of Jael, wife of Heber the Kenite, for there was an alliance between King Jabin of Hazor and the clan of Heber the Kenite. Jael came out to meet Sisera and said to him, "Turn aside, my lord, turn aside to me; have no fear." So he turned aside to her into the tent, and she covered him with a rug. Then he said to her, "Please give me a little water to drink, for I am thirsty." So she opened a skin of milk and gave him a drink and covered him. He said to her, "Stand at the entrance of the tent, and if anybody comes and asks you, 'Is anyone here?' say, 'No.'" But Jael, wife of Heber, took a tent peg and took a hammer in her hand and went softly to him and drove the peg into his temple, until it went down into the ground—he was lying fast asleep from weariness—and he died. Then when Barak came in pursuit of Sisera, Jael went out to meet him and said to him, "Come, and I will show you the man whom you are seeking." So he went into her tent, and there was Sisera lying dead, with the tent peg in his temple. So on that day, God subdued King Jabin of Canaan before the Israelites. (Judg 4:17–23)

The Kenites of these tales were a community whose ancestry was traced to an eponymous ancestor named Cain, best known to readers of the Bible for committing the world's first homicide by killing his brother Abel. Inasmuch as the in-laws of Moses are called "Kenites" in the Books of Judges and Samuel and "Midianites" in the Torah, it would appear that the two groups are identical, or at least closely related. According to Exodus 2:16 and 3:1, the Midianite father-in-law of Moses was a priest, yet the only god he ever mentions is Yahweh. According to another tradition in Exodus 18:12, he presides at a sacrificial meal attended by Moses, Aaron, and the elders of Israel. In the manner of the positive Saul traditions, the tradition that a Midianite priest officiated at Israelite sacred occasions is a marginal tradition, at odds with strong anti-Midianite traditions throughout the Bible. But over the years, numerous scholars have realized that this marginal tradition needs to be taken seriously because it suggests that the

Midianite/Kenites were responsible for bringing Yahweh worship to the group that became Israel. The suggestion is likely for a number of reasons.

First, as van der Toorn noted in a recent study, the god Yahweh is thus far not found in any Syrian or Palestinian pantheon other than Israel.[12] Unlike other gods mentioned in the Hebrew Bible, such as Kemosh, Baal, or Asherah or gods like El with whom he is often identified, Yahweh does not belong to the traditional circle of west Semitic deities. He appears first in Egyptian sources of the late second millennium B.C.E. Two Egyptian texts mention "Yahweh in the land of the Shosu bedouin" ($t3\ \check{s}3\acute{s}w\ yhw3$) as a place-name. One text comes from the first part of the fourteenth century B.C.E., another from the thirteenth century B.C.E. In the second list, from the reign of Ramses II, the name occurs in a context mentioning Seir, that is, in the area of Edom and Midian. Inasmuch as place-names were regularly referred to as the homes of divinities who lived there (cf. Bethel), the toponym "Yhw3" is probably short for "Beth-Yahweh," "House of Yahweh."

As van der Toorn points out, the Egyptian data converge with a number of marginal biblical traditions that Yahweh came from Seir, Mount Paran, Teman, and Sinai, all in or near southern areas in which Midianite/Kenites might be found. The tradition that Moses had a father-in-law who was either a Kenite or Midianite and a priest indicate that Yahweh reached Israel through Kenite/Midianite mediation.

The Kenite hypothesis in its classical form conjectured that the Israelites had come into contact with Kenite/Midianite worshipers of Yahweh in the desert on their way up from Egypt during the exodus. Geographically, this accords well with the location of the Yahweh place-names in the south in the Egyptian lists. But inasmuch as the entire episode of Israel in Egypt is allegorical, the Kenite/Midianite hypothesis must be modified. Biblical sources show us that these groups were not confined to the south. From Genesis 37:28 we learn that Midianites were active as traders in the entire area between Canaan and Egypt. More important, Judges 4:11 locates the nonsedentary, tent-dwelling group of Heber the Kenite at Kedesh in northern Israel.

The same text associates these Kenites with the father-in-law of Moses. Inasmuch as gods travel with their people, it appears that Kenites/Midianite traders brought Yahweh along with them into Transjordan and northern Israel along the caravan routes.[13] If we translate the in-law relation into the political language of clan federation, we may speak of the Kenites' federating with elements located in what was to be northern Israel, and we may speak of Saul's being crucial to this process of federation. In the process, the god Yahweh became an Israelite god, the god of what we described earlier as the *berît*, or "covenant." As the god of Saul, the nation builder of Israel, Yahweh became the national god of Israel.

There are ample analogies in the history of religion to the process that occurred in Saul's reign. Readers will immediately call to mind how Christianity triumphed after the conversion of the Roman emperor Constantine. Similarly, the triumph of Islam over Arab paganism resulted from the political successes of Muhammed. In the period roughly contemporary with the rise of ancient Israel, King Nebuchadnezzar I of Babylon (1125–1104 B.C.E.), after defeating his hated eastern enemies the Elamites, elevated the god Marduk to supremacy over all the other gods. In addition to his original supremacy over the city of Babylon, home of Nebuchadnezzar, Marduk began to claim supremacy over the gods and over the entire land.[14]

What is of special interest is that the elevation of Marduk was expressed in literature by the composition of the *Enuma Elish*, the great Babylonian epic of creation. In ancient Israel, the triumphs of Saul led to the beginnings of the composition of Israel's Torah literature for the elevation of Yahweh. The Saulide interests in early Israel used the figure of the historical Saul, zealous devotee of the religion of Yahweh, as the model for the allegorical figure of Moses. This is undoubtedly why the traditions concerning David, even those that speak of the exodus, make no reference at all to the figure of Moses.

As we saw in the previous chapters, in the course of time, allegorical figures acquired new dimensions. This was true of Moses as well, but the details of the new dimensions must be left for another occasion.

Afterword

The Greek critics who commented on Homer and his successors conceived of three levels, or kinds, of literary reality: *historia* (describing what actually happened), *plasma* (relating imaginary events as if they were real), and *mythos* (telling what never happened). The classical scholar D. C. Feeney observed that readers who interpret mythos as if it were historia or plasma mistake the genre before them.[1] If we transfer the Greek analytical categories from Homer to the Torah, we find that the Torah contains plasma and mythos but no historia. That is, even what could have occurred apparently did not.

What archaeology has demonstrated is that despite some historical semblance, the Torah's narratives are not history in the sense of events occurring in the time and place in which the biblical writers set them. It follows that the narratives of the Torah do not reflect the lives of the people who served the writers as protagonists. Instead, the stories in the Torah are allegories. They speak of the times in which they were written in the allegorical setting of a completely fictional past. By approaching the stories of the Torah as fiction, we are not, however, dismissing their historical significance. On the contrary, we are attempting to show how these politically charged texts provide historical evidence for the period in which they were composed.

In her groundbreaking study *Images, Power and Politics*, Barbara Nevling Porter shows that the royal inscriptions of Esarhaddon, king of Assyria, in the eighth century B.C.E., are precious historical artifacts precisely because they do not stick to the "facts."[2] Rather, as political documents, they reveal Assyrian attitudes, ideologies, and official policy. By identifying the different audiences to which the inscriptions were addressed, Porter is able, convincingly, to reconstruct the complexities of ancient Assyrian political life.[3]

I have tried to do something similar here. In this book, I am suggesting that the different writers of the Torah aimed their messages at particular audiences and constituencies. Their method was allegorical and their goals ideological. If we wish to know what the Torah is about, it is crucial to identify the method by which the writers attempted to achieve their goals and what those goals were. If we are correct in identifying the narratives of the Torah as allegories, then our task is to decode them.

The most prominent allegory in the Torah is the god Yahweh and what he did for Israel before it became a people in its own territorial states. The key to understanding what the narratives of the Torah tell us is to decode what "Yahweh" meant to the Torah's writers in their own age, how they used the allegory of Yahweh's deeds in the past to comment on their contemporary situation. That "Yahweh was with Abraham in all he did" means that the writer, who lived in the tenth century B.C.E., approves of Abraham's actions.

Furthermore, if Abraham is an allegory of David, the fact that "Yahweh was with Abraham in all he did" means that the writer approves of David's actions. If Yahweh personally made the earth open up to swallow Korah and his followers who sought to take the priesthood from Aaron, it means that the author writing in the fifth century B.C.E. approves of the new "Aaronide" priesthood and disapproves of dissenters unwilling to adjust to the new situation. In short, Yahweh always stands for the agenda of the individual writer. When contemporary readers try to discover the ancient agenda, they are, in fact, coming closer to understanding Yahweh.

I close by remarking on the irony inherent in my allegoresis of the Torah. Some readers will no doubt object that it is impossible to recover what really happened and that consequently, my own researches are themselves allegories of the events I have reconstructed. If so, at least I will have demonstrated the potential of my approach.

Notes

Notes to Introduction

1. Gordon Tucker and Douglas Knight, eds., *Humanizing America's Iconic Book* (Chico, Calif.: Scholars Press, 1980), 1–23. Martin Marty, "America's Iconic Book," in Tucker and Knight, *Humanizing America's Iconic Book*, 8.
2. An inscription discovered at Tel Dan in 1993 cites the "House of David" in reference to a king of Judah but not to King David himself.
3. Moshe Weinfeld, "The Creator God in Genesis I and in the Prophecy of Deutero-Isaiah," *Tarbiz* 37/2 (1968): 105–32.
4. For the Persian text, see Wilhelm Brandenstein and Manfred Mayrhofer, *Handbuch des Altpersischen* (Wiesbaden: Harrassowitz, 1964), 83.
5. The name Farnaka was held by a very high ranking economic official under Darius. Farnaka is the most prominent figure in the more than two thousand Persepolis Fortification Texts. See David M. Lewis, "The Persepolis Fortification Texts," in Helen Sancisi-Weerdenburg and Amélie Kuhrt, eds., *Achaemenid History IV Centre and Periphery* (Leiden: Nederlands Instituut voor het Nabije Oosten, 1990), 1–6.
6. See, for example, Joel Rosenberg, *King and Kin: Political Allegory in the Hebrew Bible* (Bloomington: Indiana University Press, 1986); James Kennedy, "Peasants in Revolt: Political Allegory in Genesis 2–3," *JSOT* 47 (1990): 3–14.

Notes to Chapter 1

1. For our purposes, it does not matter whether we speak of the six books as a Hextateuch or of a more original Tetrateuch (Genesis through Numbers) followed by a Deuteronomic history, of which Deuteronomy and Joshua constitute the first two books.
2. The same generally holds for the New Testament as well. Only once do we find a claim for veracity: The conclusion of the Gospel of John (21:24) states that Jesus' beloved disciple "vouches for what is written. He it is who wrote it, and we know his testimony is true." But this statement stands out because

of its singularity. By canonizing four Gospels, which often disagree about events and their chronology, rather than encouraging Gospel harmonization, the church seems not have taken historicity as its primary criterion. See Luke T. Johnson, *The Real Jesus* (San Francisco: Harper, 1996), 148.

3. Philo 1:1 (LCL, 6–7); compare the Preface by Josephus to Antiquities: "When Moses was desirous to teach this lesson to his countrymen, he did not begin . . . upon contracts and other rites between one man and another, but by raising their minds upwards to regard God and his creation of the world" (Whiston, *Josephus*, 24).

4. For a concise outline of the life and thought of Nahmanides, with a bibliography, see Leonard Kravitz, "Mose ben Nahman," *Theologische Realenzyklopädie*, vol. 23, fasc. 3/4 (Berlin: de Gruyter, 1994): 362–64.

5. For a highly readable account of the rise of modern biblical criticism, see Richard E. Friedman, *Who Wrote the Bible?* (New York: Harper & Row, 1989). Also see the convenient survey in Thomas L. Thompson, *The Origin Tradition of Ancient Israel* (Sheffield: JSOT, 1987), 11–40.

6. Julius Wellhausen, *Prolegomena to the History of Ancient Israel* (Gloucester: Peter Smith, 1973), 331.

7. See Thomas L. Thompson, *The Historicity of the Patriarchal Narratives* (Berlin: de Gruyter, 1974), 49. See Gordon Young, ed., *Mari in Retrospect* (Winona Lake, Ind.: Eisenbrauns, 1992), 316; Thompson, *Historicity*, 43. Wellhausen's theological perspective also played a role. His understanding of the development of law and its religious role in ancient Israel was firmly anchored in Martin Luther's understanding of St. Paul's critique of "the Law."

8. See Harold Louis Ginsberg, "Ugaritic Studies and the Bible," in David N. Freedman and Edward F. Campbell, eds., *The Biblical Archaeologist Reader*, vol. 2 (Garden City, N.Y.: Anchor/Doubleday, 1964), 35–58, esp. 43–44.

9. The best known of these scholars was the Assyriologist Friedrich Delitzsch (1850–1922), who gave a series of lectures in 1902 later published as *Babel und Bibel* (Babylonia and Bible), in which he argues that the Bible is not original because all the sources of Hebrew religion were to be found in Babylonia. In 1921 he published *Die grosse Täuschung* (The great deception), which was blatantly anti-Semitic in tone and, as its confrontational title indicates, "an outright attack on traditionalist biblical historiography." See Joel Sweek, "The Babel-Bibel Streit," in Lowell K. Handy and Steven W. Holloway, eds., *The Pitcher Is Broken: Memorial Essays for Gösta W. Ahlström* (Sheffield: Sheffield Academic Press, 1995), 401–19.

10. Niels Lemche, *ABD* 3: 534.

11. Compare the statement by John Bright, *A History of Israel* (Philadelphia: Westminster, 1972), 91: "We can assert with full confidence that Abraham, Isaac and Jacob were actual historical individuals." One can, of course, assert whatever one wishes.

For Albright's statement, see Louis Finkelstein, ed., *The Jews, Their History, Culture and Religion* (New York: Harper, 1960), 6. The argument of "vividness" could just as easily lead to the conclusion that Genesis was written by a talented writer of fiction rather than by a historian.

12. In Europe the primary challenge to source criticism came from form criticism. Form critics argued that the written sources identified by source criticism were themselves the product of long oral transmission, so that the time of reduction to writing could not, by itself, determine their historical reliability. Among the form critics themselves, the pioneers Hermann Gunkel and Hugo Gressmann tended to view ancient oral traditions as imaginative, whereas such scholars as Otto Eissfeldt and Martin Noth tended to assign them greater credibility. See the summary by Thomas L. Thompson, "Historiography (Israelite)," *ABD* 3: 206–12. See William Dever, "Archaeology, Syro-Palestinian and Biblical," *ABD* 1: 354–67, esp. 357–59.

13. See Rolf Rendtorff, "Postexilic Israel in German Bible Scholarship," in Michael Fishbane and Emanuel Tov, eds., *Sha'arei Talmon Studies in the Bible, Qumran and the Ancient Near East Presented to Shemaryahu Talmon* (Winona Lake: Eisenbrauns, 1992), 165–73, esp. 168, n. 10.

14. Bright, *History*, 286. No doubt Bright's "deliverance" was inspired by Byron's poem "Jerusalem Delivered."

15. Two books were primarily responsible for beginning the negative reevaluation of the biblical archaeology movement: John van Seters, *Abraham in History and Tradition* (New Haven, Conn.: Yale University Press, 1975); and Thompson, *Historicity*.

16. Nahum Sarna, *The JPS Torah Commentary Genesis* (New York: Jewish Publication Society, 1989), 390.

17. See Ephraim A. Speiser, "The Wife-Sister Motif in the Patriarchal Narratives," in Jacob Finkelstein and Moshe Greenberg, eds., *Oriental and Biblical Studies: Collected Writings of E. A. Speiser* (Philadelphia: University of Pennsylvania Press, 1967), 62–82.

18. See especially Samuel Greengus, "Sisterhood Adoption at Nuzi and the 'Wife-Sister' in Genesis," *HUCA* 46 (1975): 5–31.

19. For references to Speiser's reconstruction and the critical response, see S. David Sperling, *Students of the Covenant: A History of Jewish Biblical Scholarship in North America* (Atlanta: Scholars Press, 1992), 84, nn. 19, 21.

20. See the extensive bibliography assembled by William Dever, "Israel, History of (Archaeology and the 'Conquest')," *ABD* 3: 557–58, 546.

21. Ibid., 547, 553. Or, as Thompson has it (*The Origin Tradition*, 37), "Israelite ethnic identity came about through the process whereby the indigenous population of Palestine began to understand and identify itself as Israelite." For a balanced assessment and evaluation of the different theories of Israelite origins, resulting in a slightly more positive evaluation of aspects

of the biblical account, see Richard Hess, "Early Israel in Canaan: A Survey of Recent Evidence and Interpretations," *PEQ* 125 (1993): 125–42.

22. See Baruch Halpern, *The First Historians* (New York: Harper & Row, 1988); contrast Niels Lemche, *The Canaanites and Their Land* (Sheffield: Sheffield Academic Press, 1991), 151, n. 1.

23. The best candidates are the list of the Edomite kings and dukes (Gen 36:31–43) and the account of how Sihon conquered the territory of the first king of Moab, which deduces "historical" information from a poem (Num 21:26–31). See Baruch Levine, "The Triumphs of the Lord," *ErIsr* 20 (1989): 204–5; and some of the notices about the history of Transjordan in Deuteronomy 2–3. These items are historiographic in that they study earlier materials to find out about past events and to show that they make sense in a real time setting. Whether they are factual or correct is another matter. On the problems of Numbers 21:26–31, see John van Seters, "Once Again—The Conquest of Sihon's Kingdom," *JBL* 99/1 (1980): 117–19; J. Maxwell Miller, "The Israelite Journey through (around) Moab and Moabite Toponymy," *JBL* 108/4 (1989): 577–95; and Lawrence Geraty, "Hesbon," *ABD* 3: 181–84. For the term *historiography*, see Burke Long, review of *The Origin Tradition*, by Thomas L. Thompson, *JBL* 108/2 (1989): 328.

Notes to Chapter 2

1. See Edmund Leach, "Anthropological Approaches to the Bible during the Twentieth Century," in Gordon Tucker and Douglas Knight, eds., *Humanizing America's Iconic Book* (Chico, Calif.: Scholars Press, 1980), 75–94. The quotations are from pp. 76–77.

2. Compare James Barr's lecture to the International Society for the Study of the Old Testament on February 21, 1989, published as "The Literal, the Allegorical, and Modern Scholarship," *JSOT* 44 (1989): 3–17. One of Barr's conclusions is "The traditional categories of *literal* and *allegorical* do not fit the modern situation well; but in so far as they can be used at all, modern exposition has distinct affinities with the allegorical" (16).

3. Morris H. Abrams, *A Glossary of Literary Terms* (New York: Holt, Rinehart and Winston, 1971), 4; Erich Auerbach, *Scenes from the Drama of European Literature* (New York: Meridian, 1959), 3.

4. For the term *imposed allegory*, see Frank Talmage, "Apples of Gold: The Inner Meaning of Sacred Texts in Medieval Judaism," in A. Green, ed., *Jewish Spirituality from the Bible through the Middle Ages* (New York: Crossroad, 1986), 314.

Allegory is not confined to a particular literary form. It is best described as a "strategy which may be employed in any literary form or genre" (Abrams, *Glossary*, 5). For attempts to distinguish among different allegorical forms in early Jewish sources, see the literature cited in David I. Brewer, *Techniques and Assumptions in Jewish Exegesis before 70 C.E.* (Tübingen: Mohr, 1992), 22. The use of allegory in cuneiform literature is "extensive and largely unstudied." See Stephen Lieberman, "A Mesopotamian Background for the So-Called *Aggadic* 'Measures' of Biblical Hermeneutics," *HUCA* 58 (1987): 162.

5. On allegory in Philo, see Jenny Morris, "The Jewish Philosopher Philo," in Geza Vermes et al., *Emil Schürer, The History of the Jewish People in the Time of Jesus Christ*, vol. 3, part 2 (Edinburgh: T and T Clark, 1987), 875–80; Yehoshua Amir, "Authority and Interpretation in the Writings of Philo," in Martin Mulder, ed., *Mikra* (Philadelphia: Fortress Press, 1988), 421–53. See Hermann Büchsel, "*allēgoreō*," *TDNT* 1: 260–63; Jonathan Tate, "Allegory, Greek," *OCD*: 45–46; Saul Lieberman, *Hellenism in Jewish Palestine* (New York: Jewish Theological Seminary, 1950), 64–66; Joel Rosenberg, *King and Kin: Political Allegory in the Hebrew Bible* (Bloomington: Indiana University Press, 1986), 218, n. 31. Also see Ernest Burton, *A Critical and Exegetical Commentary on the Epistle to the Galatians* (Edinburgh: T and T Clark, 1921), 253–57.

6. In the manner of Paul, Philo treats Sarah and Hagar allegorically. For Philo, the name Sarah means "sovereignty of me," that is, "self-control" or "virtue." Inasmuch as virtue in Philo's understanding cannot be attained without preparation, Hagar is, "by interpretation" (*hermeneuthen*), the "sojourner," that is, the lower sciences of grammar, astronomy, geometry, rhetoric, music, and all the other branches of intellectual study in which one sojourns in order to prepare for virtue. See Philo 4 (LCL), 458–71; also Amir, "Authority and Interpretation," 439.

7. They have the status of "slave born in the household," and their offspring inherit the status of their slave parents. See Genesis 17:12, 13, and 27; and Leviticus 22:11 and 25:46.

8. Paul thus makes the Jews into Gentiles!

9. Sarah is not called by name here. Possibly, Paul avoids naming her because he needs to quote Sarah anonymously in verse 30 when he refers to Genesis 21:10, in which the words "Drive out the slave girl and her son" are spoken by Sarah but cited by Paul as "the scripture" (*hē graphē*).

10. In Genesis 21:9, the actions of Ishmael, the son of the slave woman, are described by the verb *meṣaḥeq*. Paul's interpretation of the verb *meṣaḥeq* as a reference to persecution is in agreement with rabbinic sources. See Julius Theodor and Chanoch Albeck, *Midrash Bereshit Rabba* (Jerusalem: Wahrmann, 1965), 568.

11. Galatians 1:13.

12. The Genesis verse is specific to the situation of Genesis 21. Both the Hebrew and the Greek text of Genesis 21:10 read: "Drive out *this* slave girl and her

son. For the son of *this* slave girl will not inherit together with my son, with Isaac." Paul's paraphrase generalizes the application of the verse by attributing the quotation to "the Scripture" rather than to Sarah and by commanding the expulsion of "the son of the slave girl," that is, by allegorical designation, "any son"—any Jew under the law and not under Christ.

13. The dangers of allegorical interpretation were also well known in Islam. Certain groups were considered heretical in their application of "inward interpretation," which was allegorical in method and imparted secretly. The *bāṭiniyya*, "inward interpreters," taught that every sacred text had a hidden meaning that was concealed in allegories and other symbolic tropes. Scripture functioned to reveal truths to those who knew the code and to conceal them from those who did not. See Marshall G. S. Hodgson, "Bāṭiniyya," in *EncIslam* 1: 1098–1100.

14. Augustine warns against those who take allegorical interpretation too far "as if there never existed these two women, Sarah and Hagar, nor the two sons who were born to Abraham, the one of the bond woman, the other of the free, because the apostle says that in them the two covenants were prefigured. . . . We yet believe the strict truth of the history" (*City of God*, book 11, p. 21; cited in Rosenberg, *King and Kin*, 14.) Note that Augustine understands the allegory as "prefiguring." For similar caveats by Philo on the danger of extreme allegoresis, see Amir, "Authority and Interpretation," 444–48; compare Peder Borgen, *ABD* 5: 338.

15. See Sarah Kamin, *Jews and Christians Interpret the Bible* (Jerusalem: Magnes, 1991), 79–80 (Hebrew section). The medieval Jewish Bible scholar Rabbi Joseph Bekhor Shor commented on Numbers 12 with a virtually direct rejoinder to Origen: The fact that God spoke to Moses "mouth to mouth" results in "breaking the arm of the gentiles who say that whatever our teacher Moses said is allegory (Hebrew: *allegoriya*), . . . and not what he [actually] said, and who turn prophecy into something else [that is, falsehood], and remove the word from its meaning entirely." See Yehoshaphat Nebo, ed., *The Commentaries to the Torah by Rabbi Joseph Bekhor Shor* (Jerusalem: Mossad Harav Kook, 1994), 259; and Kamin, *Jews and Christians*, 73. In the same passage, Bekhor Shor attacks unnamed Jewish allegorists for figuratively interpreting certain commandments. For example, they read the commandment of phylacteries as "it shall be for a sign on your hand" (Exod 13:16) in light of "set me as the seal upon your heart, as the seal upon your arm" (Cant 8:6) and thereby fail to observe the injunction literally. Some of these same readers also questioned the need to observe other commandments literally. See Nebo, *Commentaries*; and Kamin, *Jews and Christians*, 95.

16. For what follows I am greatly indebted to Professor Moshe Greenberg of the Hebrew University for sending me his article "Did Job Really Exist? An Issue

of Medieval Exegesis," in Michael Fishbane and Emanuel Tov, eds., *Sha'arei Talmon Studies in the Bible, Qumran and the Ancient Near East Presented to Shemaryahu Talmon* (Winona Lake, Ind. : Eisenbrauns, 1992), 3*–11* (in Hebrew; English Abstract, iv).

17. Zerahiah could point to the book's own puns on Job (Iyyob) and "enemy" (*Oyeb*) in Job 13:24, 33:10.

18. Text from Greenberg, "Did Job Really Exist?" 6–8. I have deviated from Greenberg's translation in minor details.

19. "Torah," "Prophets," and "Sacred Writing" are the three traditional Jewish divisions of the Hebrew Bible often referred to by the Hebrew acronym *TANAKH.* From the introduction to Joseph ibn Kaspi's commentary (in Hebrew: my translation) on Job edited by Y. Last, cited by Greenberg, "Did Job Really Exist? " 9, n. 26.

20. See Ephraim Kupfer, "Kaspi, Joseph ben Abba," *EncJud* 10: 809–11.

21. *Maskiyyot Kesef*, 39; On the biological origins of finger sacrifice, see Walter Burkert, *Creation of the Sacred: Tracks of Biology in Early Religions* (Cambridge, Mass.: Harvard University Press, 1996), 34–47.

22. Oral communication.

23. By designating them as "myths," we put them in the category of the unhistorical. The ancient Greeks used the term *mythos* to describe only those tales they held to be untrue. Grimm defines *myth* as a "story of the gods," which should be equivalent to the Greek usage indicating falsity. Among useful contemporary definitions, we cite one that is anthropological: "A sacred tale about past events which is used to justify social action in the present" (Edmund Leach, "Anthropological Perspectives," 74); and another that is literary: "A rhetorical strategy whose function is to delineate and guard a transcendent realm" (Rosenberg, *King and Kin*, 7). For a summary of other definitions of myth, see Robert Oden, *ABD* 4: 946–60. Sasson suggests that "in themselves, myths are but variant forms of allegory." See Jack Sasson, "On M. H. Pope's *Song of Songs* [AB, 7c]," *MAARAV* 1/2 (1979): 184. On the general question about the relation of myth to myth makers, see Paul Veyne, *Did the Greeks Believe in Their Myths?* (Chicago: University of Chicago Press, 1988).

24. A fine example of this approach is by Elaine Pagels, *The Gnostic Gospels* (New York: Random House, 1979). Pagels showed how the rival orthodox and gnostic myths about the origins of the world corresponded to the orthodox-gnostic conflicts over the earthly church's hierarchical character.

25. For similar reasons, Jewish scholars in the Middle Ages regularly interpreted classical rabbinic texts allegorically. See Talmage, "Apples of Gold," 333–37.

26. Of particular interest is the work of Rosenberg, *King and Kin*, 48–68. For a provocative reading of Genesis 2–3 as a political allegory of peasants in revolt, see James Kennedy,"Peasants in Revolt: Political Allegory in Genesis

2–3," *JSOT* 47 (1990): 3–14. It is irrelevant to this study whether or not the Garden of Eden story was written as an allegory or a myth, but for a survey of opinions, see Rosenberg, *King and Kin*, 2–12.

27. See, for example, Exodus 9:30 and Samuel 7:22, 25.

28. The phrasing of Genesis 2:14, "and the fourth river is the Euphrates," without the identifying marks given to the other rivers, indicates the audience's presumed greater familiarity with the Euphrates.

29. See Hosea 14:4. The identical words, in the form *giṣṣu daddaru*, can be found in the annals of Sargon II (722–705 B.C.E.; see *CAD D*, 17–18). The word *daddaru* seems restricted to Standard Babylonian, the dialect of the Assyrian annals, which provides further evidence for our hypothetical date.

30. I am not arguing for historicism at the expense of literary analysis, but I am arguing against literary analysis that fails to investigate historical background. For example, a playwright creates a German Jewish character who names his son Adolph. If we find that the play was written in 1915, the boy's name is less significant from a literary point of view than it would be if it were written in 1943.

31. Compare Howard Wallace in *ABD* 2: 281.

32. The connection between the divine garden in Eden and the gardens of royalty is made explicit in Ezekiel 28.

33. See David Stronach, "The Garden as a Political Statement: Some Case Studies from the Near East in the First Millennium B.C.," *Bulletin of the Asia Institute*, new ser., vol. 4 (1990): 171–80. See also A. Leo Oppenheim, "On Royal Gardens in Mesopotamia," *JNES* 24/4 (1965): 328–33.

34. See *CAD K*, 406.

35. In the account of his eighth campaign, the eighth-century Assyrian king Sargon describes his destruction of the land of Urartu, whose king, Rusa, had created gardens with great trees and fruit. One student of this text described Rusa's creation as a "sort of Eden." See Carlo Zaccagnini, "An Urartean Royal Inscription in the Report of Sargon's Eighth Campaign," in Mario Fales, ed., *Assyrian Royal Inscriptions: New Horizons* (Rome: Instituto per l'oriente, 1981), 274.

36. Indeed, the story of Ahab's lawless seizure of Naboth's vineyard (1Kgs 21; cf. 2Kgs 9:25) and his execution on trumped-up charges, whatever its historical value, gives the distinct impression of innovation. Contrast Isaiah 5:8–10, which shows that by the eighth century B.C.E., the successful seizure of small farms by large landowners was taken for granted.

Notes to Chapter 3

1. John Bright, *A History of Israel* (Philadelphia: Westminster, 1972), 119. Compare Jacob Licht, "Biblical Historicism," in Hayim Tadmor and Moshe

Weinfeld, eds., *History, Historiography and Interpretation* (Jerusalem: Magnes, 1983), 113: "I have excellent reasons to believe that the Exodus was an actual event . . . such as that it is extremely unlikely for a people to invent a story about its past servitude, which is not a thing to be proud of." Compare the similar statement by Helmer Ringgren, *Israelite Religion* (Philadelphia: Fortress Press, 1966), 29; and the critique by Alan Cooper and Bernard Goldstein, "Exodus and Maṣṣot in History and Tradition," *MAARAV* 8 (1992): 19–20. Niels Lemche, *Ancient Israel: A New History of Israelite Society* (Sheffield: JSOT, 1988), 109.

2. See Brian Lewis, *The Sargon Legend: A Study of the Akkadian Text and the Tale of the Hero Who Was Exposed at Birth* (Cambridge, Mass.: ASOR, 1980).

3. Hayim Tadmor, "Autobiographical Apology in the Royal Assyrian Literature," in Tadmor and Weinfeld, *History*, 36–57.

4. Compare Peter Machinist, "Distinctiveness in Ancient Israel," in Mordechai Cogan and Israel Ephal, eds., *Ah Assyria, Studies in Assyrian History and Ancient Near Eastern Historiography Presented to Hayim Tadmor*, Scripta Hierosolymitana, vol. 33 (Jerusalem: Magnes, 1991), 211.

5. Amihai Mazar, "The Iron Age I," in Amnon Ben-Tor, ed., *The Archaeology of Ancient Israel* (New Haven, Conn.: Yale University Press, 1992), 296; on Kadesh-Barnea, see p. 282.

6. For reasons that will become clear later, I prefer *allegorical* to *mythical*.

7. *Exilic* and *postexilic* are primarily theological constructs. Most descendants of deported former Israelites remained in the diaspora, and many descendants of Israelites who had never been deported remained in the home country throughout the Neo-Babylonian period. Modern perspectives on the latter half of the first pre-Christian millennium are distorted because of the abundance of literature produced by Babylonian returnees, compared with the paucity of literary and archeological documentation of the other groups. Compare Gösta Ahlström, *The History of Ancient Palestine* (Minneapolis: Fortress Press, 1993), 804.

8. Thomas L. Thompson, *The Origin Tradition of Ancient Israel*, vol. 1 of *The Literary Formation of Genesis and Exodus 1-23* (Sheffield: JSOT, 1987), 80. See also Burke Long, review of *The Origin Tradition*, by Thomas L. Thompson, *JBL* 108/2 (1989): 327–30.

9. Thompson, *The Origin Tradition*, 80–101.

10. See Robert Carroll, "Psalm LXXVIII: Vestiges of a Tribal Polemic," *VT* 21/2 (1971): 133–50; and Machinist, "Distinctiveness," 54. See Yairah Amit, *Te'uda* 2 (1982): 139–55; and Sara Japhet, *I and II Chronicles* (Louisville: Westminster, 1993), 46–47. In addition, see Keith Whitelam, "Israel's Tradition of Origin: Reclaiming the Land," *JSOT* 44 (1989): 29–36. For a dissenting view, see Peter Machinist, "Outsiders or Insiders: The Biblical View

of Emergent Israel in Its Contexts," in Laurence Silberstein and Robert Cohn, eds., *The Other in Jewish Thought and History Constructions of Jewish Culture and Identity* (New York: New York University Press, 1994), 35–60, esp. 45–47.

11. For the eighth-century dating of Joshua 24, see S. David Sperling, "Joshua 24 Re-examined," *HUCA* 58 (1987): 119–36; compare Alexander Rofé, "Ephraimite versus Deuteronomistic History," in Daniele Garrone and Felice Israel, eds., *Storia e tradizioni di Israele scritti in onore di J. Alberto Soggin* (Brescia: Paideia, 1991), 221–35. The early attestations of the foreignness traditions militate against viewing them as exilic apologia for being an Israelite outside the land of Israel. Contrast John van Seters, "Joshua 24 and the Problem of Tradition in the Old Testament," JSOTSup, vol. 31 (1984): 139–58.

12. See Isaac Seeligmann, "A Pre-Monarchic Hymn," in Avi Hurvitz et al., eds., *I. L. Seeligmann, Studies in Biblical Literature* (Jerusalem: Magnes, 1992), 189–204.

13. See Carroll, "Psalm LXXVIII"; compare Yair Hoffman, *The Doctrine of the Exodus in the Bible* (in Hebrew) (Tel Aviv: Tel Aviv University Press, 1983). Yair Hoffman, "A North Israelite Typological Myth and a Judaean Historical Tradition: The Exodus in Hosea and Amos," *VT* 39/2 (1989): 169–82; compare Cooper and Goldstein, "Exodus and Maṣṣot," 18.

14. See Machinist, "Distinctiveness," 196–212. The concept of a counteridentity was first formulated by Amos Funkenstein to describe postbiblical Jewish history. Machinist felicitously adapted the notion to the Bible. See his "Distinctiveness," 211, and his "Outsiders," 49–54. Machinist, "Distinctiveness," 203.

15. Machinist, "Distinctiveness," 203, 209.

16. Ibid., 210. For the "radical" theories that conceded the presence of an "outside component," Machinist cites the seminal essay by George E. Mendenhall, "The Hebrew Account of the Conquest of Palestine," originally published in *BA* 25/3 (1962): 66–87; and Norman Gottwald, *The Tribes of Yahweh* (Maryknoll, N.Y.: Orbis, 1979). A similar appeal to a statistically insignificant outside component was made by S. David Sperling, "Israel's Religion in the Ancient Near East," in A. Green, ed., *Jewish Spirituality from the Bible through the Middle Ages* (New York: Crossroad, 1986), 10–11. For earlier formulations, see Carroll, "Psalm LXXVIII," both p. 139 and the works cited in n. 5.

17. Ibid., 211.

18. At most, "one must reckon with the possibility that some Semites who had left Egypt settled in the hills of Palestine." See Ahlström, *History*, 286.

19. Trude Dothan, *ABD* 5: 333 (emphasis added).

20. Machinist, "Distinctiveness," 51.

21. As noted by Jack Sasson, the Bible's testimony "is as fair on the Canaanites' Baal as *Mein Kampf* is on the Jews." See Sasson's review of *The Tenth Generation*, by George E. Mendenhall, *JBL* 93/2 (1974): 294–96. "In the historical pastiche that ancient Israel fabricated to justify its ingress, all the iniquity of the ages is heaped upon the Canaanites, who thereby became the most maligned race in history." See Donald B. Redford, *Egypt, Canaan and Israel* (Princeton, N.J.: Princeton University Press, 1992), 237.

22. See William F. Albright, "The Role of the Canaanites in the History of Civilization," in G. Ernest Wright, ed., *The Bible and the Ancient Near East* (Garden City, N.Y.: Doubleday, 1965), 452–53. The same attitude toward the Canaanite religion survives in more recent works. See the critique by Niels Lemche, *Early Israel* (Leiden: Brill, 1985), 60–61; and Niels Lemche, *The Canaanites and Their Land* (Sheffield: JSOT, 1991). Compare William Dever, "The Contribution of Archaeology to the Study of Canaanite and Early Israelite Religion," in Patrick D. Miller, Jr., Paul D. Hanson, and S. Dean McBride, eds., *Ancient Israelite Religion: Essays in Honor of Frank Moore Cross* (Philadelphia: Fortress Press, 1987), 209–47, esp. 244, n. 56.

23. Naturally, these "ethics and morals" varied from one society to the next. For example, marrying one's sister's daughter might be viewed as a meritorious act in one culture but as incest in another.

24. See Benno Landsberger, "Die babylonischen Termini für Gesetz und Recht," in Symb. Koschaker, 219–34. Compare Ephraim A. Speiser, "Authority and Law in Mesopotamia," in Jacob Finkelstein and Moshe Greenberg, eds., *Oriental and Biblical Studies: Collected Writings of E. A. Speiser* (Philadelphia: University of Pennsylvania Press, 1967), 313–23.

25. See *ANET*, 159, 165.

26. References in Tallqvist, Götterepitheta, 456–58.

27. See NJV.

28. Šurpu, 13–16. On the general topic of Mesopotamian morals, see Wilfred G. Lambert, "Morals in Ancient Mesopotamia," *JEOL* 15 (1957–58): 184–96; and Wolfram von Soden, "Religion und Sittlichkeit nach den Anschaungen der Babylonier," *ZDMG* 89/2 (1935): 143–69. Like the biblical authors, Mesopotamians "abominated" all kinds of socioethical misconduct. See William Hallo, "Biblical Abominations and Sumerian Taboos," *JQR* 76/1 (1985): 21–40; Karel van der Toorn, *Sin and Sanction in Israel and Mesopotamia* (Maastricht: van Gorcum, 1985); Jacob Klein and Yitschak Sefati, "'Abomination' and Abominations in Mesopotamian Literature and in the Bible," *Beer Sheba* 3 (1990): 131–48; Markham Geller, review of *Sin and Sanction*, by Karel van der Toorn, *JCS* 42/1 (1991): 105–17.

29. For the texts, see Raymond Faulkner, Ogden Goelet, and Eva von Dassow, *The Egyptian Book of the Dead: The Book of Going Forth by Day* (San Francisco: Chronicle, 1994).

30. See, for example, Isaiah 56:1–9 and 66:21–23. Contrast the late preexilic and premonotheistic text Deuteronomy 4:19, which allots the worship of the heavenly bodies to the Gentiles but reserves the worship of Yahweh for the Israelites. Early prophecy, even when predicting Yahweh's guidance of the Gentiles, did not expect them to abandon their divinities. See, for example, Micah 4:5: "For all the peoples shall go [to Yahweh's mountain], each in the name of his god(s), but we shall go in the name of Yahweh, our god, forever."

31. For recent reconstructions as well as surveys of earlier theories of the origin of Israelite monotheism, see Valentin Nikiprowetzky, "Ethical Monotheism," *Daedalus*, Spring 1975, 69–89; Bernhard Lang, *Monotheism and the Prophetic Minority* (Sheffield: Almond, 1983), 13–56; Sperling, "Israel's Religion," 5–31; and John Scullion, "God in the OT," *ABD* 2: 1041–48.

32. See Morton Smith, "The Common Theology of the Ancient Near East," *JBL* 71/3 (1952): 135–47.

33. The fate of Israelite religion was not unique in quality but in quantity. There is evidence that some other cults of conquered peoples attracted new adherents. See Javier Teixidor, *The Pagan God Popular Religion in the Greco-Roman Near East* (Princeton, N.J.: Princeton University Press, 1977), 12. See also Karel van der Toorn, "Migration and the Spread of Local Cults," in Karel van Lerberghe and Antoon Schoors, eds., *Immigration and Emigration within the Ancient Near East: Festschrift Edward Lipiński* (OLA 65; (Leuven: Peeters, 1995), 365–77.

34. This may be seen clearly in Jeremiah 44. The prophet (v. 3) explains the fall of Judah as a consequence of serving other gods. His compatriots in the early Egyptian diaspora (v. 18), in contrast to Jeremiah, attribute their misfortune to a misguided neglect of the cult of the queen of Heaven. Note, however, that Jeremiah's opponents do not suggest abandoning the cult of Yahweh.

35. See Jan Assman, "Aton," in Wolfgang Helck and Eberhard Otto, eds., *Lexikon der Ägyptologie* (Wiesbaden: Harrassowitz, 1975–92), vol. 1, 526–40; Donald B. Redford, "Akhenaten," *ABD* 1: 135–37.

36. See Andreas van Selms, "Temporary Henotheism," in Martinus A. Beek, ed., *Symbolae biblicae mesopotamicae Francisco Mario Theodoro de Liagre Böhl dedicatae* (Leiden: Brill, 1973), 8–20.

37. See S. David Sperling in *EncRel*, 1–8; compare Michiko Yusa in *EncRel*, 266–67.

38. Karel van der Toorn refers to Israel as a society in which "religious ritual was an essential identity marker." See Karel van der Toorn, "Saul and the Rise of Israelite State Religion," *VT* 43/4 (1993): 527.

39. Morton Smith, *Palestinian Parties and Politics That Shaped the Old Testament* (New York: Columbia University Press, 1971), 23.

40. This is an overstatement. Even though such documents as Tablets vi–vii of the Enuma Elish identify all the great gods with Marduk, no serious attempts were made to close the temples of the other gods.

41. Smith, *Palestinian Parties*, 31.

42. "Most of the people who settled in the hill country in the Iron I period came from a background of pastoralism. . . . These people, who tended flocks but apparently did not herd camels, did not originate deep in the desert, but had lived on the fringes of the settled areas, or perhaps even in the midst of the sedentary dwellers." See Israel Finkelstein, *The Archaeology of the Israelite Settlement* (Jerusalem: Israel Exploration Society, 1988), 338.

43. See Roland de Vaux, *Ancient Israel* (New York: McGraw-Hill, 1965), vol. 1, 219.

44. See Andrew D. H. Mayes and Ronald Clements, eds., *The World of Ancient Israel* (Cambridge: Cambridge University Press, 1989), 44, and their summation of Noth, 47.

45. *ABD* 3: 553; compare Ahlström, *History*, 349.

46. El Amarna letter 365.

47. For a recent summary of research on *ḫāpiru*, a much-studied term that has often been associated with "Hebrew," see Niels Lemche, *ABD* 3: 6–10. We do not know whether the *ḫāpiru* of the Amarna letters actually referred to themselves by this term.

48. For the text and comments, see Miriam Lichtheim, *The New Kingdom*, vol. 2 of *Ancient Egyptian Literature* (Berkeley and Los Angeles: University of California Press, 1976), 73–78. For recent treatments, see the bibliography in Ahlström, *History*, 45, n. 2. See also Anson Rainey,"Remarks on Donald Redford's *Egypt, Canaan and Israel in Ancient Times*," *BASOR*, August 1994, 81–85; and Michael G. Hasel, "*Israel* in the Merneptah Stele," *BASOR*, November 1994, 45–61 (with bibliography).

49. See Ahlström, *History*, 288–300.

50. For the text, see Anson Rainey, *El Amarna Tablets 359–379* (Kevelaer: Butzon and Bercker), 24–26. For analysis and context, see Anson Rainey, "Compulsory Labor Gangs in Ancient Israel," *IEJ* 20/3–4 (1970): 191–202; and William Moran, *The Amarna Letters* (Baltimore: Johns Hopkins University Press), 363.

51. For why Shunem required outside workers, see Rainey, "Compulsory Labor Gangs," 194.

52. The institution was ancient by the time of Biridiya. The earliest documentation comes from Alalakh in Syria in the eighteenth century B.C.E. See Rainey, "Compulsory Labor Gangs," 192, 202.

53. According to the Standard Akkadian dictionaries, the word *sablu* is virtually identical to the Hebrew *sebel*. See *CAD S*, 4b ("Corvée party"); and AHw.,

999 ("Arbeitskommando"). For a dissenting view, see Jean-Marie Durand, *Archives épistolaires de Mari* 1/1 (Paris: Éditions recherche sur les civilisations, 1988), 15, n. 42.

54. The two seminal works were, respectively, Mendenhall, "The Hebrew Account," and Gottwald, *The Tribes of Yahweh*. These works, followed by others by Mendenhall and Gottwald, have generated an enormous bibliography. See the references and critique in Ahlström, *History*, 344–51; and Redford, *Egypt, Canaan and Israel*, 265–68. The hypothesis has been caricatured as the "revolting peasant theory." See Anson Rainey,"Uncritical Criticism," *JAOS* 115/1 (1995): 101. For Rainey's detailed critique of the revolt hypothesis, see his review of *The Tribes of Yahweh*, by Norman Gottwald, *JAOS* 107/3 (1987): 541–43. For an outline of some of the complex possibilities, see Aharon Kempinski, "How Profoundly Canaanized Were the Early Israelites?" *ZDPV* 108/1 (1992): 4.

55. See Israel Finkelstein and Nadav Na'aman, eds., *From Nomadism to Monarchy: Archaeological and Historical Aspects of Early Israel* (Washington, D.C.: Biblical Archaeological Society, 1994), 12. For a recent study of the process from the perspective of the larger eastern Mediterranean, see Robert Drews, *The End of the Bronze Age: Changes in Warfare and the Catastrophe ca. 1200 B.C.* (Princeton, N.J.: Princeton University Press, 1993).

56. Compare the malcontents who gathered around Jephthah (Judg 1:3) and David (1Sam 22:2). Rainey, *JAOS* 107 (1987): 543.

57. See Mario Liverani, *The Politics of Abdi-Ashirta of Amurru* (Malibu, Calif.: Undena, 1979). See, for example, the story of Idrimi, king of Alalakh, translated in *ANET*, 557.

58. Finkelstein and Na'aman, *From Nomadism to Monarchy*, 13.

59. On the identification of Caphtor, see Richard Hess, *ABD* 1: 869–70.

60. See Ahlström, *History*, 310, 300–6.

61. Although there are no extant stories of settlement and new foundation in the Near East outside Israel, there are examples of the topos in Virgil's *Aeneid*, itself based on the Greek genre known in scholarly literature as "Ktisisagen," that is, "founder stories," as expected in a culture in which colonization was significant. See Moshe Weinfeld, "The Promise to the Patriarchs and Its Realization: An Analysis of Foundation Stories," in Michael Heltzer and Edward Lipiński, eds., *Society and Economy in the Eastern Mediterranean ca. 1500–1000 B.C.)* (Leuven: Peeters, 1988), 353–69. Compare Moshe Weinfeld, "The Pattern of the Israelite Settlement in Canaan," *VTSup* 40 (1988): 270–83. Given their history of colonization, perhaps the Phoenicians, too, had a genre of Ktisisagen (see Ezek 25:17 and 28:2–6) in a milieu closer to early-first-millennium Israel.

62. With what follows, compare J. Maxwell Miller, *ABD* 4: 882–93.

63. See Mazar, "The Iron Age I," 282, 297; and Lawrence Geraty, *ABD* 3: 181–84, 182.

64. For the differing views on his exact dates, see Winfried Thiel, *ABD* 5: 17.
65. The verbs *yāraš*, "took possession," and *yāšab*, "dwelled," occur in the identical sequence and context in the Moabite stone and Numbers 21:31–32.

Notes to Chapter 4

1. See Bertil Albrektson, *History and the Gods* (Lund: Gleerup, 1967).
2. We lack detailed information about cult and myth in Moab, Ammon, and Midian. It is entirely possible that the cults of these nations, which were closely related to Israel in language and culture, emphasized the political activities of their gods.
3. For a contrary view that historicization was primary in Maṣṣot, see Alan Cooper and Bernard Goldstein, "The Festivals of Israel and Judah and the Literary History of the Pentateuch," *JAOS*, January–March 1990, 19–31; compare Alan Cooper and Bernard Goldstein, "Exodus and Maṣṣot in History and Tradition," *MAARAV* 8 (1992): 16.
4. For a survey of theories of origin, see Gerhard Hasel, *ABD* 5: 850–51.
5. See Frank M. Cross, *Canaanite Myth and Hebrew Epic* (Cambridge, Mass.: Harvard University Press, 1973).
6. Redford refers to the "notion of a contract between Yahweh the god of the group and the human community" as one of "the primitive concepts of the community." See Donald Redford, *Egypt, Canaan and Israel in Ancient Times* (Princeton, N.J.: Princeton University Press, 1992), 275.
7. See the extremely lucid presentation by Delbert Hillers, *Covenant: The History of a Biblical Idea* (Baltimore: Johns Hopkins University Press, 1969).
8. In the following passage, the traditional translation, "house of bondage," does not fully convey the image. As shown by the Sabbath commandment and the commandment against coveting, the Israelite audience knew how slaves lived. That Egypt was one big slave barracks would make the audience appreciate Yahweh's generosity in removing his people from there. The Hebrew *ḥesed* has traditionally been translated as "loving kindness," but more recent study has shown that the term refers to the performance of obligations that grow out of a relation. One performs acts of *ḥesed* or demonstrates an attitude of *ḥesed* to allies or kin. As such, *ḥesed* is distinguished from *ḥen*, an act or attitude of kindness to strangers or to those to whom one is not obliged or who do not deserve it. For a recent study, see Gordon Clark, *The Word Hesed in the Hebrew Bible* (Sheffield: Sheffield Academic Press, 1993).
9. That the representatives ate and drank means that they did not suffer those harmful, or even deadly, consequences that often accompany the sight of divinity. See, for example, Leviticus 16:2 and Judges 13:22.
10. Wellhausen's debt to Pauline theology for this element of his analysis should be obvious.

11. Wellhausen does not use the term *allegory* to describe Hosea's portrayal of Israel as Yahweh's bride. For this characterization, see Harold Louis Ginsberg, "Hosea, Book of," *EncJud* 8, 1016.

12. Hosea 8:1 does, however, use *berît* in parallel with *torah*.

13. See NEB. Similarly, Moshe Greenberg, *Ezekiel 1-20* (AB) (Garden City, N.Y.: Doubleday, 1983), 270: "I pledged myself to you and entered into a covenant with you." Also see Greenberg's discussion on pp. 277–78. Proverbs 2:17, whatever its date, does not refer to the marriage relation itself as *berît*. See the commentary by David Altschuler (*Mesudat David*) printed in the standard rabbinic Bibles a.l.; compare ibn Ezra a.l.

14. See Samuel Greengus,"The Old Babylonian Marriage Contract," *JAOS* 89/3 (1969): 505–32. For references to *riksu/rikstu*, see AHw., 985; there may be some Persian influence as well, as the name of the god Mithra is the same as the word for *covenant*. The god himself is the personification of covenants, and the *mithra* between husband and wife is explicitly mentioned as early as the Avesta. See Mary Boyce, *The Early Period*, vol. 1 of *A History of Zoroastrianism* (Leiden: Brill, 1975), 27–28, 57.

15. For the Near East, especially Mesopotamia, see Thorkild Jacobsen, *The Treasures of Darkness* (New Haven, Conn.: Yale University Press, 1976), 24–47; Samuel N. Kramer, *The Sacred Marriage Rite* (Bloomington: Indiana University Press, 1969); Willem H. Römer, "Einige Überlegungen zur 'Heiligen Hochzeit' nach altorientalischen Texten," in Wilhelmus Delsman, ed., *Von Kanaan bis Kerala: Festschrift für Prof. Mag. Dr. Dr. J. P. M. van der Ploeg O. P. zur Vollendung des siebzigsten Lebensjahres am 4. Juli 1979: überreicht von Kollegen, Freunden und Schulern* (Neukirchen-Vluyn: Neukirchener Verlag, 1982), 411–28; and Jacob Klein, "Sacred Marriage," *ABD* 5: 866–70 (extensive bibliography). For the question of sacred marriage closer to Israel, at Emar in Syria, see Daniel Fleming, *The Installation of Baal's High Priestess at Emar* (Atlanta: Scholars Press, 1992), 190–92. For references to Greek sacred marriage, see the index in Walter Burkert, *Homo Necans* (Berkeley and Los Angeles: University of California Press, 1983), 327. It is misleading to speak of a "common pattern" in the sacred marriages of the ancient Near East. See Klein, "Sacred Marriage," *ABD* 5: 869.

16. See Thorkild Jacobsen, "Religious Drama in Ancient Mesopotamia," in Hans Goedicke and Jimmy Jack McBee Roberts, eds., *Unity and Diversity* (Baltimore: Johns Hopkins University Press, 1975), 65–97. The text is from pp. 66–67.

17. See John Gibson, *Canaanite Myths and Legends* (Edinburgh: T and T Clark, 1987), 72.

18. For a detailed treatment of Joshua 24 with a bibliography, see S. David Sperling,"Joshua 24 Re-examined," *HUCA* 58 (1987): 119–36; See also William

Koopmans, *Joshua 24 as Poetic Narrative* (Sheffield: JSOT, 1990); and Diana Edelman, *JNES* 52 (1993), 308–10.

19. On Shechem traditions in general, see Eduard Nielsen, *Shechem, a Traditio-Historical Investigation* (Copenhagen: Gad, 1969).

20. S. David Sperling, "Joshua 24 Reexamined," *HUCA* 58 (1987), 119–36..

21. See Lawrence E. Toombs, "Shechem (Place)," *ABD* 5: 1175–86.

22. On Judges 9, see especially Edward Campbell, "Judges 9 and Biblical Archeology," in Carol Meyers and Michael O'Connor, eds., *The Word of the Lord Shall Go Forth: Essays in Honor of David Noel Freedman in Celebration of His Sixtieth Birthday* (Winona Lake, Ind.: Eisenbrauns, 1983), 263–71.

23. See Dennis McCarthy, *Treaty and Covenant* (Rome: Pontifical Biblical Institute, 1978), 222, with the literature cited in n. 20; and Kenneth Kitchen, "Egypt, Ugarit, Qatna and Covenant," *UF* 11 (1979): 453–64; More recently, see Theodore Lewis, "Baal-Berith," *ABD* 1: 550–51. Note Lewis's caveat (550) that the designations *'el berît* and *ba'al berît* might simply refer to a god who witnessed or guaranteed treaties.

24. It has been suggested that given the presence of Indo-Aryans in the Middle East in the second millennium B.C.E., the god in Shechem might reflect some form of Mithra, the god of the covenant. Compare n. 14 to this chapter, and see Martin Mulder, "Baal-Berith," *DDD*: 266–72, esp. 269.

25. George Mendenhall, "Covenant Forms in Israelite Tradition," *BA*, September 1954, 50–76. Compare George Mendenhall and Gary Herion, "Covenant," *ABD* 1: 1179–1202 (with bibliography). Weinfeld went even further. He attempted to demonstrate the antiquity and the social reality of the unconditional grants to the patriarchs by arguing that these were based on the unconditional grants preserved on the *kudurru* boundary stones in Mesopotamia known from the mid-second millennium. See Moshe Weinfeld, "The Covenant of Grant in the Old Testament and in the Ancient Near East," *JAOS* 90/2 (1970): 184–203. Contrast Harold Louis Ginsberg, *The Israelian Heritage of Judaism* (New York: Jewish Theological Seminary, 1982), 107; and Baruch Levine, "The Epilogue to the Holiness Code," in Jacob Neusner, Baruch Levine, and Ernest Frehrichs, eds., *Judaic Perspectives on Ancient Israel* (Philadelphia: Fortress Press, 1987), 25.

The quotation marks around "suzerainty treaties" are meant as a caveat against equating political systems of the second millennium B.C.E. with medieval European feudalism. Until recently, treaties from the early second millennium were unavailable. For studies of newly discovered treaties from that period, with a bibliography, see Dominique Charpin, "Un traité entre Zimri-Lim de Mari et Ibâl-pî-El II d'Ešnunna," 139–66; Francis Joannès, "Le Traité de vassalité d'Atamrum d'Andarig envers Zimri-Lim de Mari," 167–77; Jean-Robert Kupper, "Zimri-Lim et ses vassaux," 179–84; and Jesper Eidem, "An Old Assyrian Treaty from Tell Leilan," 185–207, all from

Dominique Charpin and Francis Joannès, eds., *Marchands, diplomates et empereurs études sur la civilisation mésopotamienne offertes à Paul Garelli* (Paris: Études recherche sur les civilizations, 1991).

26. To be sure, Mendenhall and Herion (*ABD* 1: 1183) allow that "these traditions also bear the marks of later 'creative writers' who embellished and reworked the traditions from the radically different perspective of the monarchic period." Quotation from Mendenhall, "Covenant Forms," 56.

27. Delbert Hillers, *Treaty Curses and the Old Testament Prophets* (Rome: Pontifical Biblical Institute, 1964). The phrase "effect of studies" is deliberate. Hillers himself advocates an early date for the rise of the covenant concept. See Delbert Hillers, *Covenant: The History of a Biblical Idea* (Baltimore: Johns Hopkins University Press, 1969). But Hillers's comparisons of Assyrian and Aramaic treaty texts of the first millennium with biblical prophecy presuppose the rejection of a significant element in Mendenhall's argument. Compare Preben Wernberg-Møller, review of *Treaty Curses and the Old Testament Prophets*, by Delbert Hillers, *CBQ* 27/1 (1965): 68–69. Rintje Frankena, "The Vassal Treaties of Esarhaddon and the Dating of Deuteronomy," *OTS* 14 (1965): 122–54. McCarthy, *Treaty and Covenant*. Moshe Weinfeld, *Deuteronomy and the Deuteronomic School* (Oxford: Clarendon Press, 1972); also see Moshe Weinfeld, *TDOT* 2: 267. Although Weinfeld has regularly argued for the early origin of the Yahweh's covenant with Israel, his own broad comparative studies tend to undermine his arguments for an early date. In "Covenant Terminology in the Ancient Near East and Its Influence on the West," *JAOS* 93/2 (1973): 190–99, Weinfeld demonstrates the penetration of Near Eastern covenant terminology into the later Greco-Roman world. Compare Moshe Weinfeld, "The Common Heritage of Covenantal Traditions in the Ancient World," in Luciano Canfora et al., eds., *I Trattati nel mondo antico: Forma, ideologia, funzione* (Rome: "L'Erma" di Brettschneider, 1990), 175–91.

28. See Mendenhall (*ABD* 1: 1182–83) for fundamental discontinuities between the Bronze Age suzerainty treaties and the Assyrian loyalty oaths.

29. Lothar Perlitt, *Bundestheologie im Alten Testament* (Neukirchen-Vluyn: Neukirchener Verlag, 1969). For a detailed critique of Perlitt's attempt to relate the covenant of Joshua 24 to the Assyrian crisis (*Bundestheologie*, 239–84), see Sperling, "Joshua 24," 1–18; compare Moshe Weinfeld, review of Nicholson's *God and His People*, RB 98, 435.

30. On the entire question of religious conversion in preexilic Israel, see S. David Sperling, "Rethinking Covenant in Late Biblical Books," *Biblica* 70/1 (1989): 51, n. 5. Quotation from George Mendenhall, "'Change and Decay in All Around I See': Conquest Covenant and *The Tenth Generation*," *BA*, December 1987, 156. Compare George Mendenhall, "Biblical History in

Transition," in G. Ernest Wright, ed., *The Bible and the Ancient Near East* (Garden City, N.Y.: Doubleday, 1965), 40.

31. *TDOT* 2: 278. Contrast S. David Sperling, "An Arslan Tash Incantation: Interpretations and Implications," *HUCA* 53 (1982): 9, n. 70. See also Robert Oden, "The Place of Covenant in the Religion of Israel," in Patrick D. Miller et al., eds., *Ancient Israelite Religion: Essays in Honor of Frank Moore Cross* (Philadelphia: Fortress Press, 1987), 437–38.

32. See Morton Smith, "The Common Theology of the Ancient Near East," *JBL* 71/3 (1952): 135–47.

33. Compare Sperling, "Rethinking Covenant," 51–52.

34. Compare Kitchen, "Egypt, Ugarit," 462.

35. Compare Sperling, "Arslan Tash," 3, 6–7; and Lewis, "Baal-Berith," *ABD* 1: 550.

36. References in AHw., 1013–14; Mullo-Weir Lexicon, 293; Tallqvist, Götterepitheta, 149; *CAD S*, 89–92.

37. For *anākuma*, "I alone," see Moshe Held, "The Root *ZBL/SBL* in Akkadian, Ugaritic and Biblical Hebrew," *JAOS* 88/1 (1968): 94, n. 81. For the text and its date, see Rykle Borger, "Gott Marduk und Gott-König Šulgi als Propheten," *BO* 28/1–2 (1971): 3–24. See *CAD S*, 103b.

38. See Sperling, "Rethinking Covenant," 50–73.

39. Or in Redford's terminology, "primitive," see n. 6 of this chapter.

40. On the allegory of Yahweh, see the Afterword. For another biblical example of confederation through oath, see Joshua 9. See Sperling, "Joshua 24."

41. See Mendenhall and Herion, "Covenant," *ABD* 1: 1188–89.

42. See, for example, Exodus 24:1–11 and Psalms 50:5. That they also resembled sacrifices outside Israel is clear from the Akkadian text of the covenant between Matiel of Arpad and Asshur-Nirari V of Assyria (754–745), which contains a specific disclaimer that the ram was being dismembered for a sacrifice. For the text, see SAA 2:10'. On the assimilation of covenant ceremonies to sacrificial procedures, see Nahmanides to Genesis 15:10. See also Samuel Loewenstamm, "The Covenant between the Pieces: A Traditio-Historical Investigation," in Samuel Loewenstamm, *Comparative Studies in Biblical and Ancient Oriental Literatures* (Neukirchen-Vluyn: Neukirchener Verlag, 1980), 273–80.

43. This is particularly evident in Hosea 8:1, where the prophet expressly rebukes his people for breaking the covenant. Because Hosea 8:1 completely undermines Perlitt's late dating of the allegory of the national covenant, he dismisses the verse as a late interpolation influenced by the theology of Deuteronomy (*Bundestheologie*, 147). In fact, other than the need to support Perlitt's hypothesis, there is no reason at all to consider the verse deuteronomic. Note that the words for "lips" and "trumpet," *ḥk* and *šwpr*,

which occur in the Hosea 8:1 verses do not even appear in Deuteronomy. For that matter, the word for "rebelled" in Hosea 8:1, *pš'*, a word of high antiquity, is likewise not found in Deuteronomy. See Sperling, "Joshua 24," 130, n. 61; also see Weinfeld, review, *RB* 98, 432; John Day, "Pre-Deuteronomic Allusions to the Covenant in Hosea and Psalm lxxvii," *VT* 36/1 (1986): 1–12.

44. See REB. The city named Adam, known from Joshua 3:16. See Naphtali H. Tur-Sinai, *The Language and the Book II* (in Hebrew) (Jerusalem: Bialik, 1959), 327; Hans Wolff, *Hosea* (Philadelphia: Fortress Press, 1974), 105.

45. With the following, compare Albert T. Olmstead, *History of the Persian Empire* (Chicago: University of Chicago Press, 1948), 1–2.

46. The antiquarian interest of the authors of Deuteronomy is well attested. See, for example, Deuteronomy 2:10–12, 20–23; 3:9–11; and 32:8–15.

47. The most familiar example is Jeremiah 31:31. See also Sperling, "Rethinking Covenant."

48. See Michael D. Coogan, "Canaanite Origins and Lineage: Reflections on the Religion of Ancient Israel," 115–24; and Jo Ann Hackett, "Religious Traditions in Israelite Transjordan," 125–36; both in Miller, *Ancient Israelite Religion*; Jo Ann Hackett, *ABD* 1: 569–72; Jacob Hoftijzer and Gerrit van der Kooij, eds., *The Balaam Text from Deir Alla Re-evaluated* (Leiden: Brill, 1991).

Notes to Chapter 5

1. See Meindert Dijkstra, "Abraham," *DDD*, 6–10.

2. Thomas Thompson, *The Historicity of the Patriarchal Narratives* (Berlin: de Gruyter, 1974), 2.

3. See Genesis 16 and 21 for surrogacy and Genesis 31 for the household gods.

4. See H. Jacob Katzenstein and Trude Dothan, "Philistines," *ABD* 5: 326–33. Contrast, for example, Nahum Sarna, *The JPS Torah Commentary Genesis* (New York: Jewish Publication Society, 1991), 389.

5. See Morton Smith, "The Present State of Old Testament Studies," *JBL* 58/1 (1969): 20.

6. Alan R. Millard, "Abraham," *ABD* 1: 40.

7. See Sarna, *JPS Genesis*, 38.

8. Hermann Gunkel, *The Legends of Genesis* (1901; reprint, New York: Schocken Books, 1964), 19.

9. *'Apiru* is the same term written in Akkadian as *ḫāpiru*, the social designation we encountered in the Amarna letters discussed in chapter 3. The vocalization is uncertain. According to Albright, "Raham" was proposed by the Egyptologist Bernhard Grdseloff. Albright vocalized "Ruhma" but agreed that the element *rhm* is identical to the corresponding Hebrew in the name

of the patriarch. See William F. Albright, "The Smaller Beth-Shan Stele of Sethos I (1309–1290 B.C.)," *BASOR*, February 1952, 29.

10. See Genesis 9:18; 10:21; 19:37–38; 22:21. See Ernest A. Knauf, "El Šaddai—Der Gott Abrahams?" *BZ* 29/1 (1985): 100–1. In the Semitic languages, "father" ('*ab*) also has the meaning "chieftain." Compare Aharon Kempinski, "How Profoundly Canaanized Were the Early Israelites?" *ZDPV* 108/1 (1992): 4, n. 21. As Sarna notes (*JPS Genesis*, 124), the meaning of "father of a multitude" is "imposed" on the name "Abraham." It does not appear to fit grammatically or etymologically.

11. We have the same phenomenon in myth, in which gods who had originated as personified natural phenomena acquired distinctive personalities.

12. See Moshe Weinfeld,"The Davidic Empire—Realization of the Promises to the Patriarchs," *Eretz Israel* 24 (1993): 87–92.

13. His name is not changed to Abraham until chapter 17, which is when "Sarai" becomes "Sarah." Note the sequence in verse 13: "Please say that you are my sister, that it may go well with me, because of you, and that I may remain alive thanks to you." In verse 16 the phrase "go well" is repeated as a reference to the riches that Abram gained by the ruse. The medieval scholar Nahmanides disapproved of Abram's treatment of Sarai and characterized it as a "great sin." Earlier readers were equally sensitive. The writer of the Genesis Apocryphon—an ancient retelling of Genesis discovered among the Dead Sea scrolls—attributes the deception to Sarai, who suggests it to her husband in order to save his life. See Joseph Fitzmyer, *The Genesis Apocryphon of Qumran Cave I* (Rome: Pontifical Biblical Institute, 1966), 54. The language of verse 19, "I took her as my wife," is the technical terminology of marriage. Pharaoh's intentions are honorable!

14. For good aesthetic reasons, the audience is not told specifically whether or not the marriage to Pharaoh was consummated (contrast Gen 20:4, 6). Apologists as early as the author of the Genesis Apocryphon and his probable contemporary Josephus and as recently as Sarna (*JPS Genesis*, 94) protected Sarai's honor by importing the assertion that she was not violated by Abimelech (Gen 20:4, 6) into the narrative of Genesis 12.

15. Julius Theodor and Chanoch Albeck, eds., *Midrash Bereshit Rabba* (reprint, Jerusalem: Wahrmann, 1965), 385. Compare also the statement attributed to Rabbi Levi: "The Holy, be he blessed, gave Abraham a sign, so that whatever happened to him happened to his children." See Salomon Buber, ed., *Midrash Tanhuma* (reprint, Jerusalem: Ortsel, 1964), 70.

16. For a recent study, see Chaim Cohen, "Genesis 14:1–11—An Early Israelite Chronographic Source," in William Hallo, ed., *The Biblical Canon in Comparative Perspective* (Scripture in Context IV) (Lewiston, Maine: Edwin Mellen, 1991), 67–107 (for bibliographical references see p. 91, n. 2). For a detailed review and critique of scholarship on the chapter between the 1970s

and 1990, see John A. Emerton, "Some Problems in Genesis xiv," *VTSup* 41 (1990): 73–102. See also Emerton's study, "The Site of Salem, the City of Melchizedek (Genesis xiv 18)," *VTSup* 41 (1990): 45–71.

17. The text does not say that the ancient Valley of Siddim became the Dead Sea. See the commentary by Abraham ibn Ezra a.l., and contrast the overly ingenious explanation of Michael Astour, *ABD* 6: 15–16.

18. The Hebrew *melek*, "king," is synonymous with the Akkadian *šuwā'u/šu'û*, an ancient synonym of *šarru*, "king." See AHw., 1295; *CAD* Sw/3, 417.

19. According to Judges 18:29, the town of Laish received the name Dan long after the death of Joshua. See Benedict Spinoza, *A Theologico-Political Treatise*, trans. Robert Elwes (reprint, New York: Dover, 1951), 124.

20. See Yehoshaphat Nebo, *Perushe Rabbi Yosef Bekhor Shor 'al Ha-torah* (Jerusalem: Mossad Harav Kook, 1994), 27.

21. See 2 Samuel 17:11; also Cohen, "Genesis 14:11," 68.

22. See Dale Manor, "Kadesh-Barnea," *ABD* 4: 1–3.

23. Yohanan Muffs, "Abraham the Noble Warrior: Patriarchal Politics and Laws of War in Ancient Israel," *JJS* (1982): 82.

24. See ibid., 94; Moshe Weinfeld, *The Book of Genesis with a New Commentary* (in Hebrew) (Tel Aviv: Gordon, 1975), 68.

25. On these criticisms, see Hayim Tadmor,"The People and the Kingship in Ancient Israel: The Role of Political Institutions in the Biblical Period," *Cahiers d'histoire mondiale* 11 (1968): 46–68; Peter Machinist, "Hosea and the Ambiguity of Kingship in Ancient Israel," in Chaim Stern, ed., *Signs of Democracy in the Bible* (Chappaqua, N.Y.: Temple Bethel of Northern Westchester, 1994), 25–63.

26. See John van Seters, "The Terms 'Amorite' and 'Hittite' in the Old Testament," *VT* 22/1 (1972): 64–81; S. David Sperling, "Joshua 24 Re-examined," *HUCA* 58 (1987), 125–26. The ancient textual versions differ over the cities named. See R. Kyle McCarter Jr., *ISamuel* (AB) (New York: Doubleday, 1980), 142.

27. The episode had a rich afterlife in the Qumran scrolls, Josephus, Philo, and the New Testament. See Jannes Reiling, "Melchizedek," *DDD*, 1047–53. Many scholars consider these verses an interpolation because they follow the introduction of the king of Sodom and precede the dialogue between him and Abraham. See Emerton, "Site of Salem," 64. Without them, however, Abraham's oath by Yahweh-El-Elyon has no context.

28. See, for example, Lansing Hicks, "Melchizedek," *IDB* 3: 343; and John A. Emerton, "The Riddle of Genesis xiv," *VT* 21/4 (1971): 403–39.

29. See Ernest A. Knauf, "King Solomon's Copper Supply," in Edward Lipiński, ed., *Phoenicia and the Bible* (Leuven: Peeters, 1991), 183.

30. Joshua 10:3.

31. See George Ramsey, "Zadok," *ABD* 6: 1034–36 (with bibliography).

32. The verse is an excellent example of the author's desire to entertain an audience. The word *šebaʿ* in Hebrew means both "seven" and "oath." Verse 30 leads the audience to expect "Well of Seven" as the etiology of Beersheba, but verse 31 dashes that expectation.

33. Sarna, *JPS Genesis*, 148.

34. Gunkel, *Legends*, 20. For the parallel story of the dispute over a well involving Abimelech, Isaac, and Phicol, see Genesis 26:23–33.

35. The language of disloyalty to the future generations using the same verb as this pericope, *šqr*, is found in an Aramaic treaty of the eighth century B.C.E. See Joseph Fitzmyer, *The Aramaic Inscriptions of Sefire* (Rome: Pontifical Biblical Institute, 1967), 12.

36. I thank my lawyer friend Alan Appelbaum for apprising me of this term. Had Abraham not resolved the condition precedent, he would have forfeited the opportunity to raise it once the covenant was concluded.

37. The Hebrew *gzl* connotes "force." Perhaps they had taken control of the well. Alternatively, they might have stopped up the wells, as in the parallel story (Gen 26:18).

38. Unlike the parallel account (Gen 26:33), in which Beersheba is called "a city," in this account, it is a *māqom*, "place," possibly a sanctuary. Compare the use of *māqom* in Genesis 12:6. For an archeological summary of the site, see Dale Manor, "Beer-sheba," *ABD* 1: 641–45.

39. See Amihai Mazar, "The Iron Age I," in Amnon Ben-Tor, ed., *The Archaeology of Ancient Israel* (New Haven, Conn.: Yale University Press, 1992), 287.

40. See 1 Samuel 27:6 and compare 29:3.

41. See especially 1 Samuel 29:1–11.

42. The best-known story about David, his victory over the Philistine Goliath related in 1 Samuel 17, is attributed to another figure in 2 Samuel 21:1. The extant tale of David and Goliath is a product of the postexilic period. See Alexander Rofé, "The Battle of David and Goliath: Folklore, Theology, Eschatology," in Jacob Neusner et al., eds., *Judaic Perspectives on Ancient Israel* (Philadelphia: Fortress Press, 1987), 117–51.

43. According to Psalms 34:1, the Philistine king of Gath contemporary with David was not named Achish but Abimelech.

44. See, for example, 2 Samuel 3:10, 17:11, and 24:2.

Notes to Chapter 6

1. See George Ramsey, "Joshua (Person)," in *ABD* 3: 999–1000.

2. For examples, see Thomas Thompson, *The Historicity of the Patriarchical Narratives* (Berlin: de Gruyter, 1974), 43–50.

3. George Washington is the eponym of Washington, D.C., Washington State, and the George Washington Bridge, among others.

4. See, for example, Exodus 19:3; Numbers 23:7, 10, and 24:5; Deuteronomy 32:9; Isaiah 2:5–6; Amos 7:2, 5; and Psalms 114:1.

5. The etymological meaning of the name Israel is "God-is-Just." The author is making a pun on Hebrew *yāšār*, "just," and *yiśśar*, "he strives." For a literary treatment, including references to earlier literature, see Stephen Geller, "The Struggle at the Jabbok: The Uses of Enigma in a Biblical Narrative," *JANES* 14 (1982): 37–60.

6. Stanley Gevirtz, "Of Patriarchs and Puns: Joseph at the Fountain, Jacob at the Ford," *HUCA* 46 (1975): 51, 50.

7. The tower may have been similar to the structure at Giloh in Judah, dating from Iron Age I. See Amihai Mazar, "The Iron Age I," in Amnon Ben-Tor, ed., *The Archaeology of Ancient Israel* (New Haven, Conn.: Yale University Press, 1992), 289.

8. We do not have to assume that Penuel had lain in ruins for more than a century. Hebrew (*wayyiben*) may be elliptical for the reconstruction of the tower. In 2 Chronicles 26:9, the verb is used specifically for the construction of fortification towers. As noted by the medieval commentator David Kimhi, 1 Kings 12:25 also employs the verb (*wayyiben*) for Jeroboam's activities at Shechem, which, according to the same chapter, was thriving at the time.

9. See Bustenay Oded, apud Gershon Galil and Ephraim Stern, eds., *Melakim Aleph* (Olam Ha-tanakh vol. 10) (Tel Aviv: Davidson-Attai, 1994), 133.

10. This is in contrast to the tradition of Genesis 35:9–10, in which God changes Jacob's name without a struggle.

11. That is what *māqom* regularly means in Genesis (for example, 12:10; 22:3, 4, 14). REB translates it as "shrine." Unlike the audience, Jacob does not yet know that he has arrived at a sacred place.

12. The Hebrew term for "platform" found here is *bāmāh*, normally translated as "high place." Although the word is found in ritual contexts in other Semitic languages in addition to Hebrew, we do not know precisely what the term denotes. In the Bible, *bāmāh* often designates a cultic installation of which the writers disapproved because it competed with the Jerusalem temple.

13. See Martin Rose, "Names of God in the OT," *ABD* 4: 1001–11.

14. What follows, including the translation, is heavily dependent on Harold Louis Ginsberg, "Hosea's Ephraim, More Fool Than Knave (A New Interpretation of Hosea 12:1–14)," *JBL* 80 (1961): 339–47.

15. Hebrew *'āqab*, "cheated," is a pun on *Ya'qob*, "Jacob."

16. Hosea 4:15, 5:8, 10:5. See Ginsberg, "Hosea's Ephraim," 343.

17. For the continued worship of this divinity in the later first millennium, see Wolfgang Röllig, "Bethel," *DDD*, 332–33.

18. Numerous scholars have noted that Jeroboam's activities were performed in Yahweh's name and sanctioned by prophets of Yahweh. Jeroboam's decision

to hold the harvest festival in the eighth month corresponds closely to the climatic conditions of the northern kingdom. In general, Jeroboam's activities, including the installation of the calves, should be viewed as conservative. See Gösta Ahlström, *The History of Ancient Palestine* (Minneapolis: Fortress Press, 1993), 550–54.

19. Amos 5:6, 15:6:6; and Psalms 78:67.

20. See Donald Redford, *Egypt, Canaan and Israel in Ancient Times* (Princeton, N.J.: Princeton University Press, 1992), 108, n. 57.

21. John Wilson, "Egypt and the Bible," in Ephraim A. Speiser, ed., *World History of the Jewish People*, vol. 1 (Tel Aviv: Massadah, 1964), 339. Contrast the more recent evaluation of the Joseph story by another prominent Egyptologist: "There is no reason to believe it has any basis in fact . . . and to read it as history is quite wrongheaded" (Redford, *Egypt, Canaan*, 429).

22. See Genesis 39:14, 41:12, 42:23, 43:32, and 46:34. See Redford, *Egypt, Canaan*, 424. Redford's "compelling case for a seventh or sixth century date" is based on the motifs of the Joseph story (427–28). But an appeal to motifs is far too subjective. More to the point, the various administrative titles used in the story, such as "chief of the butlers" and "chief of the bakers," are not specific to Egypt, but none is demonstrably later than the early Israelite monarchy. Potiphar's two titles, *sāris* and *śar ha-ṭabāḥim* (Gen 37:36, 39:1), reflect two Akkadian terms already used in the second millennium, *ša rēš šurri* and *wakil ṭābiḥi*. Joseph's father-in-law is a *kohen*, a title found in Hebrew, Ugaritic, and Phoenician.

23. The story serves the writer of Matthew 2:13–15 as a typology for the flight into Egypt by Joseph, husband of Mary. On the irony of the holy family's seeking refuge in Egypt from a Jewish king, see Elaine Pagels, *The Origin of Satan* (New York: Random House, 1995), 79.

24. Compare the story of Egyptian support for the Edomite pretender against Solomon in 1 Kings 11:14–22. Shoshenq's campaign across the Sinai frontier seems to have been directed primarily against northern Israel, once Egypt realized that it was becoming too powerful on its own. For the route and historical commentary, see Yohanan Aharoni et al., *Macmillan Bible Atlas*, 3d ed. (New York: Macmillan, 1993), 91–92.

25. The historical King Idrimi ruled in the first half of the fifteenth century B.C.E. The statue on which the story is inscribed was found at an archaeological level dating about 1200. For a detailed philological treatment, see Edward Greenstein and David Marcus, "The Akkadian Inscription of Idrimi," *JANES* 8 (1976): 59–96. See also Gary Oller, "Idrimi," *ABD* 3: 381–82.

26. Early Jewish tradition seems to have recognized the typology. In the synagogue liturgical calendar, Ezekiel 37:15–28 is read on the same Sabbath as Genesis 44 is.

27. See Mordechai Cogan and Hayim Tadmor, *IIKings* (AB) (New York: Doubleday, 1988), 311, 328–30.
28. For details, see ibid., 152–64.

Notes to Chapter 7

1. For a summary, see John R. Spencer, "Aaron," *ABD* 1: 1–6.
2. These verses follow a genealogy in which Moses and Aaron are given the same father and mother. (Contrast Exodus 4:14, in which the notice of the relation between Moses and Aaron is to be translated as "Aaron, your fellow Levite.") Miriam does not occur together with Moses and Aaron in a genealogy until Numbers 26:59. In Exodus 2, the older sister who watches the baby Moses is unnamed, and no mention is made of Aaron. In Exodus 15:21, "Miriam the prophet" is identified as "the sister of Aaron," but not of Moses.
3. The literature on the episode is vast. For a bibliography, see John R. Spencer, "Golden Calf," *ABD* 2: 1065–69; and Nicholas Wyatt, *DDD*, 347.
4. In biblical Hebrew, *'edut*, "pact," is functionally equivalent to *berît*, "covenant." Compare Deuteronomy 9:9: "The stone tablets, tablets of the covenant," with *berît* in place of *'edut*.
5. See John Brinkman, "Political Covenants, Treaties, and Loyalty Oaths in Babylonia and between Assyria and Babylonia," in Carlo Zaccagnini, ed., *Trattati*, 81–111. There is an apparent discovery of *adê* some five centuries earlier in a broken context (82).
6. See ibid., 96–97. As Brinkman observes, because the self-descriptive section of the treaty has not been preserved, we do not know for certain whether it is an *adê* agreement.
7. For the comparison between the "gods to go before" in Exodus 32:1 and the divine *ālik maḫri*, "the god who goes before," known from Akkadian sources, see Tallqvist, Götterephitheta, 18.
8. Both the Hebrew and the Akkadian expressions mean literally "go at the face."
9. See Wyatt, *DDD*, 333–34.
10. Amihai Mazar, "The Iron Age I," in Amnon Ben-Tor, ed., *The Archaeology of Ancient Israel* (New Haven, Conn.: Yale University Press, 1992), 293.
11. Moses Aberbach and Leivy Smolar, "Aaron, Jeroboam and the Golden Calves," *JBL* 86 (1967): 129–40. The quotation is from p. 129. Some of their comparisons are drawn from biblical traditions concerning Jeroboam and Aaron outside these two chapters.
12. From the perspective of the southern writers, Jeroboam's sin taints the entire history of the northern kingdom. Jeroboam becomes what one German scholar called an "Unheilsherrscher," a king whose misdeeds bring untold misfortune. See Carl Evans, "Naram-Sin and Jeroboam: The Archetypal *Un-*

heilsherrscher in Mesopotamian and Biblical Historiography," in William Hallo et al., eds., *Scripture in Context II* (Winona Lake, Ind.: Eisenbrauns, 1983), 96–124.

13. Also note that the prophet Samuel had two wicked sons, one of whom was named Abijah (1 Sam 8:2).

14. The Greek word literally means "image." The Septuagint, the ancient Jewish translation of the Torah into Greek, uses *eidōlon* to translate the Hebrew *pesel*, "graven image," in the Decalogue (Exod 20:3).

15. On the background of Shiloh in the context of Jeroboam's revolt, see Martin A. Cohen, "The Role of the Shilonite Priesthood in the United Monarchy of Ancient Israel," *HUCA* 36 (1965): 59–98.

16. See Oded apud Galil and Stern, eds., *Melakim Aleph* (Tel Aviv: Davidson-Attai, 1994), 138.

17. Hosea 8:5–6.

18. Stanley Gevirtz, " *ḥereṭ* in the Manufacture of the Golden Calf," *Biblica* 65 (1984): 377–81.

19. Samuel Loewenstamm, *Comparative Studies in Biblical and Ancient Oriental Literatures* (Kevelaer: Butzon & Bercker, 1980), 242–45, 510.

20. For the terminology of "braiding" as well as the general treatment of the story, see Baruch Levine, *Numbers 1-20* (AB) (New York: Doubleday, 1993), 405–32.

21. This contradicts the notice in Numbers 26:11: "the sons of Korah did not die."

22. Ezra and Nehemiah date events to specific Persian kings. In contrast, Chronicles relates events from creation to the proclamation of Cyrus. But 1 Chronicles 29:7 relates anachronistically that David collected temple funds in darics, the coin named for Darius the Great (522–486).

23. For full documentation, see S. David Sperling, "Pants, Persians and the Priestly Source," in Robert Chazan et al., eds., *Festschrift Baruch Levine*, in press.

24. On Josiah, see Robert Althann, "Josiah," *ABD* 3: 1015–18.

25. For example, the same list that mentions the "sons of Korah" also names the "sons of Bezal," probably a short form of "Bezalel," a name that means "in God's protection." According to Exodus 35:30, Bezalel was one of the two leading artisans named by Yahweh to carry out the design and construction of the desert tabernacle. For a survey of the Arad discoveries, see Gary Herion and Dale Manor,"Arad," *ABD* 1: 331–36.

Notes to Chapter 8

1. Karel van der Toorn, "Saul and the Rise of Israelite State Religion," *VT* 43 (1993): 519–42.

2. Joseph Blenkinsopp, "The Quest of the Historical Saul," in James W. Flana-

gan and Anita W. Robinson, eds., *No Famine in the Land, Studies in Honor of John L. McKenzie* (Missoula, Mont.: Scholars Press, 1975), 93. For a summary and bibliography of scholarship relating to Saul, see Diana Edelman, "Saul," *ABD* 5: 989–99.

3. Jeremiah 29:26 uses the same word found in our passage, *mitnabbbe'*, "prophesy," in hendiadys with *mešuggā'*, "madman." See also 2 Kings 9:11 and Hosea 9:7.
4. See Sharon R. Keller, "Nudity in the Hebrew Bible" (forthcoming). I thank Prof. Keller for a prepublication copy.
5. For details, see Philip Stern, *The Biblical Ḥerem: A Window on Israel's Religious Experience* (Atlanta: Scholars Press, 1991).
6. For the contrary view that the tale is early, see ibid., 165–77.
7. See S. David Sperling, "Blood," *ABD* 1: 763–65.
8. See Isaiah 1:11 and Psalms 50:13.
9. Leviticus 19:26.
10. Mordecai Margulies, ed., *Midrash Wayyikra Rabbah* (New York: Jewish Theological Seminary, 1993), p. 586.
11. For alternative ways of saying in biblical Hebrew "this was the first altar that he built," see V. Philips Long, *The Reign and Rejection of King Saul* (Atlanta: Scholars Press, 1989), 122.
12. See Karel van der Toorn, "Yahweh," *DDD*, 1712–30 (with bibliography).
13. See ibid., 1716–17.
14. See Wilfred G. Lambert, "The Reign of Nebuchadnezzar I: A Turning Point in the History of Ancient Mesopotamian Religion," in William S. McCullough, ed., *The Seed of Wisdom: Essays in Honour of Theophile J. Meek* (Toronto: University of Toronto Press, 1964), 3–13. Compare William W. Hallo, "Exodus and Ancient Near Eastern Literature," in Gunther Plaut, ed., *The Torah: A Modern Commentary* (New York: Union of American Hebrew Congregations, 1981), 373.

Notes to Afterword

1. D. C. Feeney, *The Gods in Epic: Poets and Critics of the Classical Tradition* (New York: Oxford University Press, 1991).
2. Barbara Nevling Porter, *Images, Power and Politics: Figurative Aspects of Esarhaddon's Babylonian Policy* (Philadelphia: American Philosophical Society, 1993).
3. See especially ibid., chaps. 4, 5, 6. See also Peter Machinist, "Literature as Politics: The Tukulti-Ninurta Epic and the Bible," *CBQ* 38 (1976): 455–82; Peter Machinist, "Assyrians on Assyria in the First Millennium B.C.," in Kurt Raaflaub, ed., *Anfänge politischen Denkens in der Antike* (Munich: Oldenbourg, 1993), 77–104.

Bibliography

Aberbach, Moses, and Leivy Smolar. "Aaron, Jeroboam and the Golden Calves." *JBL* 86: 129–40.

Abrams, Morris II. *A Glossary of Literary Terms*. New York: Holt, Rinehart and Winston, 1971.

Aharoni, Yohanan, Michael Avi-Yonah, Anson F. Rainey, and Ze'ev Safrai. *The Macmillan Bible Atlas*. Rev. 3d ed. New York: Macmillan, 1993.

Ahlström, Gösta. *The History of Ancient Palestine*. Minneapolis: Fortress Press, 1993.

Albrektson, Bertil. *History and the Gods*. Lund: Gleerup, 1967.

Albright, William F. "The Role of the Canaanites in the History of Civilization." In *The Bible and the Ancient Near East*, ed. G. Ernest Wright, 438–87. Garden City, N.Y.: Doubleday, 1965.

———. "The Smaller Beth-Shan Stele of Sethos I (1309–1290 B.C.)." *BASOR* 125 (February 1952): 24–32.

Althann, Robert. "Josiah." *ABD* 3: 1015–18.

Amir, Yehoshua. "Authority and Interpretation in the Writings of Philo." In *Mikra*, ed. Martin Mulder, 421–53. Philadelphia: Fortress Press, 1988.

Amit, Yairah. "The Position of the Exodus Tradition in the Book of Chronicles." In *Studies in Bible: A Memorial Volume in Memory of Joshua Meir Grintz* (Te'uda 2), ed. Benjamin Uffenheimer, 139–55. Tel Aviv: Hakkibutz Hammeuhad, 1982.

Assman, Jan. "Aton." *Lexikon der Ägyptologie* 1: 526–40.

Auerbach, Erich. *Scenes from the Drama of European Literature*. New York: Meridian, 1959.

Barr, James. "The Literal, the Allegorical and Modern Scholarship." *JSOT* 44 (June 1989): 3–17.

Bartlett, John R. "The Conquest of Sihon's Kingdom: A Literary Re-examination." *JBL* 97/3 (1978): 347–51.

Blenkinsopp, Joseph. "The Quest of the Historical Saul." In *No Famine in the Land, Studies in Honor of John L. McKenzie*, ed. James W. Flanagan and Anita W. Robinson, 75–99. Missoula, Mont.: Scholars Press, 1975.

Borgen, Peder. "Philo of Alexandria." *ABD* 5: 333–42.

Borger, Rykle. "Gott Marduk und Gott-König Šulgi als Propheten." *BO*, January–March 1971, 3–24.

Boyce, Mary. *The Early Period.* Vol. 1 of *A History of Zoroastrianism.* Leiden: Brill, 1975.

Brandenstein, Wilhelm, and Manfred Mayrhofer. *Handbuch des Altpersischen.* Wiesbaden: Otto Harrassowitz, 1964.

Brewer, David I. *Techniques and Assumptions in Jewish Exegesis before 70 C.E.* Tübingen: Mohr, 1992.

Bright, John. *A History of Israel.* Philadelphia: Westminster, 1972.

Brinkman, John. "Political Covenants, Treaties, and Loyalty Oaths in Babylonia and between Assyria and Babylonia." In *Il Tratatti nel mondo antico forma ideologia funzione,* ed. Luciano Canfora, Mario Liverani, and Carlo Zaccagnini, Rome: "L'Erma" di Bretschneider, 1990.

Buber, Salomon, ed. *Midrash Tanhuma.* Reprint. Jerusalem: Ortsel, 1964.

Büchsel, Hermann. "allēgoreō." *TDNT* 1: 260–63.

Burkert, Walter. *Creation of the Sacred: Tracks of Biology in Early Religions.* Cambridge, Mass.: Harvard University Press, 1996.

———. *Homo Necans.* Berkeley and Los Angeles: University of California Press, 1983.

Burton, Ernest. *A Critical and Exegetical Commentary on the Epistle to the Galatians.* Edinburgh: T and T Clark, 1921.

Campbell, Edward. "Judges 9 and Biblical Archeology." In *The Word of the Lord Shall Go Forth: Essays in Honor of David Noel Freedman in Celebration of His Sixtieth Birthday,* ed. Carol Myers and Michael O'Connor, 263–71. Winona Lake, Ind.: Eisenbrauns, 1983.

Carroll, Robert. "Psalm LXXVIII: Vestiges of a Tribal Polemic." *VT* 21/2 (1971): 133–50.

Charpin, Dominique. "Un Traité entre Zimri-Lim de Mari et Ibâl-pî-El II d'Ešnunna." In *Marchands, diplomates et empereurs: Études sur la civilisation mésopotamienne offertes à Paul Garelli,* ed. Dominique Charpin and Francis Joannès, 139–66. Paris: Éditions recherche sur les civilisations, 1991.

Clark, Gordon. *The Word Hesed in the Hebrew Bible.* Sheffield: Sheffield Academic Press, 1993.

Clements, Ronald. *The World of Ancient Israel.* Cambridge: Cambridge University Press, 1989.

Cogan, Mordechai, and Hayim Tadmor. *IIKings.* New York: Doubleday, 1988.

Cohen, Chaim. "Genesis 14:1–11—An Early Israelite Chronographic Source." In *The Biblical Canon in Comparative Perspective* (Scripture in Context IV), ed. K. Lawson Younger, William Hallo, and Bernard F. Batto, 67–107. Lewiston: Edwin Mellen, 1991.

Cohen, Martin A. "The Role of the Shilonite Priesthood in the United Monarchy of Ancient Israel." *HUCA* 46 (1965): 59–98.

Coogan, Michael. "Canaanite Origins and Lineage: Reflections on the Religion of Ancient Israel." In *Ancient Israelite Religion*, ed. Miller et al., 115–24.

Cooper, Alan, and Bernard Goldstein. "Exodus and Maṣṣot in History and Tradition." *MAARAV* 8 (1992): 15–37.

———. "The Festivals of Israel and Judah and the Literary History of the Pentateuch." *JAOS*, January–March 1990, 19–31.

Cross, Frank M. *Canaanite Myth and Hebrew Epic*. Cambridge, Mass.: Harvard University Press, 1973.

Day, John. "Pre-Deuteronomic Allusions to the Covenant in Hosea and Psalm LXXVIII." *VT* 36/1 (1986): 1–12.

Dever, William. "Archaeology, Syro-Palestinian and Biblical." *ABD* 1: 354–67.

———. "The Contribution of Archaeology to the Study of Canaanite and Early Israelite Religion." In *Ancient Israelite Religion*, ed. Miller et al., 209–47.

———. "Israel, History of (Archaeology and the Israelite 'Conquest')." *ABD* 3: 545–58.

Dijkstra, Meindert. "Abraham." *DDD*: 6–10.

Dothan, Trude, and H. Jacob Katzenstein. "Philistines." *ABD* 5: 326–33.

Drews, Robert. *The End of the Bronze Age: Changes in Warfare and the Catastrophe ca. 1200 B.C.* Princeton, N.J.: Princeton University Press, 1993.

Durand, Jean-Marie. *Archives épistolaires de Mari*. Paris: Éditions recherche sur les civilisations, 1988.

Edelman, Diana. Review of *Joshua 24 as Poetic Narrative*, by William Koopmans. *JNES* 52/4 (1993): 308–10.

———. "Saul." *ABD* 5: 989–99.

Eidem, Jesper. "An Old Assyrian Treaty from Tell Leilan." In *Marchands, diplomates et empereurs: Études sur la civilisation mésopotamienne offertes à Paul Garelli*, ed. Dominique Charpin and Francis Joannès, 185–207. Paris: Éditions recherche sur les civilisations, 1991.

Emerton, John A. "The Riddle of Genesis XIV." *VT* 21/4 (1971): 403–39.

———. "The Site of Salem, the City of Melchizedek (Genesis XIV 18)." *VTSup* 41 (1990): 45–71.

———. "Some Problems in Genesis XIV." *VT Sup* 41 (1990): 73–102.

Evans, Carl. "Naram-Sin and Jeroboam: The Archetypal *Unheilsherrscher* in Mesopotamian and Biblical Historiography." In *Scripture in Context II*, ed. William W. Hallo, James C. Moyer, and Leo G. Perdue, 94–124. Winona Lake, Ind.: Eisenbrauns, 1983.

Falkner, Raymond, Ogden Goelet, and Eva von Dassow. *The Egyptian Book of the Dead Going Forth by Day*. San Francisco: Chronicle, 1994.

Feeney, D. C. *The Gods in Epic: Poets and Critics of the Classical Tradition*. New York: Oxford University Press. 1991.

Finkelstein, Israel. *The Archaeology of the Israelite Settlement*. Jerusalem: Israel Exploration Society, 1988.

Finkelstein, Israel, and Nadav Na'aman, eds. *From Nomadism to Monarchy: Ar-*

chaeological and Historical Aspects of Early Israel. Washington, D.C.: Biblical Archaeological Society, 1994.

Finkelstein, Louis. *The Jews, Their History, Culture and Religion.* New York: Harper, 1960.

Fishbane, Michael, and Emanuel Tov, eds. *Sha'arei Talmon Studies in the Bible, Qumran, and the Ancient Near East Presented to Shemaryahu Talmon.* Winona Lake, Ind.: Eisenbrauns, 1992.

Fitzmyer, Joseph. *The Aramaic Inscriptions of Sefire.* Rome: Pontifical Biblical Institute, 1967.

———. *The Genesis Apocryphon of Qumran Cave I.* Rome: Pontifical Biblical Institute, 1966.

Fleming, Daniel. *The Installation of Baal's High Priestess at Emar.* Atlanta: Scholars Press, 1992.

Frankena, Rintje. "The Vassal Treaties of Esarhaddon and the Dating of Deuteronomy." *OTS* 14 (1965): 122–54.

Friedman. Richard E. *Who Wrote the Bible?* New York: Harper & Row, 1989.

Galil, Gershon, and Ephraim Stern, eds. *Melakim Aleph.* Tel Aviv: Davidson-Attai, 1994.

Geller, Markham. Review of *Sin and Sanction in Israel and Mesopotamia,* by Karel van der Toorn. *JCS* 42/1 (1991): 105–17.

Geller, Stephen. "The Struggle at the Jabbok: The Uses of Enigma in a Biblical Narrative." *JANES* 14 (1982): 37–60.

Geraty, Lawrence. "Heshbon." *ABD* 3: 181–84.

Gevirtz, Stanley. "Of Patriarchs and Puns: Joseph at the Fountain, Jacob at the Ford." *HUCA* 46 (1975): 33–54.

Gibson, John. *Canaanite Myths and Legends.* Edinburgh: T and T Clark, 1987.

Ginsberg, Harold Louis. "Hosea, Book of." *EncJud* 8: 1010–23.

———. "Hosea's Ephraim, More Fool Than Knave (A New Interpretation of Hosea 12:1–14)." *JBL* 80/1 (1961): 339–47.

———. *The Israelian Heritage of Judaism.* New York: Jewish Theological Seminary, 1982.

———. "Ugaritic Studies and the Bible." In *The Biblical Archaeologist Reader.* Vol. 2, ed. David N. Freedman and Edward F. Campbell, 35–58. Garden City, N.Y.: Anchor/Doubleday, 1964.

Gnoli, Gherardo. "Mithra." *EncRel* 9: 579–80.

Gottwald, Norman. *The Tribes of Yahweh.* Maryknoll, N.Y.: Orbis, 1979.

Greenberg, Moshe. "Did Job Really Exist? An Issue of Medieval Exegesis." In *Sha'arei Talmon Studies in the Bible, Qumran, and the Ancient Near East Presented to Shemaryahu Talmon,* ed. Michael Fishbane and Emanuel Tov, 3*–11*. Winona Lake, : Eisenbrauns, 1992.

Greengus, Samuel. "The Old Babylonian Marriage Contract," *JAOS* 89/3 (1969): 505–32.

———. "Sisterhood Adoption at Nuzi and the 'Wife-Sister' in Genesis." *HUCA* 46 (1975): 5–31.

Greenstein, Edward, and David Marcus. "The Akkadian Inscription of Idrimi." *JANES* 8 (1976): 59–96.

Hackett, Jo Ann. "Balaam." *ABD* 1: 569–72.

———. "Religious Traditions in Israelite Transjordan." In *Ancient Israelite Religion*, ed. Miller et al, 125–36.

Hallo, William W. "Biblical Abominations and Sumerian Taboos." *JQR* 76/1 (1985): 21–40.

Hallo, William W. "Exodus and Ancient Near Eastern Literature," in Plaut, ed., *The Torah*, 367–77.

Halpern, Baruch. *The First Historians*. New York: Harper & Row, 1988.

Hasel, Gerhard F. "Sabbath." *ABD* 5: 849–56.

Hasel, Michael G. "*Israel* in the Merneptah Stele." *BASOR* 296 (1994): 45–61.

Held, Moshe. "The Root *ZBL/SBL* in Akkadian, Ugaritic and Biblical Hebrew." *JAOS* 88/1 (1968): 90–96.

Hess, Richard. "Caphtor." *ABD* 1: 869–70.

———. "Early Israel in Canaan: A Survey of Recent Evidence and Interpretations." *PEQ* 125 (1993): 125–42.

Hicks, Lansing. "Melchizedek." *IDB* 3: 343.

Hillers, Delbert. *Covenant: The History of a Biblical Idea*. Baltimore: Johns Hopkins University Press, 1969.

———. *Treaty Curses and the Old Testament Prophets*. Rome: Pontifical Biblical Institute, 1964.

Hodgson, Marshall G. S. "Bāṭiniyya." *EncIslam* 1: 1098–1100.

Hoffman, Yair. *The Doctrine of the Exodus in the Bible*. Tel Aviv: Tel Aviv University Press, 1983.

———. "A North Israelite Typological Myth and a Judaean Historical Tradition: The Exodus in Hosea and Amos." *VT* 39/2 (1989): 169–82.

Hoftijzer, Jacob, and Gerrit van der Kooij. *The Balaam Text from Deir Alla Reevaluated*. Leiden: Brill, 1991.

Jacobsen, Thorkild. "Religious Drama in Ancient Mesopotamia." In *Unity and Diversity*, ed. Hans Goedicke and Jimmy Jack McBee Roberts, 65–97. Baltimore: Johns Hopkins University Press, 1975.

———. *The Treasures of Darkness*. New Haven, Conn.: Yale University Press, 1976.

Japhet, Sara. *I and II Chronicles*. Louisville: Westminster, 1993.

Joannès, Francis. "Le Traité de vassalité d'Atamrum d'Andarig envers Zimri-Lim de Mari." In *Marchands, diplomates et empereurs: Études sur la civilisation mésopotamienne offertes à Paul Garelli*, ed. Dominique Charpin and Francis Joannès, 166–77. Paris: Éditions recherche sur les civilisations, 1991.

Johnson, Luke T. *The Real Jesus*. San Francisco: Harper San Francisco, 1996.

Kamin, Sarah. *Jews and Christians Interpret the Bible*. Jerusalem: Magnes, 1991.

Keller, Sharon R. "Nudity in the Hebrew Bible." (forthcoming).

Kempinski, Aharon. "How Profoundly Canaanized Were the Early Israelites?" *ZDPV* 108/1 (1992): 1–6.

Kennedy, James. "Peasants in Revolt: Political Allegory in Genesis 2–3." *JSOT* 47 (1990): 3–14.

Kitchen, Kenneth. "Egypt, Ugarit, Qatna and Covenant." *UF* 11 (1979): 453–64.

Klein, Jacob. "Sacred Marriage." *ABD* 5: 866–71.

Klein, Jacob, and Yitschak Sefati. "The Concept of 'Abomination' in Mesopotamian Literature and the Bible." *Beer Sheba* 3 (1990): 131–48.

Knauf, Ernest A. "El Šaddai—Der Gott Abrahams?" *BZ* 29/1 (1985): 97–103.

———. "King Solomon's Copper Supply." In *Phoenicia and the Bible*, ed. Edward Lipiński, 167–86. Leuven: Peeters, 1991.

Koopmans, William. *Joshua 24 as Poetic Narrative*. Sheffield: JSOT, 1990.

Kramer, Samuel N. *The Sacred Marriage Rite*. Bloomington: Indiana University Press, 1969.

Kravitz, Leonard. "Mose ben Nahman." In *Theologische Realenzylopaudie*, ed. Gerhard Krause and Gerhard Muller. Vol. 23, fasc. 3/4: 362–64. Berlin: W. de Gruyter, 1977–.

Kupfer, Ephraim. "Kaspi, Joseph ben Abba." *EncJud* 10: 809–11.

Kupper, Jean-Robert. "Zimri-Lim et ses vassaux." In *Marchands, diplomates et empereurs: Études sur la civilisation mésopotamienne offertes à Paul Garelli*, ed. Dominique Charpin and Francis Joannès, 179–84. Paris: Éditions recherches sur les civilisations, 1991.

Lambert, Wilfred G. "Morals in Ancient Mesopotamia." *JEOL* 15 (1957–58): 184–96.

———. "The Reign of Nebuchadnezzar I: A Turning Point in the History of Ancient Mesopotamian Religion." In *The Seed of Wisdom: Essays in Honour of Theophile J. Meek*, ed. William S. McCullough, 3–13. Toronto: University of Toronto Press, 1964.

Landsberger, Benno. "Die babylonische Termini für Gesetz und Recht." In Symb. Koschaker: 219–34.

Lang, Bernhard. *Monotheism and the Prophetic Minority*. Sheffield: Almond, 1983.

Leach, Edmund. "Anthropological Approaches to the Bible during the Twentieth Century." In *Humanizing America's Iconic Book*, ed. Gene Tucker and Gordon Knight, 75–94. Chico, Calif.: Scholars Press, 1980.

Lemche, Niels. *The Canaanites and Their Land*. Sheffield: JSOT, 1991.

———. *Early Israel*. Leiden: Brill, 1965.

———. "Habiru, Hapiru." *ABD* 3: 6–10.

———. "Israel, History of (Premonarchic Period)." *ABD* 3: 526–45.

Levine, Baruch. "The Epilogue to the Holiness Code; A Priestly Statement on the

Destiny of Israel." In *Judaic Perspectives on Ancient Israel*, ed. Ernest Frerichs, Baruch Levine, and Jacob Neusner, 9–34. Philadelphia: Fortress Press, 1987.

―――. *Numbers 1-20*. New York: Doubleday, 1993.

―――. "The Triumphs of the Lord." *ErIsr* 20 (1989): 202–14.

Lewis, Brian. *The Sargon Legend: A Study of the Akkadian Text and the Tale of the Hero Who Was Exposed at Birth*. Cambridge: ASOR, 1980.

Lewis, David M. "The Persepolis Fortification Texts." In *Achaemenid History IV Centre and Periphery*, ed. Heleen Sancisi Weerdenburg and Amélie Kuhrt, 1–6. Leiden: Nederlands instituut voor het nabije oosten, 1990.

Lewis, Theodore. "Baal-Berith." *ABD* 1: 550–51.

Licht, Jacob. "Biblical Historicism." In *History, Historiography and Interpretation*, ed. Hayim Tadmor and Moshe Weinfeld, 107–20. Jerusalem: Magnes, 1983.

Lichtheim, Miriam. *The New Kingdom*. Vol. 2 of *Ancient Egyptian Literature*. Berkeley and Los Angeles: University of California Press, 1976.

Lieberman, Saul. *Hellenism in Jewish Palestine*. New York: Jewish Theological Seminary, 1950.

Lieberman, Stephen. "A Mesopotamian Background for the So-Called *Aggadic* 'Measures' of Biblical Hermenetics." *HUCA* 58 (1987): 137–225.

Liverani, Mario. *The Politics of Abdi-Ashirta of Amurru*. Malibu, Calif.: Undena, 1979.

Loewenstamm, Samuel. *Comparative Studies in Biblical and Ancient Oriental Literatures*. Neukirchen-Vluyn: Neukirchener Verlag, 1980.

Long, Burke. Review of *The Origin Tradition of Ancient Israel*, by Thomas Thompson. *JBL* 108 (1989): 327–30.

Machinist, Peter. "Assyrians on Assyria in the First Millennium B.C." In *Anfänge politischen Denkens in der Antike*, ed. Kurt Raaflaub, 77–104. Munich: Oldenbourg, 1993.

―――. "Distinctiveness in Ancient Israel." In *Ah, Assyria Studies in Assyrian History and Ancient Near Eastern Historiography Presented to Hayim Tadmor* (Scripta Hierosolymitana 33), ed. Mordechai Cogan and Israel Ephal, 196–212. Jerusalem: Magnes, 1991.

―――. "Hosea and the Ambiguity of Kingship in Ancient Israel." In *Signs of Democracy in the Bible*, ed. Chaim Stern, 25–63. Chappaqua, N.Y.: Temple Bethel of Northern Westchester, 1994.

―――. "Literature as Politics: The Tukulti-Ninurta Epic and the Bible." *CBQ* 38/4 (1976): 455–82.

―――. "Outsiders or Insiders: The Biblical View of Emergent Israel in Its Contexts." In *The Other in Jewish Thought and History Constructions of Jewish Culture and Identity*, ed. Robert Cohn and Laurence Silberstein, 35–60. New York: New York University Press, 1994.

Manor, Dale. Beer-Sheba. *ABD* 1: 641–45.

————. "Kadesh-Barnea." *ABD* 4: 1–3.

Manor, Dale, and Gary Herion. "Arad." *ABD* 1: 331–36.

Margulies, Mordecai. *Midrash Wayyikra Rassah*. New York: Jewish Theological Seminary, 1993.

Marty, Martin. "America's Iconic Book." In *Humanizing America's Iconic Book*, ed. Douglas Knight and Gene Tucker, 1–23. Chico, Calif.: Scholars Press, 1980.

Mazar, Amihai. "The Iron Age I." In *The Archaeology of Ancient Israel*, ed. Amnon Ben-Tor, 258–301. New Haven, Conn.: Yale University Press, 1992.

Mazar, Benjamin. *World History of the Jewish People III*. Givatayim: Jewish History Publications and Rutgers University Press, 1971.

McCarter, R. Kyle Jr. *ISamuel*. New York: Doubleday, 1980.

McCarthy, Dennis. *Treaty and Covenant*. Rome: Pontifical Biblical Institute, 1978.

Mendenhall. George E. "Biblical History in Transition." In *The Bible and the Ancient Near East*, ed. G. Ernest Wright, 27–58. Garden City, N.Y.: Doubleday, 1965.

————. "'Change and Decay in All Around I See': Conquest, Covenant and *The Tenth Generation*." *BA* 39/4 (1987): 152–57.

————. "Covenant Forms in Israelite Tradition." *BA* 17/3 (1954): 50–76.

————. "The Hebrew Account of the Conquest of Palestine." *BA* 25/3 (1962): 66–87.

————. *The Tenth Generation: The Origins of the Biblical Tradition*. Baltimore: Johns Hopkins University Press, 1973.

Mendenhall, George E., and Gary Herion. "Covenant." *ABD* 1: 1179–1202.

Miller, J. Maxwell. "The Israelite Journey through (around) Moab and Moabite Toponymy." *JBL* 108/4 (1989): 577–99.

————. "Moab." *ABD* 4: 882–93.

Moran, William. *The Amarna Letters*. Baltimore: Johns Hopkins University Press, 1992.

Morris, Jenny. "The Jewish Philosopher Philo." In *Emil Schürer, the History of the Jewish People in the Time of Jesus Christ*. Vol. 3, ed. Geza Vermes and Fergus Millar, 809–89. Edinburgh: T and T Clark, 1987.

Muffs, Yohanan. "Abraham the Noble Warrior: Patriarchal Politics and Laws of War in Ancient Israel." *JJS* 33 (1982): 81–107.

Mulder, Martin. "Baal-Berith." *DDD*, 266–72.

Nebo, Yehoshaphat. *The Commentaries to the Torah by Rabbi Joseph Bekhor Shor*. Jerusalem: Magnes, 1991.

Nicholson, Ernest. *God and His People, Covenant and Theology in the Old Testament*. Oxford: Oxford University Press, 1986.

Nielsen, Eduard. *Shechem, a Traditio-Historical Investigation*. Copenhagen: Gad, 1969.

Nikiprowetzky, Valentin. "Ethical Monotheism." *Daedalus*, Spring 1975, 69–89.

Oden, Robert. "Myth and Mythology." *ABD* 4: 946–56.

———. "The Place of Covenant in the Religion of Israel."In *Ancient Israelite Religion Essays in Honor of Frank Moore Cross*, ed. Patrick D. Miller Jr., Paul D. Hanson, and S. Dean McBride, 429–47. Philadelphia: Fortress Press, 1987.

Oller, Gary H. "Idrimi." *ABD* 3: 381–82.

Olmstead, Albert T. *History of the Persian Empire*. Chicago: University of Chicago Press, 1948.

Oppenheim, A. Leo. "On Royal Gardens in Mesopotamia." *JNES* 24/4 (1965): 328–33.

Pagels, Elaine. *The Gnostic Gospels*. New York: Random House, 1979.

Perlitt, Lothar. *Bundestheologie im Alten Testament*. Neukirchen-Vluyn: Neukirchener Verlag, 1969.

Plaut, W. Gunther, ed. *The Torah: A Modern Commentary*. New York: Union of American Hebrew Congregations, 1981.

Porter, Barbara Nevling. *Images, Power and Politics: Figurative Aspects of Esarhaddon's Babylonian Policy*. Philadelphia: American Philosophical Society, 1993.

Rainey, Anson F. "Compulsory Labor Gangs in Ancient Israel." *IEJ* 20/3–4 (1970): 191–202.

———. *El Amarna Tablets, 359–379*. Neukirchen-Vluyn: Neukirchener Verlag, 1978.

———. "Remarks on Donald Redford's *Egypt, Canaan and Israel in Ancient Times*." *BASOR*, August 1994, 81–85.

———. Review of *The Tribes of Yahweh*, by Norman Gottwald. *JAOS* 107/3 (1987): 541–43.

———. "Uncritical Criticism." *JAOS* 115/1 (1995): 101–4.

Ramsey, George W. "Joshua (Person)." *ABD* 3: 999–1000.

———. "Zadok." *ABD* 6: 1034–35.

Redford, Donald. "Akhenaten." *ABD* 1: 135–37.

———. *Egypt, Canaan and Israel in Ancient Times*. Princeton, N.J.: Princeton University Press, 1992.

Reiling, Jannes. "Melchizedek." *DDD*, 1057–53.

Rendtdorff, Rolf. "Postexilic Israel in German Bible Scholarship." In *Sha'arei Talmon Studies in the Bible, Qumran, and the Ancient Near East Presented to Shemaryahu Talmon*, ed. Michael Fishbane and Emanuel Tov, 165–73. Winona Lake, Ind.: 1992.

Ringgren, Helmer. *Israelite Religion*. Philadelphia: Fortress Press, 1966.

Rofé, Alexander. "The Battle of David and Goliath: Folklore, Theology, Eschatology." In *Judaic Perspectives*, ed. Frerichs et al, 117–51.

Rofé, Alexander. "Ephraimite versus Deuteronomistic History." In *Storia e tradizioni di Israele scritti in onore di J. Alberto Soggin*, ed. Daniele Garrone and Felice Israel, 221–35. Brescia: Paidea, 1991.

Röllig, Wolfgang. "Bethel." *DDD*, 332–33.

Römer, Willem. "Einige Überlegungen zur 'Heiligen Hochzeit' nach altorientalischen Texten." In *Von Kanaan bis Kerala: Festschrift für Prof. Mag. Dr. Dr. J. P. M. van der Ploeg O.P. zur Vollendung des siebzigsten Lebensjahres am 4. Juli 1979: überreicht von Kollegen, Freunden und Schulern*, ed. Wilhelmus Delsman, 411–28. Neukirchen-Vluyn: Neukirchener Verlag, 1982.

Rose, Martin. "Names of God in the OT." *ABD* 4: 1001–11.

Rosenberg, Joel. *King and Kin: Political Allegory in the Hebrew Bible*. Bloomington: Indiana University Press, 1986.

Sarna, Nahum. *The JPS Torah Commentary Genesis*. New York: Jewish Publication Society, 1989.

Sasson, Jack. "On M. H. Pope's *Song of Songs* [AB 7C]." *MAARAV* 1/2 (1979): 177–96.

———. Review of *The Tenth Generation*, by George E. Mendenhall. *JBL* 93/2 (1974): 294–96.

Scullion, John. "God in the OT." *ABD* 2: 1041–48.

Seeligmann, Isaac L. "A Pre-monarchic Hymn." In *I. L. Seeligmann Studies in Biblical Literature*, ed. Avi Hurvitz, Sara Japhet, and Emanuel Tov, 189–204. Jerusalem: Magnes, 1992.

Selms, Adrianus van. "Temporary Henotheism." In *Symbolae biblicae mesopotamicae Francisco Mario Theodoro de Liagre Böhl dedicatae*, ed. Martinus Beek, 8–20. Leiden; Brill, 1973.

Smith, Morton. "The Common Theology of the Ancient Near East." *JBL* 71/3 (1952): 135–47.

———. *Palestinian Parties and Politics That Shaped the Old Testament*. New York: Columbia University Press, 1971.

———. "The Present State of Old Testament Studies." *JBL* 78/1 (1969): 19–35.

Soden, Wolfram von. "Religion und Sittlickeit nach den Anschauungen der Babylonier." *ZDMG* 89/2 (1935): 143–69.

Speiser, Ephraim A. "Authority and Law in Mesopotamia" and "The Wife-Sister Motif in the Patriarchal Narratives." In *Oriental and Biblical Studies: Collected Writings of E. A. Speiser*, ed. Jacob J. Finkelstein and Moshe Greenberg, 313–23 and 62–82. Philadelphia: University of Pennsylvania Press, 1967.

———, ed. *World History of the Jewish People*. Vol. 1. Tel Aviv: Massadah, 1964.

Spencer, John R. "Aaron." *ABD* 1: 1–6.

———. "Golden Calf." *ABD* 2: 1065–69.

Sperling, S. David. "An Arslan Tash Incantation: Interpretations and Implications." *HUCA* 53 (1982): 1–10.

———. "Blood." *ABD* 1: 763–65.

———. "God in the Hebrew Scriptures." *EncRel* 6: 1–8.

———. "Israel's Religion in the Ancient Near East." In *Jewish Spirituality from the Bible through the Middle Ages*, ed. Arthur Green, 5–31. New York: Crossroad, 1986.

———. "Joshua 24 Re-examined." *HUCA* 58 (1987): 119–36.

———. "Rethinking Covenant in Late Biblical Books." *Biblica* 70/1 (1989): 50–72.

———. *Students of the Covenant: A History of Jewish Biblical Scholarship in North America*. Atlanta: Scholars Press, 1992.

Spinoza, Benedict Baruch. *A Theologico-Political Treatise*, trans. Robert H. M. Elwes. Reprint. New York: Dover, 1951.

Stern, Philip. *The Biblical Herem: A Window on Israel's Religious Experience*. Atlanta: Scholars Press, 1991.

Stronach, David. "The Garden as a Political Statement; Some Case Studies from the Near East in the First Millennium B.C." *Bulletin of the Asia Institute*, new ser., vol. 4 (1990): 171–80.

Sweek, Joel. "The Babel-Bibel Streit." In *The Pitcher Is Broken: Memorial Essays for Gösta V. Ahlström*, ed. Lowell K. Handy and Steven W. Holloway, 401–19. Sheffield: Sheffield Academic Press, 1995.

Tadmor, Hayim. "Autobiographical Apology in the Royal Assyrian Literature." In *History, Historiography and Interpretation: Studies in Biblical and Cuneiform Literatures*, ed. Hayim Tadmor and Moshe Weinfeld, 36–57. Jerusalem: Magnes, 1983.

———. "The People and the Kingship in Ancient Israel: The Role of Political Institutions in the Biblical Period." *Cahiers d'histoire mondiale* 11 (1968): 46–68.

Talmage, Frank. "Apples of Gold: The Inner Meaning of Sacred Texts in Medieval Judaism." In *Jewish Spirituality from the Bible through the Middle Ages*, ed. Arthur Green, 313–55. New York: Crossroad, 1986.

Tate, Jonathan. "Allegory, Greek." *OCD*: 45–46.

Teixidor, Javier. *The Pagan God Popular Religion in the Greco-Roman Near East*. Princeton, N.J.: Princeton University Press, 1977.

Theodor, Julius, and Chanoch Albeck. *Midrash Bereshit Rabba*. Jerusalem: Wahrmann, 1965.

Thiel, Winfried. "Omri." *ABD* 5: 17–20.

Thompson, Thomas. *The Historicity of the Patriarchal Narratives*. Berlin: de Gruyter, 1974.

———. "Historiography (Israelite)." *ABD* 3: 206–12.

———. *The Origin Tradition of Ancient Israel*. Vol. 1: *The Literary Formation of Genesis and Exodus 1-23*. Sheffield: JSOT, 1987.

Toorn, Karel van der. "Migration and the Spread of Local Cults." In *Immigration and Emigration within the Ancient Near East: Festschrift Edward Lipiński* (OLA 65), ed. Karel van Leberghe and Antoon Schoors, 365–77. Leuven: Peeters, 1995.

———. "Saul and the Rise of Israelite State Religion." *VT* 43/4 (1993): 519–42.

———. *Sin and Sanction in Israel and Mesopotamia*. Maastricht: van Gorcum, 1985.

———. "Yahweh." *DDD*, 1712–30.

Tucker, Gene, and Douglas Knight, eds. *Humanizing America's Iconic Book*. Chico, Calif.: Scholars Press, 1980.

Tur-Sinai, Naphtali H. *The Language and the Book II*. Jerusalem: Bialik, 1959.

van Seters, John. *Abraham in History and Tradition*. New Haven, Conn.: Yale University Press, 1975.

———. "Joshua 24 and the Problem of Tradition in the Old Testament." In *In the Shelter of Elyon: Essays in Honor of Gösta W. Ahlström*, JSOTSup 31, ed. W. Boyd Barrick and John R. Spencer, 139–58. Sheffield: JSOT, 1984.

———. "Once Again—The Conquest of Sihon's Kingdom." *JBL* 99/1 (1980): 117–19.

———. "The Terms 'Amorite' and 'Hittite' in the Old Testament." *VT* 22/1 (1972): 64–81.

de Vaux, Roland. *Ancient Israel*. New York: McGraw-Hill, 1965.

Veyne, Paul. *Did the Greeks Believe in Their Myths?* Chicago: University of Chicago Press, 1988.

Wallace, Howard. "Eden, Garden of." *ABD* 2: 281–83.

Wernberg-Møller, Preben. Review of *Treaty Curses and the Old Testament Prophets*, by Delbert Hillers. *CBQ* 27/1 (1965): 68–69.

Weinfeld, Moshe. "Berîth." *TDOT* 2: 253–79.

Weinfeld, Moshe. *The Book of Genesis with a New Commentary*. Tel Aviv: Gordon, 1975.

Weinfeld, Moshe. "The Common Heritage of Covenantal Traditions in the Ancient World." In *Il Tratatti nel mondo antico forma ideologia funzione*, ed. Canfora et al., 175–91.

Weinfeld, Moshe. "The Covenant of Grant in the Old Testament and in the Ancient Near East." *JAOS* 90/2 (1970): 184–203.

Weinfeld, Moshe. "Covenant Terminology in the Ancient Near East and Its Influence on the West." *JAOS* 93/2 (1973): 190–99.

Weinfeld, Moshe. "The Creator God in Genesis 1 and in the Prophecy of Deutero-Isaiah." *Tarbiz* 37/2 (1968): 105–32.

Weinfeld, Moshe. "The Davidic Empire: Realization of the Promises to the Patriarchs." *ErIsr* 24 (1993): 87–92.

Weinfeld, Moshe. *Deuteronomy and the Deuteronomic School*. Oxford: Clarendon Press, 1972.

Weinfeld, Moshe. "The Pattern of the Israelite Settlement in Canaan." *VTSup* 40 (1988): 270–83.

Weinfeld, Moshe. "The Promise to the Patriarchs and Its Realization: An Analysis of Foundation Stories." In *Society and Economy in the Eastern Mediterranean ca. 1500–1000 B.C.*, ed. Michael Heltzer and Edward Lipiński, 353–69. Leuven: Peeters, 1988.

Weinfeld, Moshe. Review of *God and His People*, by Ernest Nicholson. *RB* 98/3 (1991): 431–36.

Wellhausen, Julius. *Prolegomena to the History of Ancient Israel*. Reprint. Gloucester, Mass.: Peter Smith, 1973.

Whitelam, Keith. "Israel's Tradition of Origin: Reclaiming the Land." *JSOT* 44 (1989): 29–36.

Wilson, John. "Egypt and the Bible." In *World History of the Jewish People*. Vol. 1, ed. Ephraim A. Speiser, 338–41. Tel Aviv: Massadah, 1964.

Wolff, Hans. *Hosea*. Philadelphia: Fortress Press, 1974.

Young, Gordon, ed. *Mari in Retrospect*. Winona Lake, Ind.: Eisenbrauns, 1992.

Yusa, Michiko. "Henotheism." *EncRel* 6: 266–68.

Zaccagnini, Carlo. "An Urartean Royal Inscription in the Report of Sargon's Eighth Campaign." In *Assyrian Royal Inscriptions: New Horizons*, ed. Mario Fales, 259–95. Rome: Instituto per l'oriente, 1981.

Index

Aberbach, M., 107, 162n.11
Abimelech, 86–90
Abraham, allegory of David, 82–90;
   origin of name, 78; paradigm of
   salvation through faith, 31–32
"Absalom and Achitophel" (poem by
   Dryden), 39–40
Ahab, 144n.36
Aharoni, Yohanan, 118
Ahlström, Gösta, 145n.7
Ahuramazda (Zoroastrian divinity), 5
Albright, W. F.: on Canaanite religion,
   48; on historicity of Genesis, 20;
   on name of Abraham, 156n.9
allegoresis, 32, 35–37, 39, 40;
   opposed to allegorizing, 28
allegory, 27; co-existing with literal
   and historical meaning, 34;
   definition of, 28; displacing literal
   meaning, 31; in Greek sources,
   141n.5; "imposed," 28; of
   Yahweh's marriage to Israel, 64,
   140 n.4. See also typology
Amalek, 123
Amarna, letters from, 24, 52–53
Amiram, Ruth, 118
Amit, Yairah, on exodus traditions in
   Chronicles, 44
Amorites, 58, 60, 76; as designation
   of "Philistines," 85

Amos (Hebrew prophet): and exodus
   traditions, 45; migration
   traditions, 57; ritual and morality,
   49
anti-Semitism, in biblical scholarship,
   138n.9, 139n.13
Appelbaum, A., 159n.36
Arad, 118, 163n.25
Arameans, 57, 76, 84
archaeology, and Israelite religion,
   147n.22; biblical, rise and fall of,
   17–24
Aten (Egyptian divinity), 50, 51,
   148n.35
Augustine (Saint), 142n.14
autobiographical apology (literary
   genre), 42–43

Baal (Syro-Palestinian divinity), 66,
   107, 147n.21
Baal-Berit, temple of, 68
Babel und Bibel, 138n.9
Balaam, borrowed figure from
   Transjordan, 73
bamah (employed in cult), 160n.12
Barr, James, on literal and allegorical
   biblical exposition, 140n.2
bāṭiniyya (Arabic: "inner
   interpreters"), 142n.13
Beersheba, 76, 83, 88–89

Bekhor Shor, Joseph, 142n. 15

berît (Hebrew: "covenant"), 62, 65, 87

Bethel, 95–96, 97, 104–5, 135, 160n. 17

Bible as icon, 1–2

Blenkinsopp, J., 123, 163n. 2

blood, 129, 164n. 7

Book of the Dead, The, 49

Brewer, David, 141n. 4

Bright, John, biblical historian, 41; on historicity of biblical patriarchs, 138n. 11; on historicity of Moses, 121

calf, golden, 105–12, 162nn. 3, 11

Carroll, R., on origin of exodus traditions, 45, 145n. 10

Cohen, C., 157n. 16

Cohen, M. A., on Shilonite priesthood, 163n. 15

conversion, 154n. 30

Cooper, A., 145n. 1, 146n. 13; historicization of festivals primary, 151n. 3

counter-identity, 46

covenant, with Yahweh not monotheistic, 70–72; legalistic interpretation of, 63–65; primitive, 151n. 6. *See also* Redford, D.; Wellhausen, J.

criticism, biblical: form, 139n. 12; literary, 41–42

David: allegorically identified with Abraham, 82–90; and Goliath, 159n. 42

Day, John, 156n. 43

Delitzsch, F., on Bible as great deception, 138n. 9

Dever, W., 52, 147n. 22

Dryden, J., 39–40. *See also* "Absalom and Achitophel"

Durand, J.-M., 150n. 53

Edelman, D., 164n. 2

Eden, Garden of, 37–39, 144n. 35

edut (pact), 105–6

El-Berit (divinity), 68

Elohim (Hebrew god), 105; meanings of word, 96, 104

Ezekiel (Hebrew prophet): on Joseph story as typology, 100; on priesthood, 115

Farnaka (Persian name), 7, 137n. 5. *See also* Parnach

Feeney, D. C., 135–36

Finkelstein, I., 149n. 42, 150n. 55

Fleming, D., 152n. 15

Friedman, R. E., on rise of modern biblical criticism, 138n. 5

Funkenstein, A., 146n. 14

Galatians, Chapter 4 of Paul's epistle to, 29–30

garden, royal, as political statement, 144n. 33

Geller, S., 160n. 5

Genesis 12, as typology, 80–81

Genesis 14, 80–86, 157n. 16

Genesis 21, read allegorically by Paul, 30

Geraty, L., 59, 150n. 63

Gevirtz, S., 93, 111, 163n. 18

Ginsberg, H. L., 138n. 8, 152n. 11, 160n. 14

gişşu daddaru (Akkadian: "thorn and thistle"), 144n. 29

Goldstein, B., 145n. 1, 146n. 13, 151n. 3

Gottwald, N., peasant revolt theory, 56; critique of, 150n. 54. *See also* Rainey, A.

Greenberg, M., 142n. 16, 143n. 18, 152n. 13

Greengus, S., on wife-sister motif, 139n. 18. *See also* wife-sister (biblical motif)

Greenstein, E., 161n. 25

Gunkel, H., "life-settings," 78

gzl (Hebrew: "take by force"), 159n. 37

Hagar (biblical character), as Pauline allegory, 29–30

Hallo, W., 147n. 28, 164n. 14

Halpern, B., 25, 140n. 22

ḥāpiru (social class), 53, 156n. 9

Hebrews, epistle to, Chapter 5: 1–4, 103

Held, M., 155n. 37

ḥerem (Hebrew and Moabite: "utter extermination"), 127–28

ḥesed (Hebrew: "loyalty"), 72, 87, 151n. 8

Heshbon (city), 58–59

Hillers, D., on covenant, 151n. 7, 154n. 27

Hoffman, Y., 146n. 13

Hoffmann, D., 11, 14

Hosea (Hebrew prophet): allegory of Israel and Yahweh as wife and husband, 64–66; ambiguity toward kingship, 158n. 25; on covenant, 72–73; Ephraim as fool, 160n. 14

Hyksos, 54, 98

icon. *See* Bible as icon

Idrimi, king of Alalakh, 99, 150n. 57, 161n. 25

Jacob, allegory of Jeroboam, 93–97; as eponym, 92; wrestling with angel, 92–93

Jacobsen, T., 66, 152n. 15

Japhet, S., exodus traditions in Chronicles, 44

Jeroboam I, 91, 93–97, 99, 105

Jeroboam II, 101–2

Jesus and Pharisees (Matthew 22:41–46), 31

Job, allegoresis of, 34–36

John 21:24, 137n. 2 (chapter 1)

Johnson, Luke T., 138n. 2

Johnson, R. F., 121

Joshua, book of: Chapter 24, 45, 47, 67–71; studies, 152n. 18, 154n. 29

Joshua (character): background article, 159n. 1; covenant mediator, 67; originally local champion, 91

Josiah, king of Judah, 117

Judah (character), 99; as northern allegory, 101–2; as read typologically by Ezekiel, 100

Judges, book of, Chapter 9, 153n. 22

Kadesh, 81, 83

Kadesh-Barnea: excavations, 43; prominence in exodus traditions, 43

Kamin, Sara, 142n. 15

Kara, Joseph, 130

Kaspi, Joseph ibn, 34–36, 40

Keller, S., 164n. 4

Kenites, 131–34

Kennedy, J., Garden of Eden allegory, 143n. 26

Klein, J., 147n. 28, 152n. 15

Knauf, E. A., 158n. 29; on Jerusalem temple, 86

Koopmans, W., 152n. 18

Korah: opposition to Aaron, 112–19; sons of, 118

Kravitz, L.: on Kaspi, 35–36; on Nahmanides, 138n. 4

Lambert. W. G., 164n. 14

Leach, E., Bible to be read synchronically, 27

Lemche, N.: critique of attitudes

Lemche, N. *(Continued)*
toward Canaanite religion,
147n.22; legendary character of
exodus, 41
Levine, Baruch: "braiding," 163n.20;
historiography, 140n.23
Leviticus Rabbah, 130
Lewis, B., 145n.2
Lewis, D., 137n.5
Liverani, M., 150n.57
Loewenstamm, S., 111

Machinist, P., 145nn.4, 10, 146nn.14,
16, 158n.25, 164n.3; Israelite
counter-identity and
distinctiveness, 46–47
Malachi (Hebrew prophet), and
Torah of Moses, 14
maqom (Hebrew: "place,"
"sanctuary"), 159n.38, 160n.11
Marcus., D., 161n.25
Marduk (Babylonian god), 71, 134,
155n.37
Mari (ancient Syrian city), 18, 55–56
Marty, M., 1, 137n.1
mas (Hebrew: "forced labor"),
54–55. See also *sebel*
Matthew, book of: Chapter 2:13–15,
161n.23; Chapter 22:41–46,
31
Mazar, A., 43, 89, 145n.5, 160n.7
Megiddo, 55; battle of, 54
Melchi-zedek, 85–86, post-biblical
sources, 158n.27
Mendenhall, G., 154n.30, 155n.41;
theory of peasant revolt, 57;
Rainey's critique of theory, 150n.
54
Merneptah (Egyptian pharaoh): stela
of, 53; studies of, 149n.48
meṣaḥeq (Hebrew: "persecute"),
141n.10

Mesha, king of Moab, 58. *See also*
Moab
Millard, A., argument for historical
Abraham, 77
Miller, J. M., 150n.62
Miriam (character), 33, 45, 103, 104;
as prophet, 43, 162n.2
Mithra (Indo-Iranian god), 152n.14
Moab: claims to Moabite territory,
58–60; Moabite stone, 58
monolatry, not unique to Israel,
50–51
monotheism: and covenant, 70;
differing views in Bible, 4–5;
opposed to monolatry, 50–51;
theories of origin, 148n.31
morals, Mesopotamian, 147n.28
Moses, 121–34; reputed author of
Torah, 14–16
Muffs, Yohanan, 83, 158n.23
myth, definitions of, 143n.23

Na'aman, N., 150n.55
Nahmanides: argument for Mosaic
authorship, 15; disapproval of
Abraham's behavior, 157n.13
Nathan (Hebrew prophet), 85
Nevi'im (Hebrew: "Prophetic
books"), chronological span of, 6

Oden, R.: on covenant, 155n.31; on
myth, 143n.23
Origen, 32–33, 36, 40

Pagels, E., 161n.23; on Gnostic
myths as related to Church
hierarchy, 143n.24
Parnach, 7. *See also* Farnaka (Persian
name)
patriarchs, historicity of, 75–76
Paul (Saint), 8–9, and allegory, 29–34
Perlitt, L., 69, 154n.29, 155n.43

Persian Empire, 44; Zoroastrianism of, 5
Philistines, 22, 123; Aegean origin of, 47, 76; dealings with David, 86–90; free of Egyptian rule, 57
Philo, 8, 15, 29, 34, 141n.5
Porter, B. N., 135–36
Post-exilic, inadequacy of term, 43

Quenstadt, J., 11

Rainey, A., 149nn.50, 51, 52; critique of peasant revolt theory, 150n.54

Redford, D., 147n.21; characterization of covenant as "primitive," 151n.6; on story of Joseph, 161nn.21, 22
Rendtorff, R., 139n.13
Rofé, A., 146n.11, 159n.42
Rosenberg, J., political allegory in Bible, 141n.5, 142n.14, 143nn.23, 26
sacred marriage, 66, 152n.15
Samaria, 45
Samuel (Hebrew prophet), 123–27
Sarah/Sarai (character), 75, 80, 141nn.6, 9, 157n.13
Sargon of Agade, 42
Sargon of Assyria, 38
Sarna, N., on Philistines in Genesis, 22
Sasson, J., 143n.23, 147n.21
Saul: among the prophets, 123–25; founder of Israelite state religion, 163n.1; model for Moses, 122
sea peoples, 54, 56, 57
sebel (Hebrew: "forced labor"), 149n.53. See also mas
Seeligman, I., 146n.12
Sefire (town), 106
Sennacherib (Assyrian king), 21

Shechem, (city), 45, 67–68, 153nn.19, 20
Shishak/Shoshenq, first named Pharaoh in Bible, 99; support of dissidents, 161n.24
Shurpu (Babylonian ritual text), 49
Sihon, 58
Sikil, 57. See also sea peoples
Smith, M., 148n.32; Yahweh-alone party, 51–52
Smolar, L., 107, 162n.11
Solomon, 86, 99
Speiser, E. A., 23–24
Sperling, S. D., 146nn.11, 16, 152n.18, 154nn.29, 30, 163n.23
Spinoza, 82, 158n.19
šqr (Hebrew/Aramaic: "be false," "disloyal"), 159n.35
Stephen (Saint), speech of, 108
stone, for inscribing treaties, 106
Stronach, D., 144n.33

Tadmor, H., 42, 158n.25
Thompson, T.: origin traditions, 43–44, 145n.8; patriarchal traditions, 76
Thutmose III, 54
Toorn, K. van der, 122, 128, 133, 163n.1, 164n.12
trousers, for priests, 116
typology, 8, 80. See also allegory

Ugarit (ancient Syrian city), 18

van Seters, J., 139n.5, 140n.23, 158n.26

Weber, M., 71
Weinfeld, M., 5, 137n.3; on covenant, 70, 154n.27
Wellhausen, J.: covenant, legalistic character of, 63–65; documentary

Wellhausen, J. *(Continued)*
    hypothesis, 16–17; on literacy, 17;
    theological perspective of, 138n.7
wife-sister (biblical motif), 22–24, 76
Wyclif, J., 27

Yahweh (Hebrew god): as allegory,
136; background of, 164n.12; as
    great king, 69; as sole god, 50
Yahweh-Elohim (Hebrew god), 37
Yamm (Syrian sea god), 62

Zadok (priest), 86, 158n.31
Zerahiah of Barcelona, 33–34, 40

About the Author

S. David Sperling was ordained as a rabbi at Jewish Theological Seminary and received his Ph.D. at Columbia University. He has taught at SUNY–Stony Brook and Barnard College and is currently Professor of Bible and Chair of the Faculty at Hebrew Union College–Jewish Institute of Religion. He serves on occasion as Adjunct Professor at New York University.

Dr. Sperling's scholarly publications have been in biblical religion and history, comparative Semitic studies, and the history of biblical scholarship. He has served on the editorial board of the *Association for Jewish Studies Review* and is now a member of the editorial board of the *Hebrew Union College Annual*. He lives in New York City with his wife Rabbi Judith Lewis and their children, Deborah and Benjamin.